COMPARATIVE EDUCATION
THROUGH THE LITERATURE

To
J.A.L.
who has made
both real and near
countries from afar

COMPARATIVE EDUCATION
THROUGH THE
LITERATURE

A bibliographic guide

THELMA BRISTOW
*Senior Assistant Librarian
in charge of Research and Comparative Education,
The Library,
University of London
Institute of Education*

and

BRIAN HOLMES
*Reader in Comparative Education
University of London
Institute of Education*

ARCHON BOOKS

LONDON
BUTTERWORTHS

Published in the United States of America
by
Archon Books
The Shoe String Press, Inc.
60 Connolly Parkway
Hamden, Connecticut 06514

©
Butterworth & Co. (Publishers) Ltd.
1968

Suggested U.D.C. number: 016:37·012·5

Printed in Great Britain at the
St Ann's Press, Park Road, Altrincham

INTRODUCTION

This highly selective bibliographic guide is primarily intended for librarians and lecturers in university departments and colleges of education who are building up a section in the library or developing courses in comparative education. It should help beginning students and provide a basis on which more advanced students can build.

No attempt has been made to achieve comprehensiveness, indeed the mass of material now appearing makes such an aim difficult to achieve. The arrangement of material and the choice of examples have been made with teaching comparative education in mind. Librarians should be able to build up their own collection in the way that suits best the courses they serve.

It is essentially a beginner's guide in that it includes only works in English and those which, on the whole, are fairly easily obtainable. Much valuable literature exists in French, Spanish and German, none of which has been annotated. An attempt has been made, however, to indicate how books not mentioned here can be tracked down through bibliographies and abstracting services.

The selection of items is based fundamentally on the experiences of the authors in building up a library of Comparative Education at the University of London Institute of Education and participating in teaching the subject at four levels—the initial training course, the academic diploma, the M.A. degree by examination, and the research degrees of M.Phil. and Ph.D. Attention has also been given to the needs of lecturers in Colleges of Education preparing to teach comparative education at the B.Ed. level.

The arrangement of material moves from the general to the particular—from texts suitable for beginning students to literature of a more specialized nature and then to basic research tools. The authors are aware that each teacher will wish to follow his own line in developing courses and in relating the material in Chapters 2, 3 and 4 to the general texts given in Chapter 1 they hope that one of the various methodologies in comparative education can be used as a starting point from which to build coherent courses.

Chapter 1 deals with the most widely used general textbooks; not all of them are equally suitable for beginning students and several

INTRODUCTION

approaches are represented. Chapter 2 lists in historical perspective some of the creative writing from the British Commonwealth which may help teachers and students to sketch in some of the background to education in those countries. The choice of novels from a vast number is designed to illustrate the use which can be made of this kind of insight. In Chapter 3, books providing factual data about national systems of education are listed and annotated. These are largely descriptive accounts of the main features of a national system of education. They should not be regarded as completely different from several of the books included in Chapter 4. These are publications which either through the juxtaposition of data or through the analysis of a selected stage of, or problem in, education provide more explicit comparisons. As well as these cross-cultural and cross-national studies, books dealing with one aspect of education in a single country are put in as case studies. It should be noted that while for the purpose of classification distinctions are drawn between area, cross-national and case studies they all combine to provide comparative investigations. The index should be used for finding several references to the same work in different contexts; (q.v.) indicates that the work concerned appears elsewhere in the text.

The last chapter offers a guide to the tools of comparative education librarianship and research. Here again the material is illustrative and does not pretend to be comprehensive. It should enable students to embark on both modest research projects and to follow up more detailed research if required.

Finally it should be noted that the rate of publication of books which could legitimately be included in such a bibliography is so great that it has been impossible to ensure that the most recent books have been included. Every attempt has been made to note up-to-date publications but publishing schedules inevitably mean that as this book goes through the press the number and seriousness of omissions will grow. We apologize, but cannot help but welcome a state of affairs that augurs well for comparative education.

The authors jointly accept responsibility for the selection and annotation of material. Each has contributed to the book as a whole in accordance with particular professional responsibilities. The selection, choice of themes and annotations of the material on imaginative literature was, however, the work of Thelma Bristow alone. The Index was compiled by Jan Van der Wateren, assistant in the Research and Comparative Education Library of the University of London Institute of Education. All the non-fictional books mentioned in this bibliography are, in fact, to be found in this

INTRODUCTION

departmental library which, as a separate department of the University of London Institute of Education Library, was a result of the initiative taken just after the second world war by the then Director, Sir Fred Clarke, and J. A. Lauwerys, Professor of Comparative Education in the University of London.

Institute of Education, London.

Thelma Bristow
Brian Holmes

CONTENTS

Introduction v

1. Teaching Comparative Education 1
   General Textbooks 4

2. Imaginative Writing and Comparative Education 9
   General Background Books 12
   New Zealand 13
   Australia 14
   Canada 18
   Africa 19
   India 21

3. National Area Studies in Comparative Education 24
   Major Reference Works 24
   National Area Studies 30
   Africa 33
   The Americas 37
   Asia 44
   Australasia 51
   Europe 54
   Middle East 70
   Indexes to Periodicals 73

4. Cross-Cultural and Case Studies 87
   World Cross-Cultural Studies 89
   Regional Cross-Cultural Studies 100
   Case Studies 106
   Useful Bibliographies 110

5. Library Tools and Research in Comparative Education 112
   Research Trends 112
   Library Tools 116
   Preparing for Research 127

Index 137

1
TEACHING COMPARATIVE EDUCATION

The stated objectives of Comparative Education are sufficiently wide to justify a variety of teaching approaches. The nineteenth-century pioneers wanted to study foreign systems of education in order to improve their own. Some of them hoped to develop through comparative education a science of education. Others looked to historical traditions in order to explain why educational systems were as they were. All of them appreciated the need to collect information about foreign schools so as to describe them; they all recognized that an interpretation of these facts was desirable; and consequently all the pioneers of comparative education studied education in its relationship with other aspects of the society in which it was found.

The teaching of Comparative Education today reflects these basic assumptions. Perhaps for initial courses the most important justification for Comparative Education is that it helps students better to understand their own system and therefore makes a real contribution to their professional training. At the same time it should be recognized that many young teachers have a keen interest in international affairs and wish to see their own work in relation to what is going on elsewhere. Teachers of the subject, too, are usually motivated by a desire to relate their own experience to the teaching of education. Some teachers of Comparative Education have long experience in foreign countries—in the case of British teachers, often in the former colonial territories in Africa, Asia and the West Indies. Young people are still encouraged to spend some time abroad in voluntary service. The Peace Corps offers similar opportunities to young Americans whose country through A.I.D. and other programmes has since 1945 been committed to helping economically underdeveloped countries to develop more adequate systems of education. The cultural competition between the former colonial powers and the USA has not always helped these nations to pursue policies appropriate to their own needs.

Another group of potential teachers in Comparative Education has emerged from educators with a knowledge of foreign languages. Initially their interest has been in a particular country and its culture.

France is an obvious example but as Russian language and regional studies develop, interest in the education system of the USSR will also grow. For various reasons the schools of the USA attract a great deal of attention. More research has been undertaken and results published than in most countries. Moreover, the forces which have changed the USA educational pattern are operating more and more strongly elsewhere. At the same time Americans have always, and still do, take a keen interest in European and, recently, Soviet education.

A third group of teachers are those with a particular interest in a level or type of education. In the first half of the nineteenth century those concerned with the development of primary education were particularly anxious to study the Prussian system of primary schools. In the second half of the century the development of German technical and vocational education in the Scandinavian countries was looked at by foreign educators for the lessons they could learn from it. Since the second world war examples of 'comprehensive schools' have attracted world-wide attention.

Finally, in the contemporary world many social scientists have taken the study of education very seriously. First of all it has become politically important. Secondly, it is now 'big business' in most countries, and thirdly it has become a subject of study because of its social implications.

The literature in Comparative Education reflects these interests. Since the second world war it has grown rapidly so that in English there are several established general textbooks from which to choose. The approach varies. One category of general textbook favours an area approach. In separate chapters a description is given of national systems of education in their social context. These descriptions are often accompanied by explanation and interpretation. Another group look at levels and aspects of education and treat these comparatively. A third group of authors tend to describe in separate chapters the implications (in a number of countries') of particular factors or determinants. Finally, some authors have written with the intention of laying some foundations of methodology in Comparative Education and have illustrated their viewpoint in national case studies and cross-cultural comparisons.

It would be a mistake to assume that these various categories are mutually exclusive. Practically all the authors share many of the basic assumptions upon which their disciplined study is based. Pioneering books in the English language are: Matthew ARNOLD, *The Popular Education in France*, London, Longman Green, Longmans & Roberts, 1861, and other works; Henry BARNARD,

National Education, Systems, Institutions and Statistics of Public Instruction in Different Countries (several parts, New York, E. Steiger, 1872—and other works); Victor COUSIN, *Report on the State of Public Instruction in Prussia* (trans. Sarah Austin), London, Effingham Wilson, 1836, and *On the State of Education in Holland as Regards Schools for the Working Classes and for the Poor*, London, John Murray, 1838; Joseph KAY, *The Social Conditions and Education of the People in England and Europe*, London, Longman, Brown, Green & Longmans, 1850; William Torrey HARRIS, *Annual Report of the Commissioner of Education for the Year 1888-89*, Washington, 1891; Horace MANN, *Seventh Annual Report of the Board of Education*, Boston, Dutton & Wentworth, 1844, now reproduced; and M. E. SADLER, 'The Unrest in Secondary Education in Germany and Elsewhere' in *Board of Education Special Reports on Educational Subjects*, Vol. 9, *Germany*, London, HMSO, 1902.

Many of the earlier important writings in Comparative Education appeared in the form of accounts presented in annual reports or as the result of special enquiries. Towards the end of the nineteenth century many countries began to commission such reports and they are a mine of information.

University studies in Comparative Education were developed early in the twentieth century and between the wars at Columbia University, New York at Teachers' College and at the University of London at King's College and the Institute of Education. I. L. KANDEL published his classic *Comparative Education*, Cambridge, Mass, Houghton Mifflin in 1933. It remained one of the few general textbooks until after the second world war. Since then the literature has grown very considerably.

At least three general approaches in Comparative Education are reflected in this more recent literature. These are:

(*a*) Area Studies—National Systems

(*b*) Cross-cultural studies of:
    (i) a stage or level of education
    (ii) a type of educational institution, and
    (iii) an educational and/or socio-economic problem

(*c*) Case Studies

Some description of the scope of each kind of study is perhaps desirable.

Area Studies describe and interpret a fairly wide range of aspects of educational systems in various countries. Individual authors tend to select data on the basis of what they think is important but often fairly well established patterns are followed. International agencies such as Unesco and the International Bureau of Education draw up questionnaires in order to collect comparable educational data from national educational authorities.

Cross-Cultural Studies are not generally intended to give general descriptions of national systems. Rather they pick out a level of education, e.g. primary, and examine aspects of it in a number of countries. Socio-economic problems, e.g. those which arise because of social class differences, are also used as starting points for cross-cultural studies.

Case Studies provide depth studies of a level of education or socio-economic/political problem in a given country. Usually such studies assume that the reader has a fairly thorough knowledge of the educational system of that country and of its social background.

Reference will be made later to the various sources of literature in these three general areas. Here attention is drawn to a number of well-known general textbooks in Comparative Education which teachers of the subject may wish to use as basic books in any course. They are not all equally suitable for young students or for those with no background in Comparative Education. Choice of any one of them will depend upon the teacher's own point of reference, the experience and background of the students and the main purpose for which the course is intended. A predominantly *Area Studies* approach is perhaps most suitable for beginning students.

General Textbooks

None of the general textbooks given here falls exclusively into any of the categories mentioned earlier. Each includes elements of *Area Studies, Cross-Cultural Studies* and *Case Studies.* The regions covered in any depth vary as do the aspects of education treated. The following are among the best known books in English. There are several in German notably by Froese, Hilker and Schneider.

Some indication is given below of the scope, manner of treatment, the educational topics covered and the countries mentioned in selected English-language books.

G. Z. F. BEREDAY, *Comparative Method in Education*, New York, Holt, Rinehart & Winston, 1964.

Topic Coverage; legislation effecting school reform, indoctrination through education, scientific potential, teacher performance, control of school curriculum, the value of language and visits abroad, and the importance of cultural bias in Comparative Education.

Cross-Cultural Studies; involve two, three and four countries. Part 1 is devoted to methodology and Part 3 to preparation for study, and Part 4 to resources.

Case Studies; Poland, USA, USSR, England, France, Germany and Colombia.

Bibliography; notes and bibliography for every chapter, and a very extensive list of centres of research and teaching and printed sources.

J. F. CRAMER and G. S. BROWNE, *Contemporary Education*, New York, Harcourt, Brace & World, 1965 (2nd edn).

Topic Coverage; brief historical introduction, role of Church, State and local authorities in education in Part II. Pre-school, primary, secondary, higher, adult and youth education and teacher training are described in Part III. Comparable data are provided for each country and the book may be used in an *Area Studies* approach.

Main Countries; USA, England, France, Australia, Canada, USSR and West Germany.

Area Studies; Japan, Communist China and India.

Cross-Cultural Studies; administration, control and finance of schools and the operation of school systems.

Bibliography; at the end of the book and arranged under general references and by country.

N. HANS, *Comparative Education*, London, Routledge & Kegan Paul, 1963.

Topic Coverage; language policy; education in multi-racial societies, industrial development, the Christian churches, the Catholic orders, the English Public schools, the Dissenting Academies, the pioneers of humanism, socialism and nationalism. Federal, State and local educational authorities; primary, secondary, technical, adult and higher education. The treatment in every case is *historical*.

Main Countries; England, USA, France, USSR. Reference, in context, to New Zealand, South Africa, French Colonial territories, Belgium, Canada, Switzerland, Norway, China, Latin America, Ireland, Spain, Holland and Italy.

Area Studies; England, USA, USSR and France are provided.

Cross-Cultural Studies; based on natural factors (Racial, Linguistic, Geographic and Economic) religious factors (Catholic, Anglican, Puritan) secular factors (Humanism, Socialism, Nationalism and Democracy).

Bibliography; selected bibliography in English and French at end of volume.

B. HOLMES, *Problems in Education*, London, Routledge & Kegan Paul, 1965.

Topic Coverage; Part I is devoted to methodology. The problem of educating for democracy; aspects of economics and education; the agencies of administration and control; teacher education; secondary school curriculum; the structure of secondary education; and moral education.

Main Countries; in addition to USA, USSR, Japan and U.K. reference is made to European nations and developing countries in context of problems studied.

Cross-Cultural Studies; problems arising in economics, politics and administration in relation to educational policy.

Case Studies; USA (teacher education), U.K. (organization of secondary education), USSR (the school curriculum) and Japan (moral education).

Bibliography; notes and references for each chapter: selected bibliography at end.

A. M. KAZAMIAS and G. B. MASSIALAS, *Tradition and Change in Education*, New Jersey, Prentice-Hall, 1965.

Topic Coverage; features of European Feudal and Ottoman Islamic societies and the changes ensuing in the nineteenth century; the expansion of education during the twentieth century and the structure of these school systems; the administration, organization and curricula of modern schools. Examinations, pupil enrolments, political elites, etc.

Main Countries; primitive societies, Hellenic patterns, England, USA, France, USSR, Turkey, West Germany, Greece, Tanganyika and Japan.

Cross-Cultural Studies; treated historically in Part 2 of recruitment, selection and equality of opportunity, and in Part 3 of the structure of educational systems. Part 4 deals with education and problems of political culture.

Bibliography; notes and references throughout the text, no bibliography.

E. J. KING, *Other Schools and Ours*. New York, Holt, Rinehart & Winston, 1967 (3rd edition).

Topic Coverage; each system is described as a *Case Study* but basic information is provided together with diagrammatic representations and photographs. On-going reforms are interpreted in the light of historical antecedents. The organization of each system is described and changes noted. Interpretation of each system

GENERAL TEXTBOOKS

is largely in terms of national character as seen against the total social background.

Area Studies; Denmark, France, Great Britain, USA, USSR, India and Japan.

Bibliography; selected bibliography at the end of the volume.

V. MALLINSON, *An introduction to the Study of Comparative Education*, London, Heinemann (new edn), 1965.

Topic Coverage; the stages of education are studied in relation to the national character of the people served by a national system of education. The treatment is largely historical with recent information provided under the headings listed below. Diagrammatic representations of education are given at the end of the volume.

Main Countries; Belgium, France, Germany, Holland, Italy, Norway, Denmark, USA, England, USSR.

Cross-Cultural Studies; progressive education, the aims of education, the administration of education, the training of teachers, primary education, secondary education, and technical and vocational education.

A. H. MOEHLMAN and J. S. ROUCEK (eds), *Comparative Education*, New York, Dryden, 1952.

Topic Coverage; historical introductions, general social background, stages of education, e.g. primary, secondary, higher, adult, and administration. Details and organization of material in each chapter determined by features of individual systems. No firm classification of data to facilitate comparisons.

Area Studies; USA, Latin America, Mexico, U.K., British Commonwealth, France, Italy, Germany, Scandinavia, Czechoslovakia, Soviet Union, Africa, Arab countries, Turkey, India, China, Japan.

Bibliography; annotated bibliography at the end of each chapter.

I. N. THUT and Don ADAMS, *Educational Patterns in Contemporary Societies*, New York, McGraw-Hill, 1964.

Topic Coverage; heavily historical treatment and interpretation of the control, expansion and structural changes in education. Emphasis in each chapter is appropriate to the particular country, general cover makes each description something more than a Case Study. Diagrams throughout facilitate comparisons.

Main Countries; Spain, Germany, France, England, USSR, China, Japan, Latin America, India and North America. East Asian and European traditions and some problems in underdeveloped nations are described.

Area Studies; representative Western (including European education in fifteenth century), Oriental and newly emerging patterns.

Bibliography; fairly extensive references, pamphlets and periodicals are listed at the end of each chapter.

All these general textbooks include chapters on the aims, methods and history of Comparative Education. The space devoted to these aspects varies considerably.

Other books which could serve as general background books with a comparative and historical bias in an introductory course are:

William BOYD, *The History of Western Education*, 7th edn revised and enlarged by E. J. KING, London, A. & C. Black, 1964.

J. S. BRUBACHER, *A History of the Problems of Education*, 2nd edn, New York, London etc., McGraw-Hill, 1966.

Martin MAYER, *The Schools*, New York, Harper, 1961.

A. E. MEYER, *The Development of Education in the Twentieth Century*, New York, Prentice-Hall, 1949.

A. E. MEYER, *An Educational History of the Western World*, New York and London etc., McGraw-Hill, 1965.

P. NASH, A. M. KAZAMIAS and H. J. PERKINSON, *The Educated Man:* Studies in the history of educational thought, New York, London etc., Wiley, 1965.

In subsequent chapters ways will be suggested of building up a body of literature on the basis of the approach presented in selected general textbooks in Comparative Education.

2
IMAGINATIVE WRITING AND COMPARATIVE EDUCATION

Comparative Educationists have never been satisfied simply to describe foreign educational systems and point to differences and similarities between them. They have been anxious to explain why in one country the schools are organized in a certain way, the curriculum follows a particular pattern, teachers use characteristic methods of teaching and examinations are conducted in the way they are: and why, in other countries, differences in these and other respects can be observed.

Several ways of explaining why things are as they are have been developed. Among them one way depends upon the realization that the traditions of a nation are built into the individuals that make it up. These traditions and traits, unique to members of a community or nation, predispose those responsible for educational policy to make certain choices. If the 'French' are different from the 'English' and both are different from the 'Germans', 'Italians' or 'Americans' how can these differences be studied? And how can such studies be made relevant in comparative education? Several attempts have been made.

Vernon MALLINSON in *An Introduction to the Study of Comparative Education* (q.v.) uses the concept of 'national character' to explain why systems of education differ. The common identity of ideas and ambitions is, according to Mallinson, built up over the centuries, fixes the mentality of a people and makes it possible for them to act with a common purpose.

I. L. KANDEL in *The New Era in Education—A Comparative Study*, London, Harrap, 1955, also discusses the value of national character studies in Comparative Education. Many authors have compared, as he does, the eloquence of the Italian with the German's love of abstract thought, with the clarity and precision with which the Frenchman writes and talks with the Englishman's unwillingness to theorize and with the American's pragmatism.

A systematic review of the literature relating to national character and how it may be studied is presented in H. C. J. DUIJKER, and

IMAGINATIVE WRITING AND COMPARATIVE EDUCATION

N. H. FRIDA, 'National Character and National Stereotypes' in *Confluence*, Amsterdam, North-Holland Publishing Company, 1960. Here the various meanings given to national character are described as (i) psychological traits, (ii) modal personality, (iii) basic personality structure, (iv) systems of attitudes, values and beliefs held in common, (v) behavioural characteristics, and (vi) the cultural products, e.g. literature, art, philosophy, of a nation. Each definition leads to its own modes of study.

Impressionistic studies of national character abound. Of interest to comparative educationists are: G. GORER, *The American People—a Study in National Character*, New York, Norton, 1948; D. J. ENRIGHT, *The World of Dew*, London, Secker & Warburg, 1955, and F. MARAINI, *Meeting with Japan*, London, Hutchinson, 1959 (both on Japan); S. de MADARIAGA, *Englishmen, Frenchmen, Spaniards*, London, Oxford University Press, 1928, and A. SIEGFRIED, *The Character of Peoples*, London, Cape, 1952 (Italy, France, England, Germany, Russia, and USA).

B. HOLMES in 'Rational Constructs in Comparative Education' in *International Review of Education*, Hamburg, Unesco Institute, Vol. 11, No. 4, 1965, has suggested ways in which a system of attitudes, values and beliefs may be drawn up for a selected country using philosophical sources. PLATO's *Republic*, for example, provides with Judaic-Christian literature, a rationale for Europe as a whole. National differences can be studied through selected writings of LOCKE (England), DESCARTES (France), HEGEL (Germany), MARX (USSR) and DEWEY (USA). The arbitrariness of the choice should be noted and the extent to which such an approach makes it possible to place on-going debates in any country in a coherent framework should be recognized.

Such debates reflect national problems and the proposed solutions to them. They are symptomatic of social change. Historians, social scientists, and educationists have all paid attention to the analysis of change. In the USA historians of education such as E. P. CUBBERLEY, *The History of Education*, Cambridge, Mass, Houghton Mifflin, 1948, have seen the school as the instrument change. L. A. CREMIN in *The Transformation of the School*, New York, Vintage, 1961, and *The Genius of American Education*, New York, Vintage, 1966, has set himself the task of re-interpreting the American school in the history of the country. The move to look for sources other than those written by educationists is reflected in Maxime GREENE, *The Public School and the Private Vision—A Search for America in Education and Literature*, New York, Random House, Studies in Education, 1965. The author considers the extent to which literary criticism and educational history present two different views. She mentions Nathaniel HAWTHORNE, Henry David THOREAU and Hermann MELVILLE as literary figures and compares their views with those of educationists James J. CARTER, Horace MANN and William Torrey HARRIS.

There is another whole field of publications which may be used as a way into comparative education for students—imaginative writing which may be used as the basis of an area study, a cross-cultural study or as a case study. Comparative educationists are just beginning to see the possibilities of this study. In an article in the *British Journal of Educational Studies*, Vol. XI, No. 2, May 1963, pp. 125–141, L. SPOLTON says 'post-war fiction can also give insights into comparative education'. He compares the American 'Blackboard Jungle' with the English 'Spare the rod' among other novels.

At the Comparative Education Society in Europe, U.K. Section, Conference held at Reading in September 1966 Vernon MALLINSON read a paper on literary studies in the service of Comparative Education. He dealt mainly with the literary novels of Europe and worked out a useful table to demonstrate their comparative possibilities. He has also brought out a book which should be useful in this type of study. *Modern Belgian Literature 1830–1960*, Heinemann, 1966. This Society hopes to produce an annotated list of similar novels considered useful to lecturers teaching in Colleges of Education.

It is impossible to do more in this volume than select a few books from the vast field of imaginative writing which may be used in comparative education studies. It should be noted that the insight of the novelist into the most serious problems facing a nation may be as penetrating as that of any sociologist. His understanding of human personality may be as perceptive as that of the psychologist. His awareness of a nation's traditions may be as illuminating as that of the historian. In short, imaginative literature can add greatly to an understanding of educational problems and the social milieu in which they find expression.

Here in selecting novels from British Commonwealth countries Thelma BRISTOW has concentrated attention on the way in which they deal with social change thus illustrating how this kind of literature may be used in the study of a selected problem in particular countries.

In fact social change has provided the dynamic for the new literature coming out of emergent and rapidly developing countries. It is often lively, colourful and sufficiently documentary in nature to appeal to young students embarking on a study of the countries concerned. Surprisingly there are several guides and aids to this literature which facilitate extended studies.

GENERAL BACKGROUND BOOKS

A. L. MCLEOD (ed), *The Commonwealth Pen:* an introduction to the literature of the British Commonwealth, Ithaca, New York, Cornell University, 1961 gives an account of the national literature of several commonwealth countries and compares older developments with the beginnings of West African, Malayan, Caribbean, and South African literatures. Each of the ten chapters is written by a specialist from the country concerned and competent to discuss the principal writers and their works and to evaluate them in relation to English literature. J. PRESS (ed), *Commonwealth Literature:* unity and diversity in a common culture, London, Heinemann, 1965 consists of extracts from the proceedings of a conference held at Bodington Hall, Leeds, 9–12 September 1964 under auspices of the University of Leeds. The *National Book League's Imaginative Literature from the Commonwealth*, An annotated list, London, N.B.L., 1965 is a useful booklet to take along to the Public Library to help choose novels about other countries. A new journal called *The Journal of Commonwealth Literature*, London, Heinemann and University of Leeds, No. 1, 1965 includes an annual bibliography of Commonwealth literature and reviews and is published on behalf of the Association of Commonwealth Literature and Language Studies at the University of Leeds. The *British National Bibliography* lists novels from other countries each week. The *Yearbook of World Affairs*, London, Stevens, includes a report on contemporary literature. Using these sources it is possible to find all the novels that are fairly readily available in many Public Libraries and in London libraries of the various Commonwealth offices.

One fascinating aspect of literature from commonwealth countries is that it is possible to study the founding and development of a country over a period of less than 200 years, in most cases. Often actual live source material may be found in the way of letters and diaries in the attics of grandparents who have had relatives go away to 'England overseas'. It is thus possible to study culture contact, the development of nationalism, emigrant problems, social change, the problems of women and marriage in an 'uncivilized' environment, and a variety of other manageable comparative problems. There are numerous guides into the writings of the commonwealth countries. It may be wise to restrict a study to samples from several countries and deal with the novel only; but poetry, drama, and autobiography all offer penetrating insights.

New Zealand

The following may be read in conjunction with novels:
M. TURNBULL and Ian A. MCLAREN *The Land of New Zealand*, Longmans, 1964. This is a companion volume to *The Changing Land* by M. TURNBULL. Both give a good background picture of the country. Of more specific interest is J. E. RITCHIE, *The Making of a Maori:* a case study of a changing community, Wellington, Reed, 1963.

The guide into the literature is:
Joan STEVENS, *The New Zealand Novel*, 2nd edn, 1860–1965, Wellington, Reed, 1966. This deals with the New Zealand novel beginning with the early days of the troubles between the Maori and the settlers and concludes with the 1960's. It is intended as a teaching book and has an appendix which gives notes for critical discussions of six novels and topics for study and discussion. The author states that her criterion for choosing a New Zealand novel relates to the country, or to its people or to the experience of life as human beings met with in those islands. Her four categories of novels, recording, exploiting, preaching and interpreting, follow the historical development of the country. The early novel is mostly of the exploiting type and deals with sensational events drawn from the Maori wars. Such is G. A. HENTY, *Maori and the Settler*, 1891. A novel of the recording type is T. COTTLE's *Frank Melton's Luck*, 1891. This is a description of station life in New Zealand. In *A South Sea Siren*, 1895 George CHAMIER writes of philosopher Dick Raleigh living in a small settlement amused by the attempts of gentleman farmers to set up an old world in the new with little knowledge or experience. The 'preaching' novels are often by women, such as *The Heart of the Bush* by Edith GROSSMAN, 1910. The heroine has had an expensive English education and is torn between marrying the polished Englishman or the uncultured colonial. The novel portrays her choice of the lonely bush farm life. Eventually she and her materialistic husband find a peculiar 'New Zealand' happiness when English imported culture and excessive material prosperity are both set aside.

Katherine MANSFIELD evokes the spirit of New Zealand in her short stories but feels too 'a conflict between two worlds which leads to craving for Europe to enrich New Zealand culture'.[1]

The Story of a New Zealand River by Jane MANDER also deals with the woman's place in a pioneering community, the absence of

---

[1] Alan MULGAN, *Great Days in New Zealand Writing*. Wellington, Reed, Chap. 7, p. 63.

books and ideas, the dead weight of material interests, the awakening and broadening of a woman's nature hitherto sheltered by a class structure which stifled her own human nature.

In the interpreting category John MULGAN in *Man Alone* 'sees in the typical New Zealand figure not only the image of western man between the wars but an image of the human predicament' (p. 61) seen through the eyes of an Englishman. The interpretation of human experience is 'comparative' but not insular. Frank SARGESON writes mainly short stories. One contained in *A Man and his Wife* is called *The Making of a New Zealander*. Some critics regard him as the first New Zealand national writer. Roderick FINLAYSON writes about the Maori and the conflict between racial values. *Pencarrow* by Nelle SCANLAN in 4 volumes is the story of a family and New Zealand development over a period of 100 years. It is social and economic history as seen through the imagination of the novelist. Sylvia Ashton WARNER has become well known for *Spinster* and *Teacher;* she writes about teaching in a one-room Maori school. *Maori Girl* by Noel HILLIARD shows the effect of urban life on the simple country girl, her fight to make a decent life for herself and her disintegration when she is deserted by the boy she loves.

Landfall is a New Zealand quarterly—in its September 1966 number the retiring editor comments on the gap between literature and life in New Zealand and notes that the historical approach is all too evident. From the point of view of the comparative education student this has the advantage that a good over-all view of the development of New Zealand can be gained from its novels.

Australia

An interesting comparison could be made between the novels of Australia and New Zealand which give distinctly different flavours resulting, not only from the description of the two countries, but also from the variation in their literary developments. Is it the different social background that makes the differences in development? Does a convict heritage, covering a greater range of class background than that of the immigrant to New Zealand, produce a more diverse artistic development? Do the tougher geographical features and the subsequent economic struggle, effect this development? Do mining, gold rushes, industrial development both reduce and yet expand man's artistic development? Australia seems to have an earlier literary development as opposed to merely producing books, on the other hand poetry now seems to be growing fast in New Zealand; a great many comparative approaches are possible but as far as the Australian scene is concerned the following five books provide background reading.

David HORNE, *The Lucky Country*, Australia in the sixties, Penguin Books, 1964 vividly describes all aspects of present-day Australia, includes a fairly critical chapter on education, comments on the intellectual and artistic life and on social change. The author has travelled and worked abroad. He looks at Australia against developments in other countries and in relation to her own historical and social context and assesses her possible place in the future international scene.

A. F. DAVIES and S. ENCEL, *Australian Society*, London, Pall Mall Press, 1965 includes a chapter on education.

G. P. H. DUTTON (ed), *The Literature of Australia*, Melbourne, Penguin Books, 1964.

Vance PALMER, *The Legend of the Nineties*, Melbourne University Press (Paperback) 1963 is concerned with the legend of the Australian nineties as a period of artistic and political activity, the sudden awareness of the people of being a nation seemed to set some creative forces into motion.

Colin RODERICK, *An Introduction to Australian Fiction*, Sydney and London, Angus and Robertson, 1950 presents a survey of Australian fiction from the beginnings up to 1949. Student and general readers will find the arrangement according to types of novels (a similar arrangement will be followed here) and a concluding synopsis of basic reading in Australian fiction useful.

The first fifty years of settlement in Australia produced few novels. Time was needed to adjust and reconcile land with people. The convicts and their jailers, followed by free settlers (often retired army officers who came to exploit the land) were determined to return to England eventually. They were often defeated by the hard conditions. The writing when it did begin falls into several clearly defined groups which more or less follow the historical development of the country.

Convictism—The first Australian novel was the work of a convict Henry SAVERY who wrote *Quintus Servinton*, 1830. He was a Bristol merchant transported for forgery, and his novel is based upon his life in prison. He gives detailed descriptions of life aboard the transport boat and of the many troubles that assailed convicts and their wives who followed them there. It is not as horrific as *For the Term of his Natural Life* by Marcus CLARKE which appeared first as a serial in the *Australian Journal*, 1870–77. This sensational novel is based on the Tasmanian convict records and makes exciting if

IMAGINATIVE WRITING AND COMPARATIVE EDUCATION

depressing reading. It is made the more poignant by all the documentary evidence quoted at the back of the book which is now published in the *World's Classics* series by the Oxford University Press, 1956.

Bushranging—The numerous escaped convicts were known as 'Bolters' who lived in the bush, plundered settlers and became known as 'bushrangers'. The best known writer in this group is Rolf BOLDREWOOD. He was a police magistrate and therefore both read evidence of the bushrangers' activities and dealt with them in court. *Robbery Under Arms*, 1881, is best known as a straightforward adventure story simply told but always pointing out the lawlessness of the behaviour of the participants.

Pastoralists—The early pastoralists, hard at work making homesteads and grazing their animals, clashed with the aborigines and had little time to write. The next generation began to chronicle some of the happenings of pioneer life. Gold began to attract more immigrants. Clashes between individuals and government made for dramatic situations. Changing social trends appeared in novels. One of these is *Clara Morison:* a tale of South Australia during the gold fever, 1854 by Catherine SPENCE who migrated to Australia from Scotland in 1839. Based upon her own experiences it gives a picture of middle class life in Adelaide 1851–53 and describes how the gold diggings affected life in South Australia.

Immigrants—An interesting novel of a later period is *No Escape*, 1932, by Velia ERCOLE the daughter of an Italian immigrant. It tells of an Italian who cannot adjust to life in Australia while he is married to an Italian girl but when she dies and he marries an Australian the problem is solved to such an extent that when he enlists in the army in World War I he finds he is more at home with a British than with an Italian soldier.

Henry KINGSLEY went to Australia for a while during the early immigrant period. He wrote *The Recollections of Geoffry Hamlyn*, 1859, describing pastoral life from the English colonizer's point of view. *The Head Station*, 1885, by Mrs Campbell PRAED has become a classic; it depicts the way of life in settlements which were still at that period replicas of the estates of the English gentry. Australian settlers still looked to London for cultural inspiration.

It was not until the nineties and the Sydney *Bulletin* writers that Australia began to establish a cultural ethos of her own. Little publishing was established in the country itself, most writers had come from and returned to Great Britain and their orientation was British. The *Bulletin* published short stories, essays, poems, articles that were essentially Australian. It was founded in 1880 by J. F. ARCHIBALD and when A. G. STEPHENS became editor in 1896 and

AUSTRALIA

encouraged short story writers, social criticism and national feeling found a medium of communication. One of these writers was Henry LAWSON who loved Australia and fought for democratic freedom in his poetry and short stories. He was 'a man of the people' and representative of this period. *While the Billy Boils*, 1896 is one of the best known of his works of which there are various collections.

Social Criticism—Another well-known writer is Joseph FURPHY. Under the pseudonym of 'Tom Collins' he wrote *Such is Life*, 1903. He believed in the 'brotherhood of man' above all and was critical of any situation that menaced it. Yet another *Bulletin* contributor was Steele RUDD; some of his contributions were collected together and published as *On our selection*, 1899. Each chapter depicts a scene in the life of a settler's family. He pays tribute to the men and women who fought their way through the Bush-land and made Australia Australia.

Another group of novels are concerned with 'Larrikinism'. Larrikins were men who had known the old convict rings, formed groups and became the urban criminal delinquents. Louis STONE, *Jonah*, 1911 is concerned with the leader of a larrikin gang.

Aborigines—There are many stories about the *aborigines*. Mrs Aeneas GUNN wrote *The Little Black Princess of the Never Never*, 1905 which marks a change in the white man's attitude to the aborigines. Katherine PRITCHARD's *Coonardoo*, 1929 and Xavier HERBERT's *Capricornia*, 1938 are both sympathetic stories about relationships between white and black. A recent book by A. W. REED, *Myths and Legends of Australia*, 1965 consists of short stories and some poems based on the aborigines' myths classified into various groups illustrating the variety and colour of their fantasy world.

Historical and Social Change—There are various *chronicle* novel writers; among them Martin BOYD's *The Monteforts*, 1928 is a lively history of a century as well as a family in *Brent of Bin Bin, Up the Country*, 1928, *Ten Creeks Run Back to Bool Bool*, 1927-28; the last volume brings the story up to comparatively modern times. Louis KAYE in *Tybal Men*, 1931 describes through three generations a family who owned a sheep farm which finally has to be changed to a wheat producing farm to provide food for the town that has grown up around it. The chief characters in the novel have to solve all the real problems of social change.

A modern writer that shows the impact of social change on his characters is Randolp STOW. His latest novel *The Merry-go-round in the Sea*, 1965 is a story of a boy, Rob Coram, growing up as part of a large Australian family in a small town and the country around it during the second world war years. The feeling, atmosphere, and history of Australia are made very vivid through the experiences of the boy and his much-loved cousin who goes away to the war and is taken prisoner by the Japanese. He survives torture and returns to the country and family whose memory and spirit have nourished him during his prison camp experiences. He becomes disillusioned and restless and finally leaves for England. Rob realizes that everything is changing around him, that Western Australia is becoming part of the pattern of urban living and that everything that he has loved is fast disappearing. The story concludes with him as an adolescent on the threshold of life: 'The world the boy had believed in did not, after all exist. The world and the clan and Australia had been a myth of his mind, and he had been all the time, an individual' (p. 283). He is reminded of the merry-go-round of his childhood and his cousin's words written in his autograph book when he returned from the war, 'Thy firmness makes my circle just, and makes me end, where I began'. The individual artist is born but yet he is part of the very structure of his background.

One cannot conclude these comments on the Australian novel without reference to Patrick WHITE who is to the novel what abstract painting is to art, he has pruned and cut away everything obvious or unnecessary and left the basic forms and feeling of Australian life in literature, particularly in *The Tree of Man*, 1961 which is about a young man who wrests a home out of a wilderness near one of the growing cities of Australia. And *Voss*, 1957 who sets out with a small van to cross the Australian continent for the first time.

A study of Australian education could be made in depth as well as breadth if all the material mentioned here were used in conjunction with the material given in Chapter 3. On the other hand, the novels, with the background books suggested at the beginning of this section, would make an interesting study for a student just beginning to study education in other countries in a comparative way.

Canada

Canadian literature could be looked at in relation to that of Britain, France and the United States. All these countries have a vast literature of their own. It is not proposed to look at the novel in Canada here as, fortunately, a new bibliographical guide was published in 1966: R. E. WATTERS and I. F. BELL (compilers), *On Canadian Literature 1806–1960*, a check list of English-Canadian literature, its authors and language, Toronto University Press, 1966.

It is interesting to observe though, the Canadian novels often pose similar problems to those shown in Australian and New Zealand fiction. A recent Canadian novel is a good example of this.

George RYGA, *Ballad of a Stone-picker*, London, Joseph, 1966 is the story of two brothers illustrating two aspects of life, that of the body and that of the spirit or mind. One brother stayed at home in Canada to wrest a living out of the soil, the other went away to England to be educated and develop his mind, he lost his contact with his roots, became disintegrated and eventually killed himself. The struggle with the conditions of nature make a man of the other brother. Should the two parts of man be split in this way? This is perhaps the problem of early days in Canada that in order to develop the land the intellect had to be allotted another, perhaps secondary place. This ambivalent attitude to the intellectual as opposed to manual, as well as the 'lessons of toil' and proximity of the soil have perhaps affected the development of education in these commonwealth countries:—a distrust of the highly academic:—a positive belief in the wider curriculum than that of the parent country.

Africa

Such is not the case with the continents of Africa and India. In fact most of the literature coming from these countries put a very high premium on education and many of their novels are directly concerned with the acquisition of education. Possibly the imaginative writing coming out of Africa is more directly concerned with comparative education than from any other commonwealth countries. All are concerned with education and illustrate social change brought about by education. A most useful guide into this writing has recently been published.

Anne TIBBLE, *African/English Literature*, a short survey and anthology of prose and poetry up to 1965, London, Owen, 1965. It is intended for schools and universities in order to illustrate the diversity and liveliness of African writing. It begins with a short historical outline of Africa and a survey of its languages. The literature of each area (South Africa, French-speaking Africa, East and West Africa) is discussed showing its development from traditional oral texts and the influences of Western ideas. The books and writers discussed show the conflict between tribal society and modern urbanized society. The second part of the book consists of passages by leading Africans from the earliest known writer in 1793 to the present day. Most have been written during the last twenty years. Part three is a bibliography of African writers and their work. The preface is introduced with the following quotation from Peter ABRAHAMS' *The Blacks:* 'If the men inauguring the new ways have the sense and patience to preserve the finer qualities of the old ways and fuse these with the new, then we can expect something magnificently new out of Africa'. This book follows this theme and makes fascinating reading.

The African writers' series paperbacks make it comparatively easy to obtain these writings in England at a low cost. They are all useful from the point of view of social change but *The African* by William CONTON, 1964 and Chinua ACHEBE's three novels are all particularly relevant. *The African* is a fictionalized autobiography of Kisimi Kamara who comes from an imaginary African state. He tells of growing up in a village in Northern Nigeria, his education from missionaries, how he came to England to study at Durham, where he fell in love with a South African girl who was killed probably for caring for him, how he returned to his country to teach and became involved in the formulation of a new political movement, became a Muslim in order better to fit into his own society. He became involved in a Pan-Africa Federation, then disappeared into South Africa to avenge the death of his girl friend but finally learns compassion rather than vengeance. Discussions and situations that relate to many of the debates in comparative education abound, they are simply presented in the course of normal living. 'I hope you won't consider it too personal if I ask you how and where you learned your English?' asked Mrs Morris. 'Not at all. We speak it as a lingua franca at home. We have many languages and many tribes so it's just as well that English has been kept as the medium of instruction in the schools. It links us both with each other and with so much of the outside world.' He goes on later to talk about 'pidgin English'. There is too a dual quality about the writing which shows an intellectual awareness of the problems of an emerging country. Kisimi has been celebrating with a school friend their successful passing of an examination and concludes the description of the happy occasion with these words, 'Both of us realized the symbolism of our position in place and time: buffeted by confused crosscurrents of native and alien cultures, standing excitedly on the fringes of academic life. We stood there for a moment, silent and thoughtful'.

Chinua ACHEBE comes from East Nigeria. His three novels, *Things Fall Apart, No Longer at Ease* and *Arrow of God*, all in *The African writers' series*, illustrate the struggle between the values that remain in rural society and the values of modern urban society. In

Things Fall Apart he writes about traditional village society and the coming of the white invader on his 'iron horse', a bicycle. The village society is gradually changing, the missionaries convert and educate some. The old prejudices like the traditional ones of casting away twin babies have to be challenged by new beliefs, compassion is not a simple matter and Christianity if it is not an elusive truth has much to prove. This novel illustrates the gap between the African and white man's viewpoints. It also illustrates the gap between standards of behaviour in different societies and in the same society.

No Longer at Ease is about the grandson of Obi of the previous novel. This Obi grows up in a Nigeria near independence with new towns and industrial development. He returns from England to Lagos. It is about the confusion of values, new progress, new corruptions. He is involved in taking bribes. The book stresses the need for strength of mind and charity of spirit to keep abreast of the morass of social change. How can the 'brave man' of tradition become the modern man needing psychological insight as a necessary equipment for wise action? *Arrow of God*, 1964 is about an earlier period—1931. It is concerned with village people's sense of community as well as their unity with natural forces. Achebe seems to be emphasizing this link with nature as an antidote to modern planned community life. Yet hasn't the white man the answer to the 'good life' or does the answer lie somewhere between the two societies? Is this cross-cultural development the beginning or the end of an exploration for the truth?

There are many other writers that might be discussed, they all possess that dual quality that make them exciting reading, as well as a positive optimism as Leon DAMAS says in his poem 'Somehow we survive': 'Somehow we survive and tenderness, frustrated, does not wither'.

India

India is an old country with a long literary tradition. Literature in English is largely a problem of translation or is a product of cross-cultural influences. Fortunately there are a number of publications on the Indian novel in English.

D. M. SPENCER, *Indian Fiction in English, an annotated bibliography*, Philadelphia, University of Pennsylvania Press and London, O.U.P., 1960 consists of an introductory essay on Indian society, culture and fiction and an annotated list of fiction and autobiography.

IMAGINATIVE WRITING AND COMPARATIVE EDUCATION

K. R. S. IYENGAR, *Indian Writing in English*, Bombay and London, Asia Publishing House, 1962.

M. E. DERRETT, *The Modern Indian Novel in English, a comparative approach*, Université Libre de Bruxelles, Editions de L'Institut de Sociologie, 1966.

A most interesting writer and very relevant from the point of view of Comparative Education is V. S. NAIPAUL. He is of Indian origin brought up in the West Indies, writing of Indians living in the West Indies. An interesting novel *A House for Mr Biswas*, London, Deutsch, 1961 deals with the problem of an East Indian Hindu settlement in Trinidad. The central figure, Mr Biswas, is a gentle thoughtful man, son of a labourer. He has a gift for sign writing which leads him into a marriage with the younger daughter of a matriarchal household where there is neither peace nor privacy. His longing for independence of mind is such that it drives him along devious routes that lead to many failures until he finally achieves a house of his own just before his early death. As well as being an epic of a small man contending with many hardships and mishaps, many of his own making, this is a detailed cross-cultural study of Hindu life in the West Indies. It leaves the reader with a quite extraordinary feeling of having been in two worlds at the same time. The language is evocative of the West Indies and at the same time all the traditions and restraints of a large Indian family is so apparent that it leaves an exhaustion that must have been part of the reason for the early demise of Mr Biswas.

In an M.Phil thesis written for The Institute of Education, University of London, G. BROUGHTON says 'In the context of Naipaul's Trinidadian novels, there sounds a certain irony in Macaulay's Minute of 1835, the instrument which lay behind the subsequent English language policy of British India: "We must at present do our best to form a class of persons Indian in blood and colour, but English in tastes, in opinions, in morals and in intellect". This ideal of a new class of native leader educated to pass on to his less fortunate countrymen his newly acquired knowledge is exceeded by the new kind of interpreter represented by Naipaul. A direct product of Macaulay's Minute, his thinking transcends the narrow tastes and opinions of Englishmen, for he has been educated out of nationalism, class, cast and creed: he speaks not from ruler to ruled, but as man to men'.[1]

If, as a result of bringing imagination, as well as factual knowledge

---

[1] G. BROUGHTON, *A Critical Study of the Development of V. S. Naipaul as a Novelist as reflected in his four West Indian novels*, p. 91. Unpublished M.Phil. Thesis, University of London, 1967.

and intellectual thought, to the study of education in other countries, students also transcend the narrow tastes and opinions of their own countries and come to understand people as individuals, then the novel and other imaginative literature will have proved to have a place in the study of comparative education.

3
NATIONAL AREA STUDIES IN COMPARATIVE EDUCATION

In this chapter literature useful in building up a comprehensive picture of education in any selected country will be discussed. It should be remembered that the classification previously suggested is not intended to differentiate one type of study from another. Consequently many of the books referred to here would also be useful in *Cross-Cultural* and *Case Studies*. Indeed the manner in which material about individual countries is organized in some publications and series is designed to facilitate cross-cultural comparisons even though these are not always made explicit. General textbooks which might serve as a basis on which to mould this kind of study are CRAMER and BROWNE, *Contemporary Education* (q.v.), KING, *Other Schools and Ours* (q.v.) and THUT and ADAMS, *Educational Patterns in Contemporary Studies* (q.v.).

The tradition of collecting data about education has been mentioned. It is often said to stem from the work of Marc-Antoine Jullien de Paris *Esquisse d'un Ouvrage sur l'Education Comparée*, Geneva, International Bureau of Education, 1962. In this work, first published in 1817, the author asked a series of questions designed to gather together information, both qualitative and quantitative, about education in foreign countries. An English translation is edited by Stewart FRASER, *Jullien's Plan for Comparative Education*, New York, Columbia University, Comparative Education Studies, Teacher's College, Bureau of Publications, 1964. Pedro ROSSELLO has traced the growth of international agencies for the collection of educational data from the work of JULLIEN in *Les Precurseurs du Bureau International d'Education*, Geneva, International Bureau of Education, 1943. A shortened version in English appeared under the auspices of *Year Book of Education*, London, Evans Bros, 1944.

Major Reference Works by International Agencies

The publications of the International Bureau of Education in Geneva and the United Nations Educational, Scientific and Cultural Organisation in Paris constitute MAJOR REFERENCE WORKS in the field of Area Studies. None of them is suitable as a course textbook. They are essentially books to which teachers and students will turn for information about selected countries or particular aspects of education. One important feature about them is that the information presented is usually supplied by a government agency, e.g. the Ministry of Education in the country concerned.

In this field there are two types of reference work. The first provides similar data about education from a large number of countries. The lapse of time between gathering data, putting it into comparable form and publication date means that the information is bound to be somewhat out of date when it appears. The second kind of reference book attempts to keep readers up to date by providing each year a summary of changes in education from as many countries as possible.

Unesco's *World Survey of Education* is a typical and valuable example of the first kind of reference work. Over the years comprehensive information has been provided by member states about their educational systems. By 1966 four volumes had appeared. The first was published in 1951 under the title *World Handbook of Educational Organisation and Statistics*, Paris, Unesco, and in the introduction a detailed description is provided saying how the volume was conceived and produced. Each of 57 national entries comprised a short descriptive passage, bibliography, diagram, classification of school types and statistical tables. This first volume covered all stages of education. Subsequent volumes dealt with a particular stage, and were renamed.

The World Survey of Education, Handbook of Educational Organisation and Statistics, Paris, Unesco, 1955 was the first of what the Unesco secretariat hoped would be a series prepared at three-yearly intervals. Questionnaires or draft texts were sent to all States in the world. Most of the information was supplied by official agencies, and a few of the texts were prepared by the secretariat. There are 197 national or territorial chapters and these, as in subsequent volumes, constitute the major part of the volume. They are constructed on a common pattern in order to facilitate comparisons and generalizations. The introductory chapters clear the ground by discussing some methodological issues. Literacy as a measure of educational development is discussed. The percentage of the child population enrolled in school is another measure but difficult to apply; pupil-teacher ratios, the enrolment of girls, secondary school enrolments and public expenditures on education all offer possible ways of assessing the level of educational development. Some difficulties and tentative answers to them are presented in the first chapter. In the next chapter some assumptions behind comparative descriptions of educational systems are examined. At the time this volume was published 68 official national reports on education were published. They varied greatly in form and size. The analysis goes on to mention the shortage of reference books and to survey the literature in the field at that time. An attempt is made to select and describe the minimum elements of an educational system and to find ways of expressing some salient features in diagrammatic form.

Problems of statistical reporting of educational systems are dealt with in Chapter III. Five main types of sources were used for this volume: national publications of general statistics, reports dealing solely with education, reports from ministries and departments of education, replies to questionnaires addressed to educational and statistical agencies and from miscellaneous official statements. The framework used to provide information at the various levels—pre-school, primary, secondary and higher education—is discussed by describing the kind of institution to be included, age, grade and sex distribution, and the enrolment and attendance figures at these levels.

National studies are arranged under the following sub-headings: Legal basis, Administration, Organization of school system (pre-primary, primary, secondary, higher education, adult education), status of teachers and school welfare services, and in some cases trends and problems. Diagrams showing the progress of a child through the school systems are given. Statistical tables give summaries of the position in 1950/51. The data in these tables are not strictly comparable but enrolments, the number of schools and teachers (for the various levels, including higher), public expenditure on education, and the age level and distribution of pupils are given. Each chapter includes a glossary of terms and a brief bibliography.

World Survey of Education, Vol. II, Primary Education 1958 was intended as a self-contained work of reference as part of a series. As before it includes summary tables of school statistics for all levels of education using the same tabulation as Vol. I. This second volume gives a world view of primary education and a detailed picture of primary schooling in each of over 100 nations and in their colonial territories. The first aim is achieved through generalizing on the evidence of facts carefully collected as answers to questions about the extent to which children are deprived of the chance to receive primary schooling and about the progress made towards the achievement of universal primary education. The national studies are intended to give recent and accurate data about a self-contained system. The descriptive and statistical material is given in a uniform pattern to facilitate comparison. They are arranged alphabetically.

Self-governing territories are grouped after the States responsible for some or all of their administration.

Introductory international chapters trace in broad outline (1) the educational situation throughout the world between 1950 and 1954, (2) effective enrolments in all kinds of school as a proportion of the appropriate age group and (3) the progress of primary education since 1930. The statistics, graphs and diagrams aid comparisons.

The main headings in each of the national studies are (1) Historical, (2) Organization, and (3) Problems and Trends. The constitutional and legal bases of education are sketched in and a somewhat more extended description of primary schools given under pre-primary schools, curriculum and methods, examinations, teachers and welfare services. Diagrams show the agencies of control and administration and their inter-relations, and the possible routes for children through the system. Each chapter concludes with a glossary of terms, useful statistics and a brief bibliography.

The third volume of the *World Survey of Education*, Paris, Unesco was published in 1961 and dealt with *Secondary Education*. It includes over 200 national studies. The difficulties of presenting information about secondary education are greater than with primary schools. The compilers attempted, however, to present a unified and systematic presentation of the material so that comparisons can be made. Statistical tables give the position up to the year 1957/58 for all stages of education. Two particular aims of this volume were to give a world survey of secondary education and to give a more detailed view of all types of schooling or instruction at the second stage of education in each country of the world. The techniques are similar to those used in previous volumes. An additional feature of this volume is that the international section is greatly expanded. Three chapters analyse the quantitative aspects of educational change, first during the period 1953–57, then the proportion of school-age children actually in school, and finally the trends in secondary school enrolments since 1930 in selected countries. The first of four subsequent chapters describes three aspects of change in secondary education; namely (i) widening opportunities, (ii) the unifying of primary and secondary education, and (iii) the search for a balanced curriculum. Each of these themes is then taken up in a separate chapter. The last of the international chapters gives a bibliography of secondary education periodicals of about 50 national systems.

NATIONAL AREA STUDIES

World Survey of Education, Vol. IV, Higher Education, Paris, Unesco, 1966, as with others, was planned by the Unesco Secretariat and the detailed information about national systems was supplied by the educational authorities of some 200 member states. The two aims are to give a liberal view of higher education and to give condensed information about the provisions for higher education in relation to educational systems, as a whole. One difficulty has been to define higher education. In this volume it is taken to mean all types of education for which (a) the basic entry requirement is completion of secondary education, (b) the usual age of entry is about 18 years, and (c) degrees or diplomas are awarded at the end of the courses. Six introductory international chapters provide statistical surveys for the period 1957–61, the proportion of school-age attenders in relation to the appropriate age group and the progress of higher education since 1930. Chapters written by Professor Basil FLETCHER analyse the changing patterns of higher education, the human aspect of its provision and the different concepts and approaches to the planning of higher education in major regions of the world. There is a selected bibliography on higher education.

National studies provide a very brief description of the educational system as a whole, review the development of higher education by referring to legislation, administration and finance, describe the various kinds of institutions of higher education, how students are admitted to them, what range of studies is offered, what kind of research is carried out, and what are the trends and problems. As usual statistical tables give recent information about all stages of education, and educational finance. The usual diagrams show how children pass through a system of education.

The work of the International Bureau of Education in Geneva commenced in the 1930s. Since the second world war collaboration with Unesco has been close. Its publications have served the second of the two functions mentioned—namely it has kept readers informed about up-to-date changes and trends in education throughout the world. In 1966 the IBE listed some 300 publications as well as a quarterly *Bulletin of the International Bureau of Education* and an *International Card Index Service*. Important in providing recent information are the Bureau's *International Year Book of Education* and comparative reports based on the *Sessions of the International Conference on Public Education* held each year in Geneva. An *Annual Bibliography of the International Bureau of Education* is also published.

The information provided in the *International Year Book of Education* is based upon reports and evidence provided by representatives of the Ministers of Education throughout the world. The number of reports received has grown so that there were in the 1965 volume 93 national reports. Prior to this volume the general comparisons made in the year books dealt more specially with the direction of educational trends. In 1965 several changes were made in the comparative study at the beginning of the volume. A table index gives a number of categories of educational events and indicates in which national reports these may be found. Comparisons are thereby facilitated. The finance of education is then reviewed followed by the main structural changes and those which have occurred in the field of teacher shortage and training throughout the year of report. Main headings include *Administration, Quantitative Development, Structure and Organization, Curricula, Syllabus and Methods, Teaching Staff* and *Auxiliary Services.*

These *International Year Books of Education* can be used in two ways. By consulting the national reports over a period of years the trends of change in any one country's educational system can be traced. The information tends to supplement that provided in Unesco's *World Survey* (q.v.). It is also possible to see from these reports to what extent some issues are common to many countries and are being met in similar ways. There is a wealth of information, therefore, which is useful to teachers and students building up an *Area Study* and who wish to examine the trends of development in that country. Each volume also gives the names of leading officials in national ministries of education and statistical tables based on data collected by Unesco.

The annual reports of the *International Conference on Public Education* provide information based on a theme or themes of the conference, and collected from answers to questionnaires addressed to ministries of education. The use of themes makes *Cross-Cultural Studies* possible but the information is so arranged that teachers and students may find these volumes more useful in building up a comprehensive picture of education in selected countries. The topics are of variable interest but most of them relate very directly to aspects of the school system—administration, methods and content of teaching, teacher training, inspection, equipment, buildings and textbooks. The data are descriptive rather than interpretative.

Illustrative of this kind of study are the following numbered and recent publications of the IBE: 155, Secondary Teacher Training; 182, Training of Primary Teacher Training Staffs; 192, Facilities for Education in Rural Areas; 204, Primary School Textbooks; 280, Modern Languages in General Secondary Schools; and 254, Organization of Educational and Vocational Guidance. A list of

publications is given on the covers of most of the IBE publications.
A characteristic feature of the Annual Conference is that recommendations regarding educational reform are frequently given. These represent official statements of intention and have been collected in volumes entitled *Recommendations, International Conferences on Public Education,* No. 200 (1934–58), No. 222 (1934–61) and No. 246 (1934–62). These recommendations indicate the consensus of aims among educationists throughout the world in as far as such consensus exists. They constitute an international charter of education the moral authority for which rests on the fact that the recommendations are always voted upon by senior representatives of the educational authorities of the states represented at the Annual Conference.

National Area Studies

The collection of data by international agencies has certainly provided a basis in Comparative Education on which more detailed *National Area Studies* may be built. The number of books describing in some detail aspects of education in a particular country is growing fast. Two series designed to meet the needs of students may be mentioned. Pergamon Press has a series entitled *Society, Schools and Progress* which is edited by E. J. KING, and Routledge & Kegan Paul has launched a *World Education Series* edited by B. HOLMES. Both series will provide in separate volumes information on national systems of education.

The literature is, however, extensive, and relatively few national systems need be avoided through lack of suitable books. A teacher may nevertheless decide to select for special study one of the major educational systems in the world. Those of England, France, Germany, the USA and the USSR are important not only because they are found in heavily populated and highly industrialized countries but also because most other systems are derived from one or other of them. In the former colonies of Britain and France the schools reflect Imperial prototypes. Many national systems in Europe bear a resemblance to those of the German lands. Since World War II the competition between the USA and the USSR has highlighted the relative merits of the two systems of education. Any one of these systems is worthy of study.

An attempt is made here, however, to give an over-all view of the literature on education in the main areas of the world. Several methods of classifying this material are possible. Two criteria have been used, geographical location and political identity. Six land masses have been chosen and within each, nation states identified.

NATIONAL AREA STUDIES

Literature providing an over-all picture of each of the main regions are given at the beginning of each section prior to books describing in some detail the educational system of countries within the region. Relevant bibliographies conclude each section.

1. *Africa* includes books on Ghana and Nigeria.
2. *The Americas* includes books on education in Brazil, Canada, Chile, Mexico, Peru, the USA and the West Indies.
3. *Asia* draws on books about Burma, Ceylon, China, India, Japan and Pakistan.
4. *Australasia* includes literature about Australia and New Zealand.
5. *Europe* includes studies on the educational systems of Austria, Belgium, Czechoslovakia, Denmark, England, Finland, France, Germany, Greece, Ireland, Italy, Luxembourg, The Netherlands, Norway, Poland, Portugal, Rumania, Scotland, Sweden and the USSR.
6. *The Middle East* lists volumes on Iran, Israel, Turkey and the United Arab Republic.

The bibliography is obviously selective. The criteria for choosing material have been that it is

1. written in English,
2. recent, except in special cases,
3. written by comparative educationists or having a comparative basis, and
4. part of a series or published by an institution directly concerned with the study of comparative education.

These criteria are in short designed to ensure that students will be able to find up-to-date information in English and written from a comparative viewpoint. Publications in languages other than English have not been included, but wherever possible translated material has been included in order that a variety of viewpoints is available—a case in point is the USSR. Germany is an example where historical material has been given in order to cover the period prior to the post-war division of the country. Another example is pre-independence India. In the majority of cases, studies giving a general over-all picture of education have been chosen. Where the literature on education is profuse different types of material showing particular aspects of a national system have been included.

Since this and other lists are intended to help librarians and lecturers build up a comparative education library, special care has been taken to indicate all the various types of comparative education publications. Not every book is, however, listed. Where books on the same country appear in more than one series, the book in the series not previously quoted has been given. The publications of various comparative education centres have been included to show the range and approach of the particular centre, e.g. the University of Michigan, Comparative Education Dissertation Series. Once the details of one book in a series are known it should be fairly simple to track down the rest of them.

Nor is every book of an individual author given. Where a writer such as C. W. DIXON has several publications on a national system his book on Denmark has been omitted, because his most recent book on Scandinavia is included. A. NELLEMANN, *Schools and Education in Denmark*, Det Danske Selskab, 1964 is included because it is produced by the Danish Information Service. Whereas in the case of Norway, the book by H. HUUS, *The Education of Children and Youth in Norway*, Pittsburgh University Press, 1960 is included because it is one of the Pittsburgh University series, *Studies in Comparative Education*.

The annual education reports of a country have not been included. When obtainable these are obviously invaluable sources of information. Most governments make them available through their own publishing houses. Much educational information can also be found in Annual Yearbooks. The British Commonwealth countries publish yearbooks in English which include extremely useful and up-to-date data. Educational associations too often produce reports and other publications which give relevant information. Details of many of these can be found in *An International Directory of Education Associations* (Educational Studies and Documents, No. 34), Paris, Unesco, 1959.

Journals from foreign countries often have a special issue of education. Frequently it is illustrated and beginning students may find such an issue useful. In the concluding chapter a description is given of how such articles can be traced. General background books dealing with a country often contain chapters on education. In a small library it may be well to index such books analytically so that as much information as possible is brought to light in the catalogue. The smaller the collection the greater the need for exploiting every avenue of information.

The arrangement of the following annotated bibliography is: first, publications on the area as a whole, i.e. cross-cultural surveys; then books on individual countries within the area; followed by bibliographies at the end of sections that seem inadequately covered or are of particular value to comparative education.

Periodical articles are not included but there is a country index to articles in *Comparative Education* and the *Comparative Education Review* at the end of the chapter. The *International Review of Education* has been indexed from the beginning in the *British Education Index* and has therefore not been included here.

All the *Area Studies* given in this list are in the Comparative Education Library of the University of London, Institute of Education. All of them have been perused but not always read. Reviews and comments by friends and authors have helped in making annotations intended to give a brief summary of the books' contents, and some indication whether or not they have a bibliography, tables, illustrations, etc. Such information is intended to help when ordering a book or requesting it through another library. Teachers of comparative education may also find these details helpful when advising students which books will provide them with suggestions for further reading.

Inevitably, in this chapter as in others, a great many useful books have been left out. Those included should be taken not only as useful in themselves but as indicative of the kind of books which are available in building up satisfactory accounts of education in various countries.

AFRICA

Section 1. General

D. G. BURNS, *African Education, an Introductory Survey of Education in Commonwealth Countries*, London, Oxford University Press, 1965 was written for Africans training to be teachers who want to find out about education in other countries of Africa. It begins with an analysis of the social determinants of education in Africa—the change in social customs, the behavioural development of children and the important factors in planning. Chapters are devoted to the primary school, secondary, further and higher education, the training of teachers, the administration of education and the present achievements and future needs. Bibliographical references are given at the end of each chapter. The author draws on annual reports for much of his factual information.

L. G. COWAN, J. O'CONNELL and D. G. SCANLON (eds), *Education and Nation-building in Africa*, New York and London, Praegar, 1965 is a collection of documents, statements and speeches on education policy that show the need to relate education to economic growth. In the introduction which is a synopsis of the five parts of the book, the editors show the important place that education has had in the development of Africa as a whole and show the need for rethinking educational development in many independent African countries. Part I deals with education in the colonial framework; Part II with education and the nationalist parties including the relation between church and state; Part III discusses education and economic development and with the education, training and status of the teaching profession; Part IV universities and higher education and Part V is on education and social change. The bibliography is divided into main groups both by types of material, documents, surveys, etc., and separate sections for individual African countries.

L. J. LEWIS, *Education and Political Independence in Africa, and other essays*, Edinburgh, Nelson, 1962 provides a description of educational problems in African countries, and Ghana particularly, in relation to their development since their independence. LEWIS emphasizes that a 'partnership' between the British and American institutions previously responsible, and the Africans, now responsible for their country's educational development, must be established.

The other essays cover higher education in the Oversea Territories 1948–58; Anglo-American university co-operation; partnership in Oversea Education; the British contribution to education in Africa; education and social growth; social and cultural problems of urbanization for the individual and the family.

L. J. LEWIS and A. J. LOVERIDGE, *The Management of Education*, London, Pall Mall Press, 1965 is intended as a guide for teachers to the problems in new and developing systems. It examines the control, administration and finance of education in relation to the law, economics and planning. There are chapters on the government of education, as well as schools and government action, and the administrative art in education. The laws re children, teacher training and voluntary agencies all receive some attention. The latter part of the book is concerned with economics and education and educational planning. A list of references and a select reading list are included.

D. G. SCANLON (ed), *Traditions of African Education* (Classics in education, No. 16) New York, Bureau of Publications, Teacher's College, Columbia University, 1964 reveals how Africa has inherited a great variety of educational systems from Europe and America and suggests that African educators have to reshape this legacy in order to plan for present-day needs. Beginning with a historical review the author analyses past German, British, French, and Belgian educational policies in Africa. The following chapters are summaries of the main reports and educational policies of those countries in Africa including the Phelps-Stokes Reports of 1922 and 1925.

Section 2. African Countries

Ghana

P. J. FOSTER, *Education and Social Change in Ghana* (International Library of Sociology and Social Reconstruction), London, Routledge & Kegan Paul, 1965. The first half of this book deals with the historical background. After looking at the traditional social structure the author assesses the European influence and goes on to look at the dynamics of educational growth—the African demands for schooling suitable to prepare them for positions in society, influenced by the colonial employment structure, which was already changing as a result of a developing society. The second part of the book deals with the contemporary scene—educational policy since 1951. The social significance of academic schools has increased and unemployment has likewise increased for those pupils educated at other schools. There is a detailed investigation of secondary school pupils, their social background, parental occupation, ethnic origins, vocational hopes. The place of formal education in processes of social mobility is demonstrated and the problems that arise in trying to develop agriculture and technology analysed. The data were collected as a result of observation and there are no documentary sources listed in the bibliography. Tables and references are included in the text. The author hopes that 'this work will not be regarded as a study of Ghanaian education alone but rather as a case study wherein some of the basic processes underlying educational growth in states newly emerging from colonial rule are delineated' (p. vii).

Nigeria

L. J. LEWIS, *Society, Schools and Progress in Nigeria* (Commonwealth and International Library), Oxford, Pergamon Press, 1965. The author states in the introduction to this book that an 'attempt is made to put the provision of education with reference to the historical, social and economic factors and in the context of a policy of development which has as its main objective the attainment of self-sustaining social and economic growth for the nation' (p. 3). A summary of the background of the country and its people is given in the first chapter. The development of education from 1571 to 1925 and from 1926 to 1960 follows in the next two chapters, and then one on the content and methodology of education. It begins with comment on the Phelps-Stokes Commission Report which advocated a policy of adaptation of education to the environment in the light of religious, social, hygienic and economic conditions. Some of the practical experiments based on this report are described and discussions on the content of syllabi and criticisms given. The difficulties of disseminating information and constantly moving staff within the colonial service are shown to have been the causes of failure in many cases. Ancillary education services—newspapers, periodicals, broadcasting, television, libraries, museums, examinations, citizenship training, external aid—are discussed in relation to the problem in Nigeria and in comparison with similar problems elsewhere. The chapter on universities and teacher education ends with emphasis on the need for the development of African studies. The chapter on problems of adaptation deals with many diverse subjects such as methods of teaching, community responsibility, the international school at Ibadan which provides educational facilities for the children of expatriate workers, the demonstration comprehensive school for Western Nigeria and the curriculum studies project. The final chapters cover organization, planning, the control of education and future needs. There is an appendix showing the educational ladder in Nigeria and a short bibliography.

O. NDUKA, *Western Education and the Nigerian Cultural Background*, Ibadan, Oxford University Press, 1964 outlines the effect of Western culture on traditional Nigerian culture in the field of education from the middle of the nineteenth century to 1960. The author works at the contributions of missionary, colonial, and nationalist education to the development of Nigerian school education and makes some recommendations, not only for educational development, but also from the economic and social aspects of the country's future. He concludes with an analysis of the *Ashby Report* and suggests results which might follow its implementation. The bibliography lacks dates of publication for most items.

Section 3. Bibliographies on Africa

M. COUCH (compiler), *Education in Africa:* a select bibliography. Parts I and II, London, University of London, Institute of Education, Education Libraries Bulletin, Supplements V and IX, 1962 and 1965. Part I of this publication is a selective bibliography on education in the British and former British territories in Africa, excluding the Republic of South Africa. It is based on the catalogue of the library of the Department of Education in Tropical Areas, Institute of Education, University of London and contains material listed to the end of 1961 and includes books, pamphlets, and articles from journals. The material is arranged first by country, then subdivided into various levels of education. There is an author index. Part II is on French-speaking territories (former French and Belgian colonies), Portuguese and Spanish territories; Ethiopia and Eritrea; Liberia; and General African references 1962–64. The arrangement is chronological under each country with an author index.

SCHOOL OF ORIENTAL AND AFRICAN STUDIES, *Asia and Africa*. A select bibliography for schools, compiled by E. H. S. SIMMONDS, 2nd edn, London, S.O.A.S., 1963 is intended, as stated in the preface, as an aid to schools in their selection of appropriate and reliable books on Asian and African subjects. Books included cover history, geography, economics, political and social problems and the literature and arts of the various regions as well as some autobiographies and accounts of family life. Although intended as a guide for school libraries it is also a useful background list for training college students.

B. A. YATES, *A Bibliography on Special Problems in Education in Tropical Africa*, Comp. Ed. Rev., Vol. 8, No. 3, Dec. 1964, pp. 307–319 is annotated and is intended for the general reader. The selected material covers traditional methods, the role of education in modernization, technical and vocational education, education of women, teachers and their training, language education, community development and educational assistance to Africa. There is also an annotated list of periodicals on African education. The bibliography contains a number of references to books on childhood and bringing up of children in different countries of Africa such as B. KAYE, *Bringing up Children in Ghana; an impressionistic survey*, London, Allen & Unwin, 1967.

B. A. YATES, *Educational Policy and Practice in Tropical Africa; a general bibliography*, Comp. Ed. Rev. Vol. 8, No. 2, 1964, pp. 215–228 is intended for the general graduate reader in comparative education rather than the specialist. It is annotated and lists official reports and secondary sources in giving an over-all view of the history of education in Africa as well as contemporary problems.

THE AMERICAS AND THE WEST INDIES

Section 1. North American Countries

Canada

CANADA YEAR BOOK. Dominion Bureau of Statistics, Ottawa, Queen's Printer (latest edition), gives official statistics—annual of the resources, history, institutions and social and economic conditions of Canada. A whole section is devoted to education which deals with Canada as a country—most of the books and reports that come out are on one particular province. The Dominion Bureau of Statistics publishes a variety of publications including bibliographies which cover the whole of Canada and are essential to the research students studying Canadian education. This educational chapter in the Year Book gives the general educational background and includes up-to-date statistics.

DOMINION BUREAU OF STATISTICS. Education Division, Research Section, *The organization and administration of Public Schools in Canada*, 2nd edn, Ottawa, Queen's Printer, 1960, gives, according to the preface, 'The basic material used in preparing the chapters on the provinces consists of provincial school laws and regulations, reports of the Ministers and Departments of Education, reports of Royal Commissions when available, other accounts in encyclopedias, books, pamphlets'. Much statistical material is included.

J. KATZ (ed), *Canadian Education Today: a Symposium*, London, Toronto, New York, McGraw-Hill, 1956. The authors of these essays are teachers, principals, professors, superintendents, directors and university presidents and their joint work provides a contemporary conspectus of Canadian education. The essays cover various aspects of different levels of education in Canada. In this way all types of schools are covered as well as curriculum, social change, government and education and in some cases, such as curriculum, varieties between the different provinces. There is no supporting documentation or bibliography.

C. E. PHILLIPS, *The Development of Education in Canada*, Toronto, Gage, 1957 is both an historical and an interpretative account of education in Canada. It explains how the changes in education have come about since the early foundations of Canada and deals with various aspects of school administration, educational thought and practice, but not with higher education. The democratic aspect of educational development is the central theme; the place of the church, the central and regional authorities are considered in some detail. The curriculum, discipline and ethics, women's education, the teacher and the future are all touched upon. The bibliography lists material for the individual provinces as well as for Canada as a whole.

DOMINION BUREAU OF STATISTICS, Education Division, Research section. A bibliographical guide to Canadian education, Ottawa, Queen's Printer, 1964 points to the sources of bibliographical information including lists of theses, the actual bibliography is brief. Most useful for information on associations, centres and general orientation.

The United States

G. Z. F. BEREDAY and L. VOLPICELLI (eds) *Public Education in America: a new Interpretation of Purpose and Practice*, New York, Harper, 1958 is an introductory survey of education in America which highlights the causes of contemporary trends. Contributions are from seventeen well-known educationists writing on different issues. The underlying theme is how American schools have developed to meet the particular needs of the American people. Comparative studies have made them more critical of their own educational system and this volume re-appraises it in relation to sociological factors such as social class and race problems, the American school and the immigrant. Notes and book references are found at the end of each chapter.

C. A. DE YOUNG, and R. WYNN, *American Education*, 5th edn, New York and London, McGraw-Hill, 1964 gives over-all view of education in the United States for prospective teachers both in the States and other countries. The chapters are arranged under six main aspects of American education. (1) Its role in the world today. (2) Organization and administration. (3) Areas of education. (4) Personnel in education. (5) Provisions for educational materials and environment. (6) Interpretation of education. At the conclusion of each chapter there is a summary, suggested activities, that is, study methods, and an annotated bibliography. An appendix gives the Code of Ethics for the education profession adopted by the National Education Association in 1963, and a glossary of educational terms.

H. G. GOOD, *A History of American Education*, New York and London, Macmillan, 1956 presents a comprehensive and clear picture of the subject, suitable for study and general reading. Useful bibliographies and questions accompany each chapter. The development of education is traced from the time of the first British settlements in 1607 by showing how society adjusted itself to the new environment by transplanting many English ideas and building educational foundations on them. The books show how after the American Revolution in 1776 the society grew and expanded and inevitably, the parochial systems of education had to make way for State education, the private schools became public schools and the academies became colleges. The evolution of educational theories and ideas are discussed in the light of educationists involved, especially Dewey. Current educational theories and practices are covered and there is a chapter devoted to contemporary unsolved problems, such as adult education, religion and education. Finally a report on the White House Conference of 1955 is given.

E. F. HARTFORD, *Education in the United States*, New York and London, Macmillan, 1964 presents a broad comprehensive introduction to education in the USA for student teachers. It emphasizes the democratic basis of education in America by presenting the historical background followed by the development of the common school. The philosophy, institutions and programmes, the teachers, pupils and parents are all considered. The book is well illustrated and has many tables and diagrams. Each section of the book ends with a long bibliography and suggestions for discussions and ideas for individual study and a list of appropriate films.

E. J. KING, *Society, Schools and Progress in the USA* (Commonwealth International Library), Oxford, Pergamon Press, 1965 in the series 'Society, School and Progress', gives the background, achievements and present developments in American education. It is aimed at students of sociology, government and politics, as well as education, and purports to be an up-to-date survey. A major theme of the book is the place and influence of American education on the rest of the world. Ways for retaining this influence are considered. The organization and administration of education in America, including segregated education, church and private schools are discussed in relation to the historical background and hopes or pointers for the future. The attitudes and curricula found in typical American schools, with comments on how teachers feel about the quality of the school pattern, is followed by a detailed account of higher education. There have been several changes in government administration of education; the effects produced by these are discussed. Professional training of teachers and methods of extra study for them concludes the section on education. A chapter on social background follows, and deals with such matters as the attitude of parents towards children, children's attitudes towards each other from early years, and other relevant information on the influence of American family life.

V. T. THAYER, *The Role of the School in American Society*, New York, Dodd Mead and Co., 1960 reprinted 1963, presents an analysis of the public school and its function in American society. It is divided into four main sections. (1) American attitudes which explain the historical development of American education. (2) Contemporary economic and social trends. (3) Theories of learning which form cultural trends. (4) Critical issues in the contemporary educational scene. Each of these sections is broken down and bibliographies are added to each section for suggestions for further reading.

Section 2. Latin America—General

H. R. W. BENJAMIN, *Higher Education in the American Republics*, New York, McGraw-Hill, 1965 is divided into two parts. Part I begins with a comparative study of higher education followed by a history of higher education in the American Republics. The author emphasizes the regional approach to the development of education. Part II deals with the institutions, their people and their programmes. Many data are given in tables and there is factual information about all the principal institutions of higher education in each country of the region. In his conclusions the author analyses the present situation by looking at the various current provisions for higher education and investigating whether the needs of the people and a particular area's development are being satisfied through higher education. He examines trends and future possibilities and suggests improvements for higher educational programmes.

C. C. HAUCH, *The Current Situation in Latin American Education*, Washington, U.S Department of Health, Education and Welfare, Office of Education, 1963 (OE-14080 Bulletin 1963, No. 21) is a pamphlet giving a brief description of education in Latin America. It surveys the general situation and points out some of the major problems related to future development. An annotated list of references is included so that the reader can follow up the limited amount of material in English on Latin American education.

R. F. LYONS (ed), *Problems and Strategies of Educational Planning*, Lessons from Latin America, Paris, Unesco, International Institute for Educational Planning, 1965 is the product of a five-week seminar held in Paris in 1964 organized by the International Institute of Educational Planning. The participants represented a mixture of educators, economists, sociologists and political scientists. The aim of the seminar was to learn and to underline key questions and problems facing planners in all developing countries and to seek solutions. Latin America was chosen as a case study because of its considerable experience of educational planning. Five major questions were discussed. (1) What are the economic, social, political and educational conditions in Latin America which affect any educational planning; (2) how can educational planning be linked to economics and social development; (3) what internal changes are needed in education and how should educational planning facilitate these; (4) how can educational planning contribute to better co-ordination with external aid, and (5) what organization and administration is needed to implement educational planning? This study contains the most significant papers selected from those presented at the seminar.

PAN-AMERICAN UNION, Department of Educational Affairs, *Challenges and Achievements of Education in Latin America*, Report of the Eastern Regional Conference, Comparative Education Society, May 7–9, 1964, Washington, Pan-American Union, General Secretariat of the Organization of American States, 1964. The main object of the Conference was to take stock of what has been accomplished in education in Latin America. Since the whole area could not be covered in one conference, mainly challenges that were of interest in the international, as well as the national situation, were chosen. Chapters cover such topics as procedure and machinery for evaluating educational development in the Americas; the role of comparative education in international educational co-operation; a comparative historical review of education in the Americas; educational planning; the Latin American University; science education in Latin America; the ten-year plan under the Alliance for Progress; and a case study of Peru.

Section 3. Latin American Countries

Brazil

R. J. HAVIGHURST, and J. R. MOREIRA, *Society and Education in Brazil* (Studies in Comparative Education, No. 4), Pittsburgh, University of Pittsburgh Press, 1965 is based on the thesis that education is an agent for transformation as well as being shaped by social and economic forces. The material ranges from Colonial Brazil, Brazil as an Empire, Republican Brazil, the social structure, education and social mobility, socio-economic development, the state and education, the various levels of education, the family and education, the church and education, teachers and the teaching profession. Possible developments in the future are considered—such as curriculum change, demands for education and changes in attitudes and the practice of education. Standard Brazilian sources and those of foreign scholars have been used in research for this work. Much of the information about society and education was obtained from studies sponsored by the Brazilian Government Centre for Educational Research while the writers were co-directors of the research centre. Bibliographical notes are appended to each chapter and a glossary of terms in Portuguese is included.

THE AMERICAS AND THE WEST INDIES

Chile

C. C. GILL, *Education and Social Change in Chile*, Washington, U.S. Department of Health, Education and Welfare, Office of Education, 1966 (OE-14111, Bulletin 1966, No. 7) is based on data collected by the writer on two visits to Chile in 1960 and 1963. He looks at the recent Chilean educational developments and interprets them in the context of social and economic change. He introduces the study by looking at the physical and social setting, followed by a historical survey. He then looks at the organization and administration of the school system followed by a description of the various stages of education including vocational education, higher education, and teacher training. Educational aid from other countries is discussed. Progress, problems and prospects form the title of the final chapter. A number of tables and a bibliography of material, mostly in Spanish, are included.

Peru

A. R. FREEBURGER and C. C. HAUCH, *Education in Peru* (Studies in Comparative Education), Education in Peru, Washington, U.S. Office of Education, 1964 (OE-14104, Bulletin 1964, No. 33) is a booklet in the series and follows its usual pattern. The general background and educational development are reviewed and then followed by a description of the various levels of education including a section, in this case, on literacy and adult education programmes. Part III deals with the educational outlook—problems and trends and international co-operative assistance. A list of educational centres and services is included as well as a number of tables and statistics and a glossary of terms and a bibliography of English and Spanish material.

Mexico

C. N. MYERS, *Education and National Development in Mexico*, New Jersey, Princeton University, Department of Economics, Industrial Relations Section, 1965 is a part of a series on manpower, education and economic growth. It shows the relationship between economic growth and secondary and higher education. It indicates that in Mexico's history education has been the cause and the consequence of national development and that unless investment in education is planned it may hinder rather than promote progress. The author is of the opinion that Mexico cannot be looked at as a whole because the regional differences in development are so great, but one result of this area approach should be a better picture of the national development and needs of the country as whole.

NATIONAL AREA STUDIES

Section 4. Bibliographies on Latin America

L. S. KENWORTHY, *Studying South America in Elementary and Secondary Schools*, New York, Columbia University, Teacher's College, Bureau of Publications, 1962 is a booklet mainly bibliographical in a series of World Affairs Guides. The author has attempted to select a few salient ideas to emphasize, in order to suggest the outline of a curriculum for elementary and secondary schools and to point to a wide variety of resources covering books, pamphlets and films.

Section 5. The West Indies

S. C. GORDON (Compiler), *A Century of West Indian Education: a source book*, London, Longmans, 1963 presents some of the key statements about education in the West Indies between 1833 and 1933. 'The chronological presentation has been broken down into periods. There is a general chapter on education before emancipation, then a chapter on the period of the Negro Education Grant 1835–45. The next chapter deals with development when the Imperial Government handed over responsibility for maintaining education to the old West India legislatures.' When Crown Colony government was introduced education passed over to colonial administration. Chapters following this historical approach are then under the titles: teachers, secondary education, higher education and the heritage since 1935. There is no bibliography, the reports quoted in the text are themselves sources of educational history of the West Indies.

ASIA

Section 1. General

Muhammad Shamsul HUQ, *Education and Development Strategy in South and Southeast Asia*, Honolulu, East West Centre Press, 1965 deals with development, its meaning, implications and motivations—the economic value of education—educational planning—national plans—the philosophy, goals and basic features of education. The national plans for development in Pakistan, India, Indonesia, Philippines, and China are discussed. Problems such as education for girls, wastage in education, primary education, teacher education, curriculum planning are analysed in the final chapter with particular reference to Pakistan. The bibliographical references cover both economics of education and material on education in India and Pakistan.

ASIA

J. FISCHER, *Universities in Southeast Asia: an Essay on Comparison and Development* (International Education Monographs No. 6), Columbus, Ohio State University Press, 1964 discusses the place of the University in society in Southeast Asia. The author states in the preface that 'This monograph is a preliminary essay on the possible uses in underdeveloped countries of the university as a unit for social science analysis and comparative research' (p. vii). It is not intended to give an over-all description of higher education in Ceylon, Indonesia, Burma, Thailand and The Philippines, but universities were selected on the basis of a particular criteria—to demonstrate the extent to which these universities have a role in the nation's economy and development. The appendix includes a number of tables on such items as student enrolment, ethnic origins of students and a bibliography arranged by countries.

JAPAN, Ministry of Education, Research Bureau in Co-operation with Unesco, *Education in Asia*, Tokyo, Ministry of Education, 1964 is a comprehensive study of the nineteen countries taking part in the Karachi Plan. It is intended to provide reference material which may be useful to governments replanning their educational policies, and comparative statistics data are given about education, social, class and economics. Various graphs and structural diagrams are included.

UNESCO, *Report of Meeting of Ministers of Education of Asian Member States participaing in the Karachi Plan*, Tokyo, 2–11 April 1962, Bangkok Unesco Regional Office for Education in Asia, 1962. The purpose of this meeting was 'to stimulate and co-ordinate the action of co-operating agencies in the extension of primary and compulsory education in Asia—to examine the Karachi Plan in relation to educational planning and social economic planning—to review the progress made and the problems met in implementing the Karachi Plan: to discuss future implementation, to review external aid for the Asian States concerned and to discuss problems of co-operation in relation to this. A table gives a summary of the needs of Asian States'.

Section 2. Asian Countries

Burma

K. L. NEFF, *Burma Educational Data*, Washington, U.S. Department of Health, Education and Welfare, Office of Education, 1965 is a slim pamphlet which gives the main details of the basic educational system in Burma. A short list of references reveals how little has been written on the subject but indicates that some additional material can be found.

NATIONAL AREA STUDIES

Ceylon

W. R. MUELDER, *Schools for a Nation*, Colombo, De Silva, 1962; the author, an American educationist, states in his introduction 'This writing is neither intended to be an overview nor a survey. From a background of historical perspective, Ceylon's educational modes are analysed from (1) the organization and control of the schools, (2) the financial considerations, (3) the goals and curriculum of the public school institutions' (p. 2). The historical perspective, particularly the effect of Western influence on education in Ceylon, forms the basic core of the book. The legal structure of the modern era and the organization and administration are investigated. Case studies are made of five well-known schools. In conclusion aims and objectives, and State participation in education lead to a final comment on democracy and education.

China

S. FRASER (compiler and editor), *Chinese Communist Education, Records of the first decade*, Nashville, Vanderbilt University Press, 1965 is a collection of records of Chinese education from 1955 to 1965 and gives an insight into developments under Communism. The collection is from Chinese Communist and United States Government sources. Speeches, articles and official documents are assembled in such a way that they show the plans and ideology for all aspects of education which contribute to the remaking of China. The policies designed to indoctrinate the young and change established intellectual thought are discussed. Education is seen as a means for developing complete integration of all parts of society in China both in the combining of work and education, and in changing the outlook and attitudes of all citizens, although the need for diversity in the arts is also considered. This is a very comprehensive study of all aspects of the educational field in China and includes a very extensive bibliography.

CHANG-TU HU (ed), *Chinese Education under Communism* (Classics in Education No. 7), New York. Columbia University, Teacher's College, Bureau of Publications, 1962 is a study of education under Communism in China and is introduced by an historical review which emphasizes the continuity and lack of fundamental change over 2,000 years. The author examines the philosophy and principles of communism and in the growth of communist China, the place of education and its role in political thought and production. He concludes with a discussion on totalitarianism and a section of bibliographical notes. The rest of the book consists of series of articles and excerpts by famous

Chinese writers and political leaders. For example, there is a chapter by Mao Tse-Tung 'On the relation between knowledge and practice between knowing and doing' (p. 51).

India

S. NURULLAH and J. P. NAIK, *A History of Education in India*, 2nd edn, Bombay and London, Macmillan, 1951 summarizes the history of education in British India from the Charter Act of 1698 which required the East India Company to maintain priests and schools in its garrisons, until the Independence Act of 1947 when the British left India. Although the book covers a wide field some idea of the impact on education of the social and political background is shown. Major educational controversies are dealt with in some detail. What should be the object of educational policy, the spread of Western knowledge or the preservation of Eastern culture? What medium of instruction should be used, English, Sanskrit, Arabic or the modern Indian languages? What should be the method of spreading education, the direct education of the masses or the education of a few Indians who might pass their learning on to others? What agency should carry out the educational work, the missionaries, the British Government or the Indians themselves? Macaulay's Minute of 1835, Wood's Despatch of 1854 and the reports of the Indian Education Commission 1882, the Indian Universities Commission 1902 and the Hartog Committee of 1929, are among the main documents discussed. The main periods and fields in educational development are clearly shown and tabulated with helpful sub-headings. The bibliography is organized to list important books, to indicate some of the problems of historical research into aspects that need further investigations, and to offer a few suggestions to the reader who wants to know how to set about studying a particular problem in Indian education.

G. RAMANATHAN, *Educational Planning and National Integration*, London, Asia Publishing House, 1965 is a study of the structure of education in India, and policy in relation to national integration and, its influence on educational reconstruction. The author discusses such matters as crafts in the primary school, which he thinks should be linked with the academic side of the curriculum. He favours different patterns of secondary education running side by side with the possibility of transfer from one school to another. Universities should play their part in forming a national outlook. The language question naturally forms an important section of the book and there is also a chapter on Gandhi's thoughts on it. He discusses administration and favours decentralization. He supports a Central Bureau for the study and investigation of educational problems and emphasizes the need for improved teacher training. Basic education, the teaching of English and the development of Indian languages are all given in some detail.

REVIEW OF EDUCATION IN INDIA 1947–61, New Delhi, Ministry of Education, National Council of Educational Research and Training, 1961 is the first yearbook of education in India and reviews educational developments since independence up to the close of the Second Five-Year Plan and the beginning of the Third Five-Year Plan. The purpose of the review is to assess the past and to indicate plans for the future. The different States and areas of India sent in material so that it is possible to use the review for information in the educational scene in separate States.

K. L. SHRIMALI, *Education in Changing India*, London, Asia Publishing House, 1965 is a collection of speeches on various aspects of Indian education. The author was at one time Minister of Education in India. The book gives an over-all view of education in changing India and stresses its role in the development of a democracy. The author examines the basic problems of education, which are common to many countries—the problem of expanding education, the role of education in bringing about national integration. He makes suggestions for the improvement of teacher training and the administration of education. He looks at international organizations such as Unesco and Commonwealth Co-operation in Education and assesses India's part in supporting these organizations. He discusses international understanding and the need for education for peace. Special education and sports education receive some comment. The Third Five-Year Plan, basic education and technical terminology for Indian languages form the basis of the content of the concluding chapter.

Japan
R. P. DORE, *Education in Tokugawa Japan* (International Library of Sociology and Social Reconstruction), London, Routledge & Kegan Paul, 1965 gives an account of the school education of feudal Japan and shows that the Japanese were early aware of the moral, social and political implications of education. The curricula of the schools began to vary and by the nineteenth century western influence had already penetrated the classroom. Educational institutions were adapted to the political system but they also helped to change it. A respect for ability and achievement developed which laid down the precepts for the development of modern industrial Japan. The

traditional Japanese interest in moral education and the authoritarian attitudes to teaching have also carried over into the modern scene and created some of the problems that have invited research in order to replan the system. The book is very well documented and the bibliography includes a long list of sources cited, mostly in Japanese.

H. PASSIN, *Society and Education in Japan* (Comparative Education Studies), New York, Columbia University, Teacher's College, Bureau of Publications, 1965 is the first of a series of comparative education studies edited by G. Z. F. BEREDAY and is devoted to a study of schools in one country but combines all the techniques required for area studies in comparative education. Part I is a historical study showing Japan as an undeveloped country and deals mainly with pre-Meiji and nineteenth-century Japan. Part II deals with education and society in modern Japan. There is a description of the contemporary school system and the relationship between social class, the education, and between politics and education. The rest of the book consists of translations of important Japanese documents on education intended to be illustrative of the trend of ideas, controversies and official actions, and appendices showing diagrams of the Japanese school systems of 1937–1963 and a note on Tokugawa educational statistics. A glossary of educational terms in Japanese is included and a bibliography of both Japanese and English material.

Pakistan

M. S. HUQ, *Compulsory Education in Pakistan* (Studies on compulsory education XII), Paris, Unesco, 1954 has as its chief aim the study (one of a series sponsored by Unesco covering many parts of the world) of what remains to be accomplished in the field of universal primary education in Pakistan. It is based on available data examined in collaboration with the local education officers from different parts of the country. The book gives the early historical background and developments during the British period, the present status of primary education, compulsion, the law and practice. The chapter on special factors deals with the economic position of the country, the geographical situation, social-religious factors and literacy rates. Future needs include teacher training and all relevant problems. Among other tables the appendices give extracts from education acts in Pakistan, primary pupil enrolment, salaries of teachers. There is a short list of additional reading.

Pakistan Quarterly. Special education number 1966, Vol. XIII, No. 4. The whole number is devoted to education and deals with the complete range of educational problems. Statistics are included and it is well illustrated.

F. RAHMAN, *New Education in the Making in Pakistan*, London, Cassell, 1953, is a collection of lectures and addresses by the Pakistan Minister of Education. The speeches were made during the first four years of Pakistan's independence and show the effort that was made to raise the general standard of education, to deal with illiteracy, and to provide higher education and research facilities.

A. H. K. SASSANI, *Education in Pakistan*, Washington, U.S. Department of Health, Education and Welfare, Office of Education, 1954 repr. 1958, (Bulletin 1954, No. 2) is a report based on data collected by SASSANI in 1952 and supplemented since by documentation. The information was primarily intended for officials dealing with school transfers but the material is wide enough in scope to be useful for students of comparative education. It shows the role that education plays in the life of this new Moslem State. Chapter I covers the evolution of Pakistan, its language, people, population boundaries and government. Chapter II deals with educational development from the earliest times to the present educational administration, the subsequent chapters deal with the various levels of education but more space is given to higher education and includes some details of colleges, examinations and syllabuses. Charts and tables are included and a bibliography divided into government publications and others.

Section 3. Bibliographies on Asia

'*Books in the East* an annotated booklist in English, French and Spanish of books in Western languages on Asian and Arabic countries, has been compiled for the International Federation of Library Associations by Michael FODOR and is obtainable from IFLA/FIAB, c/o British Museum, London, W.C.1, and is free for Public Libraries. The list was commissioned by UNESCO for the East-West Major Project on Mutual Appreciation of Eastern and Western Cultural Values and hopes to introduce young adults to Asia. The list, of 107 pages, contains books in Swedish, Russian, German, English, Czech, etc., most of them originally published for adults but suitable for youngsters, and covering a wide range of areas and topics, but the multitude of languages sometimes means a country may be little represented in a language you can use' (*Bookbird* 2/1966, p. 22).

AUSTRALASIA

C. S. BREMBECK and E. W. WEIDNER, *Education and Development in India and Pakistan*, a select and annotated bibliography (Michigan State University Education in Asia series 1, College of Education, International Programmes), 1961 is a bibliography listing books and articles on education and development in India and Pakistan and gives fairly long annotations for each item.

K. L. NEFF, *Selected Bibliography on Education in Southeast Asia* (Studies in Comparative Education series) Washington, U.S. Department of Health, Education, and Welfare, Office of Education, 1963 (OE-14071). All the material listed in this bibliography is in English. It is arranged under individual countries and includes articles in journals and some reports.

H. PASSIN, 'Japanese education: guide to a bibliography of materials in the English language'. *Comparative Education Review*, Vol. 9, No. 1, 1965, pp. 81–101, is an extremely comprehensive and up-to-date bibliography arranged under broad subject headings.

J. D. PEARSON, *Oriental and Asian Bibliography;* an introduction with some reference to Africa, London, Crosby Lockwood, 1966 is primarily concerned with institutions, books and libraries which relate to the Asian continent.

South and Southeast Asia, a bibliography from Educational Materials Center Division of Research Training and Dissemination, Washington, U.S. Department of Health, Education and Welfare, 1965 is intended to advise in background reading on Asia and is meant for use in schools and colleges of education. It includes novels and textbooks.

AUSTRALASIA

Section 1. Australia

AUSTRALIAN COUNCIL FOR EDUCATIONAL RESEARCH, 1930 to date is a non-governmental body, engaged on education in a wide variety of fields. It conducts surveys and enquiries, makes grants to investigators, serves as a centre for disseminating educational information. It publishes reports and results of research and is also the principal centre for preparing and distributing tests used in the schools of Australia.

A. BARCAN, *A Short History of Education in New South Wales*, Sydney, Martindale Press, 1965 deals with the period 1788 to 1965 and has a wider connotation than New South Wales since the educational system of Tasmania, Victoria and Queensland were influenced by the developments in this part of Australia. Administrative developments, the political background, the growth of the state system are all considered as well as curriculum developments, teaching methods, private and church schools, and various levels of education. The book is extremely well documented with quotations from source material, includes a critical bibliography and is also well illustrated.

R. W. T. COWAN (ed), *Education for Australians: a Symposium*, Melbourne, Cheshire, 1964 consists of essays by thirteen Australian educationists on different aspects of education in Australia. It is intended for the informed layman and the student of education and covers all the major aspects of the Australian education system relating the traditional pattern to the problems and needs for future development.

L. H. MARTIN (Chairman), *Tertiary Education in Australia;* report of the Committee on the Future of Tertiary Education in Australia to the Australian Universities Commission, Melbourne, Government Printer, 3 volumes, 1964–65 (Martin Report) is similar in its function for Australia as the Robbins Report is for Great Britain. It covers universities, teachers' colleges, technical and other institutions. There is a good deal of evidence of a democratic and sociological type as well as problems of university teaching and examining.

C. SANDERS, *Educational Writing and Research in Australia 1960–1965*, a bibliographical review, Faculty of Education, Universities of Western Australia, 1966 (mimeographed) is a collection of reviews and bibliographies that appeared in the *Review of Educational Research* published by the American Educational Research Association. It forms an extremely useful annotated bibliography to articles and books on Australian education arranged in a systematic form. It is obvious from this that a great deal of up-to-date information on Australian education may be found in the *Australian Journal of Education*.

Section 2. New Zealand

NEW ZEALAND *Official Yearbook*, Wellington Government Printer (latest edition) includes a substantial chapter on education which covers all aspects and various levels of education, as well as useful statistics.

NEW ZEALAND COUNCIL FOR EDUCATIONAL RESEARCH, 1933 to date is an organization which concentrates on New Zealand educational problems and many of its publications survey critically aspects of education and give accounts of outstanding experiments in school practice. It also acts as a clearing house for information on educational matters.

SIR GEORGE CURRIE (Chairman), *Report of the Commission on Education in New Zealand*, Wellington, Government Printer, 1962 (Currie Report) covers all aspects of education in New Zealand today and makes many recommendations for the future. The *Thomas Report* 1944 dealt with the post-primary school curriculum, and the *Parry Report* 1959 was concerned with higher education. The three reports therefore add up to a substantial amount of information.

UNESCO *Compulsory Education in New Zealand*, Paris, Unesco, 1952 (Studies on Compulsory Education) gives the historical background, the development of compulsory education, a description of the school system, rural education, the education of Maori children, teacher training, the raising of the school-leaving age, education in the island territories and correspondence education. There is a short bibliography. Although rather out of date now, this is a useful short introduction to the study of education in New Zealand.

J. E. WATSON, *Intermediate Schooling in New Zealand*, Wellington, New Zealand Council for Educational Research, 1964 is particularly concerned with the history and development of a group of schools in a predominantly agricultural country but also deals with problems relevant to many other parts of the world. These post-primary schools were established in New Zealand in 1922 and the writer recommends their continuance on the basis of evidence collected. Although this view may be at variance with reforms in many other countries the detailed investigation of the problems of secondary education in one country stimulate further thought on others. The author concludes with an appendix on intermediate schooling in other countries.

Section 3. Bibliographies on Australasia

Education within the Commonwealth, London, National Book League, 1965 is an annotated book list which was prepared for the Commonwealth Books Exhibition which was held at Marlborough House in October 1965. The list includes works published both in Great Britain and in overseas Commonwealth countries.

NATIONAL AREA STUDIES

H. ROTH, *A Bibliography of New Zealand Education*, Wellington, New Zealand Council for Educational Research, 1964 lists 4,000 references which have been published in New Zealand on New Zealand education for the last 120 years. The bibliography is arranged in a broad classification and there is a chronological guide to government papers and an author, subject and schools index.

EUROPE

Section 1. Western Europe—General

COUNCIL OF EUROPE, COUNCIL FOR CULTURAL CO-OPERATION, *School Systems: a Guide* (Education in Europe. Section 11 General and Technical Education. No. 5), Strasbourg, Council of Europe, 1965 is a guide to the school systems of Europe including Finland. 'Each chapter consists of a short description of the national school system from pre-school education up to higher education; a simplified and a detailed diagram and an explanatory list of terms in the original language and in English and French'. Statistical tables of the number of children entering and leaving school are included. The book was commissioned as a result of a number of international meetings with the object of providing a survey which could be used as a basis for comparative study, of the different types of schools in the fields of general education, technical and vocational education and teacher training.

Education in Europe, a report on education in the countries of Europe, London, National Association of Schoolmasters, 1963 is intended to make available to teachers more information on schools in Europe. The countries covered are Austria, Belgium, Denmark, France, German Federal Republic, Holland, Italy, Luxembourg, Norway, Portugal, Sweden. In each case a general outline is given of the educational system, including such matters as all the various levels of education, administration, salaries, accompanied by a plan of the education systems and a glossary of terms.

I. SVENNILSON, F. EDDING and H. L. ELVIN, *Policy Conference on Economic Growth and Investment in Education*, Washington, 1961, II. Targets for Education in Europe in 1970, Paris, Organisation for Economic Co-operation and Development, 1962. Rapid technological development has hastened the need for organized information and for human co-operation to facilitate social adjustment to rapid change. Education is becoming recognized as an instrument for growth and an important factor in national policy. The European countries are faced with the task of reforming education to meet these needs. This report surveys prospects for expansion and analyses some of the main policy problems involved. Appendices include notes on sources, statistics, and methods of compiling statistical data for individual countries, and many diagrams and tables.

J. THOMAS and J. MAJAULT, *Primary and Secondary Education; Modern Trends and Common Problems* (Education in Europe, Section 11 General and Technical Education No. 1), Strasbourg, Council of Europe, Council for Cultural Co-operation, 1963 is a survey commissioned by the Council of Europe as a result of the Second Conference of European Ministers of Education held in Hamburg in 1961 and reported to the Third Conference in 1962 and revised by 1963. It constitutes an authoritative guide to present development in primary and secondary education in the countries which are member states of The Council of Europe. The authors assume that the educational systems of Europe have the same roots and face the same problems. The main problems (1) 'being the increase in the school population and the prolongation of school attendance, (2) the adaptation of teaching to the new economic conditions that transform the labour market and consequently the nature and standard of the professions'. The educational reforms of these countries are investigated comparatively. Compulsory schooling, the primary stage, the secondary stage and especially guidance, curriculum, methods of instruction and certificates awarded are considered. Many charts and tables are used to illustrate the text. Teacher training, finance, administration and higher education are not discussed. There is no bibliography.

Section 2. Western European Countries—General
Austria

L. VON KLEMPERER, Austria. *A survey of Austrian education and guide to the academic placement of students from Austria in educational institutions in the United States of America* (World Education series), Washington, American Association of Collegiate Registrars and Admissions Officers, Committee on Foreign Students, 1961 is a report intended to help admissions officers arrive at their own decisions on the placement of individual students. For this reason a picture of the educational system of the country is needed. A historical view is followed by a description of administration and finance. Various levels of the educational system are described with reference to curricula and systems of grading and promotion. In the section on higher education there is a description of the various courses of study. The bibliography shows that very little work has been written in English on the Austrian education system.

NATIONAL AREA STUDIES

Belgium

V. MALLINSON, *Power and Politics in Belgian Education 1815 to 1961*, London, Heinemann, 1963 states in its preface that 'as one Belgian puts it, [Belgium is] a kind of miniature continent, a synthesis of Western Europe. Problems that can face the larger nations of Western Europe are all fully represented here and thrown into sharper relief' (p. x). This makes it a very useful study for comparative education and the book has been organized in such a way as to emphasize this. It begins with the Revolution of 1830. The events leading to the emergence of Belgium as a separate nation are analysed. The ideological development is traced up to 1940 and this shows that education is a vital issue to all parties. Chapter VII is about the Flemish question. The second half of the book deals with economic factors, the development of technical and commercial education, with agriculture and the Belgian Congo. The chapter on the Belgian Congo gives a historical review and the factors which lead to the withdrawal from Africa. The appendices give a list of principal dates, a diagram of the school system in 1950 and the Schools Pact of 1959. The bibliography consists mainly of original source material in French.

The British Isles

W. ALEXANDER, *Education in England: the National System, How it Works*, London, Newnes Educational Publishing Co. Ltd., 2nd edn, 1964 describes the administration of the British educational system. It deals with the powers of the Department of Education and Science, the Local Education Authorities and Parliament. The place of the church and private foundations in the financing of the schools is shown. The various types of schools and education at different levels including further education and teacher training are described in detail with relation to their legal and social background. A chapter deals with the education of special categories of children and describes the psychological and welfare services. The concluding chapter deals with the balance of power between the Central Authority and the Local Education Authorities and the place of the free press and parliamentary government. It draws attention to the general principle of the 1944 Act to protect the freedom of parents in the interests of individual children and that parents can appeal to the minister should that prove necessary. The value of this in a democratic nation is pointed out, but it is emphasized that this does not mean that it should inevitably become a pattern to be adopted by all nations. The English system of education is a result of growth—some of the principles on which it is based may be appropriate elsewhere but it is unlikely that the total pattern could work in any other country with a different background and conditions. In conclusion, changes that have taken place during the previous ten years are discussed in relation to possible future developments.

G. BARON, *Society, Schools and Progress in England* (Commonwealth International Library), Oxford, Pergamon Press, 1965 has as its purpose the presentation of a descriptive analysis of changing purposes in English education—how education during the past hundred years has met the needs of an evolving industrial society. The book covers finance and administration of education, the school system, methods of teaching, technical education, teacher training and higher education. The need to produce highly trained technologists and managers is emphasized and opportunities for education and the development of the comprehensive schools to meet the needs of contemporary society are all considered in relation to the stability of English institutions. The book is also intended as a comprehensive account of education in England for oversea readers and is written within the context of comparative studies.

S. J. CURTIS, *History of Education in Great Britain*, 6th edn, London, University Tutorial Press, 1965 is intended for students training to be teachers and administrators. It covers the period from the fourth century to the present day, and covers all aspects of education in England, Wales and Scotland. The chapter on Scotland shows some of the ways in which it has been influenced by and has influenced events in England and is useful from a comparative point of view. The concluding chapter on recent developments in British education summarizes a number of recent reports on education. There is also a selected list of official publications from 1861 to date. The bibliography is arranged by main subject groups and contains a list of individual school histories. A date chart from A.D. 397 to 1964 supplies a useful reference guide to educational developments through the ages.

W. O. LESTER SMITH, *Government of Education*, Harmondsworth, Penguin Books, 1965 is intended to answer parents' questions on the government and administration of education in England and Wales. The first chapter deals with the growth of power in the central administration. The next chapter traces the historical development of the control and direction of education from the time of the Greeks up to the contemporary scene. The second half of the book is concerned with the inter-relation of society and education. Economic influences are affecting the centralization of education. Higher education has changed and is changing social strata. The concluding chapter is on international affairs with comments on international organizations such as Unesco and the Commonwealth Education Conferences. The author feels that a development of an educational partnership may be one of the important factors for making a more unified world. There is a selected bibliography arranged under main groupings as given in the text.

F. H. PEDLEY, *The Educational System in England and Wales*, Oxford, Pergamon Press, 1964 provides a straightforward account of the educational system of England and Wales for parents, students, and others. It is divided into five parts and a conclusion, bibliography and glossary of educational terms. Part I deals with primary, secondary and further education. Part II asks the question, who controls the schools? There are chapters on the Department of Education and Science, the Local Education Authorities, Managers and Governors and teachers. Part III deals with special services such as the school health service, education for the handicapped, the welfare services and some of the common problems that parents have to meet, mostly of an administrative nature. Part IV is concerned with the Public Schools and University, particularly types of schooling and ways into the university. Part V concentrates on the rights and duties of parents and problems that arise, mostly from deviation from the normal school arrangements. The conclusion deals with the public and the schools—the demand for more uniformity in better conditions in schools and like matters.

G. BARON, *A Bibliographical Guide to the English Educational System*, 3rd edn, London University, Athlone Press, 1965 is a comprehensive, annotated bibliography of the English educational system and includes material published up to September 1964. It lists reference books, periodicals, material covering education at all levels, various aspects of education, and a chapter which covers historical and comparative studies, sociology of educational institutions, the economics of education, the administrative framework, and descriptive pamphlets and books for the general reader. Each section has a short introduction, which describes the place of the type of education or institution in the whole educational pattern. This makes it of special value to the oversea student. There is an index of authors.

T. J. McELLIGOT, *Education in Ireland*, Dublin, Institute of Public Administration, 1966 provides a comprehensive description of education in Ireland, showing how the various parts of that system evolved from the early nineteenth century. Each chapter—on primary, secondary, vocational and university education—is followed by appendices of detailed tables, statistics, etc., relevant to the particular chapter. As well as the bibliography there is a list of Acts cited in the text.

A. J. C. KERR, *Schools of Scotland*, Glasgow, Maclellan, 1962 has, according to the author, as its main purpose making Scotsmen think in a more informed way about education in Scotland. At the same time he thinks that English readers may find some interest in a brief description of Scottish education. He deals with the history, the aims, content and methods of education, the grant-aided and independent schools, the colleges of education, teachers, extracurricular activities, conclusions and recommendations. The appendices deal with a variety of matters including education in Iceland and Jewish education in Scotland. There are a number of illustrations of schools, a glossary and a very brief bibliography.

France
W. R. FRASER, *Education and Society in Modern France* (International Library of Sociology and Social Reconstruction), London, Routledge & Kegan Paul, 1963 is about the dynamics behind the French educational system. In making plans for reforming the educational system there have been various obstacles, the administrative, the professional, the cultural obstacles. Should education in an industrial society be entirely anti-elitism, what should be the place of democratization, should there be specialization or general education? How can the balance between the humanities and science and technology be maintained? What is the solution to the religious question? Debates, speeches and arguments are presented but the author offers no solutions. The book is well documented with reference to documents, periodicals and books.

W. D. HALLS, *Society, Schools and Progress in France* (Commonwealth International Library), Oxford, Pergamon Press, 1965, in the series 'Society, Schools and Progress' it is intended for sociologists, the general reading public as well as educationists by surveying French education against its social setting. In common with other books in the series the work covers firstly the historical and institutional background then social, economic, and political factors: then the administration and organization and school systems. Accounts of the Langevin-Wallon commission of 1947 and the reform proposals of 1965 are included in appendices. A short bibliography for background reading is given in addition to the references in the footnotes. This book should be considered as an interim survey since French education is at present experiencing a series of reforms unlikely to be completed until the 1970s.

G. A. MALE, *Education in France*, Washington, U.S. Department of Health, Education and Welfare, Office of Education, 1963 (OE-14091, Bulletin 1963, No. 33), begins with a description of the general characteristics of France and its education system. The history of French education since the eighteenth century places emphasis on the Napoleonic era and the changes after 1945. A chapter is devoted to the administrative structure and the relationship between the national and local control. The nursery school and kindergarten are considered in some detail. The elementary school and academic secondary education are looked at from all aspects—curriculum, teacher training, new reforms. Vocational and higher education are treated in light of the social situation and future manpower needs. Special consideration is given to guidance particularly at the age of 12 and 13 years. There is a very useful bibliography divided into government and non-government publications.

Germany—Pre-war and Federal Republic

T. ALEXANDER and B. PARKER, *The New Education in the German Republic*, New York, John Day, 1929 gives a comprehensive and detailed survey of the educational changes and experiments inside and outside the state system during the Weimar Republic. Positive developments of the time were less the result of official reform than of private initiative on the part of teachers to overcome the stifling authoritarianism of earlier times. There is very little historical introduction, which could assist the reader to understand the significance of these moves, but the discussion of the changes is detailed and sympathetic. The contrast in interpretation of the same phenomena found in this book and that written by Samuel and Thomas (q.v.) affords valuable comparisons. The book includes a short bibliography and tables explaining the school system and organization. The index is excellent.

SENATOR für VOLKSBILDUNG, *Schools in Berlin (West)*, Berlin, Goebel, 1961 is a pamphlet about German schools written for the American student, so that variations and differences between American and German schools are emphasized. The first part is on the development of the Berlin school system since 1945 followed by a chapter on the structure and analysis of the Berlin school as it exists at present. It ends with statistical tables of information on Berlin schools.

T. HUEBENER, *The Schools of West Germany: A Study of German Elementary and Secondary Schools*, New York University Press, 1962 is a report made as a result of a three-month visit to Germany which was undertaken under the auspices of the American Council of Germany. The author introduces the survey by summarizing the historical background to German education. Then follows a chapter on the present educational structure which deals with all the different types of schools and the school building. The teachers, teacher training, pupils and the parents are studied under the 'human factor'. The chapter on curriculum gives detailed samples of various subjects taught both in the secondary and elementary school. The methods of teaching are looked at through the ways of teaching foreign languages, English, religion and political education. The chapter on reform and reorganization looks at the past, present and future with especial consideration of the Rahmenplan. The bibliography lists English as well as German publications. There is a list of courses of study and official publications and a glossary of school and pedagogic terms.

R. H. SAMUEL and R. H. THOMAS, *Education and Society in Modern Germany* (International Library of Sociology and Social Reconstruction), London, Routledge & Kegan Paul, 1949 traces educational developments, and the social forces affecting it, from the early nineteenth century up to the Nazi period. The historical aspects serve largely as a background to the periods from Wilhelmenian Germany onwards. Each chapter is concerned with a particular aspect, e.g. Universities, Control and Administration, and covers the complete time-span. There is a short concluding chapter on post-1945 developments. The bibliography is divided into a short section of English books of a general nature, and a second section of more detailed works, mainly in German. Many of the historically orientated works are still relevant. This book, written in 1948, is not free from hostile bias—not unnatural at the time; but it nevertheless gives an admirable introduction to the social and historical factors which have affected German educational development.

Greece

T. C. THEOLOGIS, *Modern Greek Education*, Aberdeen, Blair, 1957 is a brochure based upon a Greek manuscript and translated and adapted by Mr THEOLOGIS. It is divided into three sections—pre-school and primary education, secondary education and higher education. There is a description of Anavryta National School—a school of the Gordonstoun type which was founded in 1949. There is a section on the Children's Colonies which were organized in 1947 for the children of the Northern Provinces and their purpose was to prevent their being kidnapped by communists. After the need for these ceased the idea of community training for children was continued in the rural youth centres. The text is interspersed with illustrations and there is a diagram of the educational administration showing the Ministry of Religious and National Culture as the umbrella organization and under this the Educational Council and within that various Inspectorates.

Italy

J. JUSTMAN, *The Italian People and their Schools* (International Education Monographs No. 1), Ohio, Kappa Delta Pi, 1958 is a report written by an American educationist as a result of a year, 1956–57, spent in Italy travelling about the country visiting schools and studying the educational scene. The study deals with people, places and activities as well as educational matters. Part I is a social commentary, and Part II summarizes and discusses present trends and problems in Italian education.

A. A. SCARANGELLO, *Progress and Trends in Italian Education* (Studies in Comparative Education), Washington, U.S. Department of Health, Education and Welfare, Office of Education, 1964 (OE-14098, Bulletin 1964, No. 21) is a pamphlet dealing with the main educational changes and trends in Italy. The description of the historical background is followed by a description of various sections—administration, teacher training, higher education in the present educational system. Part III deals with current issues, problems and trends; among these are the Latin question, the Gonella Plan for educational reform, the Fanfani Ten-Year Plan, educational television and vocational and technical training. There is a bibliography of primary sources, general sources and periodical articles, and a glossary of Italian education terms translated into English. An appendix gives the educational provisions of the Italian constitution of 1947, and another lists the Italian institutions of Higher Learning.

The Netherlands

Ph. J. IDENBURG, *Education in the Netherlands*, The Hague, Netherlands Government Information Office, 1951 sketches the educational system of the Netherlands from the point of view of organization emphasizing the decentralization of education. It also gives a short description of the central educational institutions. Otherwise the various levels of education are described and there are chapters on technical and domestic economy training, agricultural training and school hygiene. Statistical information and references for further material of this nature are listed.

EUROPE

Portugal
U.S. DEPARTMENT OF HEALTH, EDUCATION, AND WELFARE, Office of Education, International Educational Relations, *Educational data: Republic of Portugal* (Information on education around the world), Washington, U.S. Department of Health, Education and Welfare, Office of Education, 1959 (OE.14008 No. 27) is a brief survey which includes a glossary of terms and a list of references.

Spain
ORGANISATION FOR ECONOMIC CO-OPERATION AND DEVELOPMENT, *The Mediterranean Regional Project, Spain.* Paris, O.E.C.D., 1965. This book is one of a series brought out by the Mediterranean Regional Project whose aim is to relate educational planning to economic growth and social advancement. In 1961 the Spanish Government in co-operation with O.E.C.D. set up a team to study Spain's long-term needs for education particularly with relation to man-power and the resources to meet these needs. The first chapter gives a summary of the educational policy for 1964–65. Chapter II is on the present educational system and deals with organization and administration, school population, output, the quality of education and cost. Future education needs are discussed in the next chapter followed by the future development which discusses policy and needs in various sectors of education. The final chapter is on expenditure. A great many tables and statistics are included in the text.

Switzerland
Swiss Schools, Switzerland, Pro Helvetia Foundation, 1962 gives an over-all picture of Swiss schools. There is no uniform school system set up by the Federal Government but the twenty-five cantons have rights that entitle them to pass legislation on matters of culture in general, and on education in particular. The people themselves take a great interest in their schools in their own particular canton and provide for requirements and serve on committees to deal with educational matters at all levels. There are illustrations of school types in different cantons with text giving some over-all information on such matters as expenditure, public and private schools, teacher and vocational training. There are some bibliographical notes which show how little material there is in English on Swiss education.

Section 3. Eastern Europe—General

J. S. ROUCEK and K. V. LOTTICH, *Behind the Iron Curtain—The Soviet Satellite States—East European Nationalisms and Education,* with a special section devoted to Mainland China by Dr. T. H. E. CHEN. Caldwell, Idaho, Caxton Printers, 1964 presents facts about national life behind the Iron Curtain and gives a picture of the education systems of these countries. The first three chapters of the book are devoted to discussion on nationalism and education, nationalism and the East Central European Bloc, and the Communist ideology. The following chapters are on Poland, East Germany, the Baltic States, Czechoslovakia, Hungary, Rumania, Bulgaria, Yugoslavia, Albania and Mainland China. The concluding chapter is of the educational outlook in East Central Europe. Bibliographical footnotes are included and some tables.

Section 4. Eastern European Countries

Czechoslovakia

S. VODINSKY, *Schools in Czechoslovakia*, Prague, State Pedagogical Publishing House, 1965 is a book in which illustrations form an important part. They follow the text which describes the school system through from pre-primary to higher and apprenticeship schools. There are a number of statistical charts. The aim of the book is to show how much the education system is part of the social set-up in Czechoslovakia and has been since the time of Comenius.

German Democratic Republic

Education in the German Democratic Republic, Leipzig, GDR, 1962 gives factual information about the education system in the German Democratic Republic as well as the social philosophy which forms the dynamic for the educational system. The various levels of schooling are described with special reference to science training. The book is well illustrated. The bibliography only lists books in German.

Poland

G. SINGER, *Teacher Education in a Communist State: Poland 1956-1961*, New York, Bookman Associates, 1965 makes the point in the preface that it is in teacher education that the philosophy of education of a particular country can be examined and analysed, especially in a country such as Poland where the education system is centralized and Soviet orientated. Since it is the aim of the education system to bring up future citizens of the state, the political and social attitudes of the teachers are of great importance. The aim of the book is to discover the forces which shape the Polish educational system as a whole and with particular reference to teacher training since 1956. The book is divided into six parts. Part I deals with the present educational system in Poland—the organization both at

Ministry level and the school system. Part II deals with the historical background till 1956. Part III deals with the organization of teacher education. Part IV analyses the educational curricula of training institutes, as well as teaching practice and textbooks; the influence from the East and West on textbooks and the need for new ones to be written. Part V is concerned with the educational reform of 1961. Part VI gives conclusions followed by appendices of tables and statistics. The bibliography lists primary and secondary sources with English explanations. A useful periodicals list is added.

Rumania

R. L. BRAHAM, *Education in the Rumanian People's Republic*, Washington, U.S. Department of Health, Education and Welfare, Office of Education, 1964 (OE-14087, Bulletin 1964, No. 1) was compiled according to the usual pattern in this series. It begins with a description of the country's background, followed by a description of the educational system, both before and after the 1948 reforms. One chapter is on pre-primary facilities, nursery schools and kindergartens. The chapter on elementary and secondary schools contains a number of tables showing numbers of pupils, teachers, etc., in different types of schools. The chapter on vocational and technical education discusses the first Five-Year Plan. Chapters follow on higher education and the teaching profession and youth work. There is an appendix on textbooks used in the 11-year schools of general education, a glossary of Rumanian terms, a table showing changes in Rumanian education between 1954 and 1962, and a bibliography arranged by type of material.

USSR

G. Z. F. BEREDAY, W. W. BRICKMAN and G. H. READ (eds), *The Changing Soviet Schools: the Comparative Education Society, Field study in the USSR*, Cambridge, Mass, Riverside Press, 1960 is based on a study carried out in 1958 by a group of members of the Comparative Education Society, USA, when they visited the Soviet Union for the purpose of investigating the educational system. Half of their time was spent in conferences in Moscow, Leningrad, Kiev and Tashkent, the other half was used to visit schools. The first part of the book gives an account of historical, philosophical and sociological background of Soviet education. The second part describes the organization of the Soviet school system. There are reports on all types of schools but the main emphasis is on the secondary school, particularly the move towards polytechnization. The third part of the book looks at selected issues such as special education for the mental and physically handicapped and for the gifted, education outside the school, character and moral education. The extensive bibliography is arranged both by chapters and in a selected classified order.

N. GRANT, *Soviet Education*, Harmondsworth, Penguin Books, 1964 seeks, according to the author, 'to present a bird's-eye view of Soviet education today' (p. 9). He intends it to be a factual account and to keep conclusions to the minimum. His own views are drawn from impression of schools and colleges in Moscow and Leningrad made on visits in September 1962. Factual information was gathered from books and journals now available in English on Soviet education and listed in an annotated bibliography. He gives the historical background to the Soviet educational system followed by the general outline of the present system. He shows the links with economic and technological development—the polytechnization of the Soviet schools. He writes about co-education and comprehensive schooling, the relationship between the family and the school, discipline and moral education and the various youth movements. The changes in the length of schooling, boarding schools, special schools and teaching methods are looked at. Higher education and teacher training are discussed in some detail. The conclusions and comments look at Soviet education in relation to other systems.

D. LEVIN, *Soviet Education Today*, 2nd edn, London, MacGibbon and Kee, 1963. The author taught in a Moscow school for five years before the war and has visited the Soviet Union a number of times since, both as an individual and as a member of a group. She has spent long periods in a variety of schools listening to lessons and talking to teachers and educationists as well as children, both in and out of school. She writes about Soviet education in relation to Soviet society and the role that education has to play in this society. She discusses such matters as school holidays, out-of-school activities, rewards and punishments, as well as school organization and the Academy of Pedagogical Sciences. The appendices include a lesson scheme for a secondary school in 1958, curriculum analyses for 1963 in various schools, and various syllabuses. Documents are quoted in the text but there are no footnotes or bibliography.

H. B. REDL (ed. and trans.), *Soviet Educators on Soviet Education*, Glencoe (USA) Free Press, London, Collier-Macmillan, 1964. This is a collection of writings in English by both famous and less famous Soviet educators. A. S. MAKARENKO writes on 'The problems inherent in Soviet school education' (p. 145), KRUPSKAYA writes on children's literature and the young pioneers. There are essays on heredity, sex education, the family, rewards and punishment within the family, parents' committees and other like themes, concluding with 'To inspire children'. A pioneer Leader's notebook. (p. 245). The editor has added some explanatory notes which weld the book together to give a flavour of the Soviet education field.

S. M. ROSEN, *Significant Aspects of Soviet Education*, Washington, U.S. Department of Health, Education, and Welfare, 1965 (OE-14112 Bulletin 1965, No. 15,). This pamphlet represents the results of a preliminary investigation of data on the USSR made before a visit in 1963. This information was checked and added to after observations made during this visit. It deals with trends since 1958 and especially the reforms of 1964. There is a table giving the curriculum plan for a secondary general labour-polytechnical school.

USSR MINISTRY OF EDUCATION, RSFSR, *Public education in the Soviet Union 1965–1966* (XXIX International Conference on Public Education, Geneva, 1966) Moscow, Ministry of Education, 1966. This booklet in English, French, Spanish, Russian is a brief survey for the 1964–65 academic year; statistics are included. Annual.

USSR NOVOSTI, PRESS AGENCY. *The birth of a vocation: creative technical work of children in the Soviet Union*, Moscow Novosti Press Agency Publishing House (1967) is a practical account of ways of introducing technical education to young children.

Yugoslavia

V. TOMICH, *Education in Yugoslavia and the New Reform*, Washington, U.S. Department of Health, Education and Welfare, Office of Education, 1963 (OE-14089), Bulletin 1963, No. 20. There is a statement in the preface to this work which says 'The purpose of this study is to present a factual and objective summary of the present legal basis, organization, administration and programmes of secondary schools in Yugoslavia, as revealed by literature, available documents, the author's interviews and observations; and to describe briefly the development of secondary education from 1946 to 1959, presenting the significant facts and events leading to the passage of the new General Law on Education in 1958'. This new law, translated into English, is an appendix to the study. The bibliography lists a number of articles and publications in English as well as Yugoslav material.

Section 5. Bibliography on Eastern Europe

N. APANASEWICZ and S. M. ROSEN, *Eastern Europe: a Bibliography of English-language Materials*, Washington, U.S. Department of Health, Education, and Welfare, Office of Education, 1966. This bibliography covers a fairly large number of relevant articles and monographs published since the end of the 1950s. American and foreign authors whose articles are written in English or have been translated into English are included.

Section 1. Northern Europe. General

C. W. DIXON, *Society, Schools and Progress in Scandinavia*, Oxford (Commonwealth and International Library), Oxford, Pergamon Press, 1965. This book is one of a series that is intended to serve students of sociology, government and politics as well as education. Therefore the first part of the book is devoted to a description of the background, social policy and welfare, politics, traditional and contemporary policy. This is followed by chapters on education in Denmark, Norway and Sweden. In each country the author deals with the historical movements and reports that have helped to formulate reforms and contemporary policy. The last chapter is on change and progress and deals with the economics of education; kindergarten problems; the Unity school; education and training; reform of administration; national policy and planning; social problems and international co-operation. The bibliography is restricted to works published in English but the author includes the names and addresses of official bodies for obtaining original source material from the countries concerned.

H. RUGE, *Educational Systems in Scandinavia*, Oslo, Norwegian Universities Press, 1962. This is a symposium of the school system in the Scandinavian countries meant for all those connected with schools—teachers, politicians and students. It was commissioned by the Scandinavian Cultural Commission and carried out by the Expert Committee on Educational Research. The last chapter is a comparative survey of all the Scandinavian school systems. The bibliography is arranged by countries; very little of the material listed is in English.

Section 2. Scandinavian Countries

Denmark

A. NELLEMANN, *Schools and Education in Denmark* (Danish Information Handbooks), Copenhagen, Det Danske Selskab, 1964. Written for the Danish Information Service, this book commences with a short outline history of Danish schools and is followed by three chapters on the primary school. The organization, teaching, training of teachers, and statistical information on the primary school are all covered. There is a chapter on secondary education which covers the historical development and the 'New Gymnasium' in Denmark. The last chapter is on home tuition, private schools and schools in Greenland and the Faeroes. A number of illustrations are included in the text and there is a short list of books and articles in English.

Finland

R. H. OITTINEN, *Education in Finland* (Education abstracts, Feb. 1960, Vol. XII, No. 2), Paris, Unesco, 1960. This abstract follows the usual pattern in this series and begins with a brief over-all description of education in Finland. This is followed by a note on educational research by Matti KOSKENNIEME. Then follows the selected classified bibliography giving books and journals with short notes and the language in which they can be obtained.

Norway

H. HUUS, *The Education of Children and Youth in Norway* (Studies in Comparative Education No. 3), Pittsburgh University Press, 1960. The author begins with a description of the organization and administration of the whole system of education in Norway, and goes on to describe in separate chapters the various stages of education from pre-school through to higher education for teachers. Dr HUUS clarifies the differences in the various types of schools at each level. A number of tables are included in the text which help to illustrate important facts. The information is based on statistical reports and directives and publications from the Ministry, current literature and personal observation. A list of schools visited is included. The author does not attempt to evaluate the schools as such but questions are raised and problems commented on. The bibliography includes school laws, published curriculum plans, school brochures and jubilee publications and journals.

Sweden

Urban DAHLLOF, Sven ZETTERLUND, and Henning OBERG, *Secondary Education in Sweden*, Stockholm, National Board of Education Publishing Department, 1966 surveys the reforms which have been introduced into the entire Swedish educational system below university level. The authors deal with the new comprehensive school against a description of the old system of secondary education and then go on to explain how the new structure of the schools will work. The organization of the schools is given in detail as are the curricula now being introduced into the various types of school. Up to date, well organized and factual, this book provides a good general picture of education in Sweden.

M. L. MING, and G. A. MALE, *Sweden: Educational Data*, Washington, U.S. Department of Health, Education, and Welfare, Office of Education, 1965 (OE-14034-78). This pamphlet gives a brief over-all picture of education in Sweden beginning with the history of Swedish education and followed by a section on administration, finance, enrolments, reform and the new comprehensive school, and of all the various stages of education, including pre-school. Art and music education, vocational education, higher education, special education and educational television are investigated. Tables include numbers of class periods for various subjects for various age groups. There is a glossary of educational terms, and a list of universities and degrees offered at each. The bibliography lists material in English.

THE MIDDLE EAST

Section 1. General

D. LERNER and others, *The Passing of Traditional Society: Modernizing the Middle East*, Glencoe, Illinois, Free Press, 1958. Based on a survey in 1950 of seven Middle Eastern countries by a group of native teachers and advanced students under the supervision of an American, the analysis was made by the Bureau of Applied Research at Columbia University. The impact of modernization on a traditional society, a Turkish village, is shown. A survey is made of the passing of traditional society in Turkey, Lebanon, Egypt, Syria, Jordan and Iran. The appendices include the questionnaire and the method used for the survey. Notes and bibliography are arranged according to the chapters.

R. D. MATTHEWS, and M. AKRAWI, *Education in Arab Countries of the Near East, Egypt, Iraq, Palestine, Transjordan, Syria, Lebanon*. Washington, American Council on Education, 1949. 'This is a factual document—a descriptive report of personal visits to 471 schools in six countries' (p.v). It is a descriptive report and recommendations have not been included. The last section is on education and cultural change in the Arab world, otherwise the educational pattern of each country is described. Charts and tables and illustrations are included in the text. There is no bibliography.

Section 2. Middle Eastern Countries

Iran

R. ARASTEH, *Education and Social Awakening in Iran*, Leiden, Brill, 1962. The writer who was educated in Iran but has also studied in the United States of America intends this to be an objective survey of education in Iran, looked at from outside but with an inside knowledge of the system. He begins with a survey of education in ancient and medieval Iranian society which shows the emphasis on physical education, it being part of the Zoroastrian religious belief that mind and body must be at one. It shows, too, the pattern of education in village and tribal life which was part of the social pattern of the group. There is a chapter which deals with education for bureaucracy and the civil service; another on education for citizenship, another on contemporary physical education and group affiliation such as Scouting. There is a chapter on teachers as agents of change and the role of education in the reconstruction of Iran. Missionary education includes medical education provided by missionary hospitals. There is an appendix that gives the important laws affecting Iranian education. Tables accompany the text to illustrate points made. A few books are mentioned in footnotes but otherwise there is no bibliography.

Israel

J. S. BENTWICH, *Education in Israel* (International Library of Sociology and Social Reconstruction), London, Routledge & Kegan Paul, 1965. This book is about education in both an 'old' and a 'developing' country since one half of the country is made up of immigrants coming from all countries of the world. The task of education is to integrate all these people and to revive the Hebrew language and culture. The problem of retaining traditions in a technological age, particularly when this involves religious traditions, is a major issue. As well as the historical background, the present school system is described in some detail with up-to-date statistical information. A chapter is devoted to Arab education and another to agricultural education and a brief description of the youth 'Aliyah' organization and Kibbutz education. In the concluding chapter the author discusses the problem of 'ends' and indicates a solution for the survival of the Jewish people.

Turkey

A. M. KAZAMIAS, *Education and the Quest for Modernity in Turkey*, London, Allen and Unwin, 1966. This study throws light on the westernization of Turkey through the medium of education. It shows both the transformation of the Islamic private system of education to a state secular system and also the role played by education in the social and political development of Turkey. Statistics, tables and a glossary are included and bibliographical footnotes.

TURKEY, Ministry of Education, *The Report of the Turkish National Commission on Education*, English edition, Istanbul, American Board Publication Department, 1961. The purpose of this report, which was aided by the Ford Foundation, was to investigate Turkish education as a whole. The Commission composed of experienced persons from all levels of education was set up to carry out investigations both within the country and abroad, to look at the education situation within Turkey with special reference to teacher training and to see how other countries deal with this problem. Part I deals with the basic principles of education and the state of education in Turkey today with reference to the social, economic and cultural position. Part II consists of observations and recommendations on all levels of education and includes such problems as the position of women in Turkish society and their education. There are chapters on the school system but otherwise no tables or bibliography.

United Arab Republic

A. BOKTOR, *The Development and Expansion of Education in the United Arab Republic*, Cairo, The American University in Cairo Press, 1963. This book presents an up-to-date factual picture of the educational system in the UAR. The author did not intend to evaluate or make recommendations. The first chapter consists of a summary of the educational development in the UAR. There follows a description of the administration, organization of the educational system and then of the various levels of education. A number of tables are included giving comparative statistics. The chapter on higher education includes a fairly detailed analysis of faculty teaching hours. The comments in the last chapter discuss centralization and decentralization, counselling and guidance, compulsory primary education, co-education, methods of learning, teacher training, foreign languages. The bibliography includes material in Arabic and English.

INDEXES TO IMPORTANT PERIODICALS IN COMPARATIVE EDUCATION

COUNTRY INDEX of the *INTERNATIONAL REVIEW OF EDUCATION*. Issued four times a year, edited on behalf of the Unesco Institute for Education, Hamburg and published in The Hague by Martinus Nijhoff, has been indexed from its inception in the *BRITISH EDUCATION INDEX* (q.v.)

COUNTRY INDEX to *COMPARATIVE EDUCATION REVIEW*. The official organ of the Comparative Education Society. Issued three times a year. New York, Teacher's College, Columbia University. Vol. 1, 1957 to Vol. 9, 1965.

Africa

CLIGNET, R. P., and FOSTER, P. J. French and British colonial education in Africa. Vol. 8, No. 2, Oct. 1964, pp. 191–198.

FOSTER, P. Comparative methodology and study of African education. Vol. 4, No. 2, Oct. 1960, pp. 110–117.

LEWIS, L. J. Education and political independence in Africa. Vol. 5, No. 1, June 1961, pp. 39–49.

YATES, B. A. A bibliography on special problems in education in tropical Africa. Vol. 8, No. 3, Dec. 1964, pp. 307–319.

YATES, B. A. Educational policy and practise in tropical Africa: a general bibliography. Vol. 8, No. 2, Oct. 1964, pp. 215–228.

EVANS, P. C. C. American teachers for East Africa. Vol. 6, No. 1, June 1962, pp. 69–77.

Asia

BREMBECK, C. S. Education for national development. Vol. 5, No. 3, Feb. 1962, pp. 223–231.

Australia

FOSTER, A. Teacher training in New South Wales. Vol. 6, No. 3,Feb. 1963, pp. 224–229.

FRASER, S. Recent developments in Australian higher education. Vol. 5, No. 1, June 1961, pp. 27–34.

Austria

DUDLEY, L. P. International schools in Vienna. Vol. 7, No. 3, Feb. 1964, pp. 286–296.

NATIONAL AREA STUDIES

Belgium
MALLINSON, V., and DE COSTER, S. Church and state education in Belgium. Vol. 4, No. 1, June 1960, pp. 43–48.
SEIF, N. S. The teaching of modern languages in Belgium, England, Holland and Germany. Vol. 9, No. 2, June 1965, pp. 163–169.

Brazil
KIMBALL, S. T. Primary education in Brazil. Vol. 4, No. 1, June 1960, pp. 49–54.
MOREIRA, J. R. Some social aspects of Brazilian education. Vol. 4, No. 2, Oct. 1960, pp. 93–96.

Burma
FISCHER, J. Education and political modernisation in Burma and Indonesia. Vol. 9, No. 3, Oct. 1965, pp. 282–287.

Canada
ARRICALE, F. C. Varieties of church-state relations in Canadian education. Vol. 7, No. 1, June 1963, pp. 36–42.
CHEAL, J. E. Factors related to educational output differences among the Canadian provinces. Vol. 6, No. 2, Oct. 1962, pp. 120–126.
DOWNEY, L. W. The task of the public school in the United States and Canada. Vol. 4, No. 2, Oct. 1960, pp. 118–120.
KATZ, J. Comparative education and external aid programmes in Canada. Vol. 6, No. 1, June 1962, pp. 12–15.
MACDONALD, J. The social ideas of Canadian educators. Vol. 9, No. 1, Feb. 1965, pp. 38–45.
MAGNUSON, R. P. Secular trends in French Canadian education. Vol. 7, No. 1, June 1963, pp. 43–46.
NASH, P. Quality and equality in Canadian education. Vol. 5, No. 2, Oct. 1961, pp. 118–129.
ROHNER, R. P. Factors influencing the academic performance of Kwakiutl children in Canada. Vol. 9, No. 3, Oct. 1965, pp. 331–340.

Ceylon
RYAN, B. The dilemmas of education in Ceylon. Vol. 4, No. 2, Oct. 1960, pp. 84–92.

China
BIGELOW, K. W. Some comparative reflections on Soviet and Chinese higher education. Vol. 4, No. 3, Feb. 1961, pp. 169–173.
FRASER, S. E., and WEI, C. Training targets and teaching plans of advanced engineering schools in China. Vol. 8, No. 3, Dec. 1964, pp. 334–339.
HU, C. T. Higher education in mainland China. Vol. 4, No. 3, Feb. 1961, pp. 159–168.
KLEPIKOV, V., and CHABE, A. M. The preparation of school reform in China. Vol. 7, No. 1, June 1963, pp. 74–79.
LAUWERYS, J. A. Problems of educational policy in communist China. Vol. 1, No. 2, Oct. 1957, pp. 4–6.

INDEXES TO IMPORTANT PERIODICALS

Congo
YATES, B. A. Structural problems in education in the Congo (Leopoldville). Vol. 7, No. 2, Oct. 1963, pp. 152–162.

Denmark
CANFIELD, A. T. Folk high schools in Denmark and Sweden: a comparative analysis. Vol. 9, No. 1, Feb. 1965, pp. 18–24.

Ethiopia
GILLET, M. Western academic role concepts in Ethiopian University. Vol. 7, No. 2, Oct. 1963, pp. 149–151.
WODAJO, M. Postwar reform in Ethiopian education. Vol. 2, No. 3, Feb. 1959, pp. 24–30.

Europe: East
ROUCEK, J. S. Juvenile delinquency and crime in the Soviet bloc. Vol. 3, No. 3, Feb. 1960, pp. 40–47.

Europe: West
ANDERSON, D. Geographic and economic factors and the development of educational systems in Western Europe. Vol. 9, No. 2, June 1965, pp. 147–154.
FAHMY, M. S. Technical education in Western Europe. Vol. 9, No. 2, June 1965, pp. 155–162.
KETTELKAMP, G. C. Foreign language teaching in Western Europe and Central United States. Vol. 5, No. 1, June 1961, pp. 63–65.

Far East
CHU, YU-KUANG. General education and cultural change in the Far East. Vol. 4, No. 1, June 1960, pp. 35–42.

Finland
KYÖSTIÖ, O. K. Contemporary Finnish school legislation. Vol. 5, No. 2, Oct. 1961, pp. 130–135.

France
DOBINSON, C. H. French educational reform. Vol. 3, No. 1, June 1959, pp. 5–14.
FRASER, W. R. Progress in French school reform. Vol. 7, No. 3, Feb. 1964, pp. 273–278.
GUTERMAN, S. L. The 'Church-School question' in England and France. Vol. 7, No. 1, June 1963, pp. 28–35.
HANS, N. State and church in education in Italy and France. Vol. 1, No. 3, Feb. 1958, pp. 10–12.
JOLLY, R. Regional training centre for secondary school teachers in France. Vol. 2, No. 3, Feb. 1959, pp. 14–17.

German Democratic Republic
HOFMANN, E. The changing school in East Germany. Vol. 6, No. 1, June 1962, pp. 48–57.

NATIONAL AREA STUDIES

German Democratic Republic (continued)

LOTTICH, K. V. Extracurricular indoctrination in East Germany. Vol. 6, No. 3, Feb. 1963, pp. 209–211.

German Federal Republic

ANWEILER, O. The study of Soviet and East European education in West Germany. Vol. 9, No. 3, Oct. 1965, pp. 341–345.

BRICKMAN, W. W. Some review data on history of German education. Vol. 8, No. 3, Dec. 1964, pp. 281–284.

BUNN, R. F. Treatment of Hitler's rise to power in West German school textbooks. Vol. 6, No. 1, June 1962, pp. 34–43.

EDDING, F. The university enrolment in West Germany. Vol. 9, No. 1, Feb. 1965, pp. 5–10.

ENDERWITZ, H. Two German education reform schemes: the Rahmenplan and the Bremerplan. Vol. 7, No. 1, June 1963, pp. 47–50.

HAHN, W. Higher education in West Germany; reform movements and trends. Vol. 7, No. 1, June 1963, pp. 51–60.

HAHN, W. West Germany's secondary school preparation. Vol. 9, No. 3, Oct. 1965, pp. 346–355.

HILKER, F. Comparative education in the documentation and information center in Bonn. Vol. 3, No. 3, Feb. 1960, pp. 13–15.

HOFMANN, H. School psychology in Germany. Vol. 3, No. 1, June 1959, pp. 23–26.

HUEBENER, T. Proposed reforms in the German schools. Vol. 6, No. 1, June 1962, pp. 44-47.

HYLLA, E. Recent developments in education in the Federal Republic of Germany. Vol. 2, No. 1, June 1958, pp. 12–16.

KIRKPATRICK, U. The Rahmenplan for West German school reform. Vol. 4, No. 1, June 1960, pp. 18–25.

LAWSON, R. F. The English approach to educational re-orientation in post-war Germany. Vol. 8, No. 1, June 1964, pp. 58–64.

PRESTON, R. C. Issues raised by the Weisbaden-Philadelphia reading study. Vol. 7, No. 1, June 1963, pp. 61–65.

SCANLON, D. G. Some comparative reflections on German and Italian school reforms. Vol. 4, No. 1, June 1960, pp. 31–34.

SEIF, N. S. The teaching of modern languages in Belgium, England, Holland and Germany. Vol. 9, No. 2, June 1965, pp.163–169.

SHAFER, S. M. American social studies in West German schools. Vol. 8, No. 2, Oct. 1964, pp. 146–152.

SPRINGER, U. K. West Germany's turn to 'Bildungspolitik' in educational planning. Vol. 9, No. 1, Feb. 1965, pp. 11–17.

Ghana

FOSTER, P. J. Ethnicity and the schools in Ghana. Vol. 6, No. 2, Oct. 1962, pp. 127–135.

WILLIAMS, T. D. Sir Gordon Guggisberg and educational reforms in the Gold Coast 1919–1927. Vol. 8, No. 3, Dec. 1964, pp. 290–306.

INDEXES TO IMPORTANT PERIODICALS

Great Britain: England and Wales

ARMYTAGE, W. H. G. Foreign influence in English universities: four case histories. Vol. 7, No. 3, Feb. 1964, pp. 246–261.

BATT, J. Compulsory and free education: a content analysis of nineteenth-century British opinion. Vol. 6, No. 2, Oct. 1962, pp. 93–96.

BENTLEY, A. Music education in England. Vol. 9, No. 2, June 1965, pp. 186–194.

BIDWELL, C. E., and KAZAMIAS, A. M. Religion, politics and popular education: an historical comparison of England and America. Vol. 6, No.2, Oct. 1962, pp. 97–110.

CLARK, A. J. Graduate study in education at Oxford. Vol. 6, No. 3, Feb. 1963, pp. 238–242.

DALVI, M. A. A historical survey of commercial education in England 1543–1902. Vol. 9, No. 2, June 1965, pp. 170–176.

ECKSTEIN, M. Britain's white paper on education and its implications. Vol. 3, No. 1, June 1959, pp. 14–20.

GUTERMAN, S. L. The 'Church-School question' in England and France. Vol. 7, No. 1, June 1963, pp. 28–35.

HANSEN, G. B. 'Separate but Equal': some myths and realities of English secondary education. Vol. 9, No. 3, Oct. 1965, pp. 356–365.

KING, E. Comprehensive schools in England: their prospects. Vol. 3, No. 3, Feb. 1960, pp. 16–21.

KING, E. Comprehensive schools in England: their context. Vol. 3, No. 2, Oct. 1959, pp.13–19.

LLOYD, J. W. British and American education in cultural perspective. Vol. 6, No. 1, June 1962, pp. 16–24.

NOEL, E. W. Sponsored and contest mobility in America and England: a rejoinder to Ralph H. Turner. Vol. 6, No. 2, Oct. 1962, pp. 148–151.

PASSOW, A. H. After Crowther—what? Vol. 5, No. 3, Feb. 1962, pp. 175–181.

REE, H. A. The new universities in Britain. Vol. 8, No. 1, June 1964, pp. 94–97.

SEIF, N. S. The teaching of modern languages in Belgium, England, Holland and Germany. Vol. 9, No. 2, June 1965, pp. 163–169.

STEPHENS, W. B. The new deal for higher technical education in England. Vol. 4, No. 1, June 1960, pp. 55–60.

Great Britain: Scotland

JACOBSON, E. S. Junior secondary education in Scotland. Vol. 5, No. 3, Feb. 1962, pp. 208–211.

Greece

KAZAMIAS, A. M. The 'Renaissance' of Greece secondary education. Vol. 3, No. 3, Feb. 1960, pp. 22–27.

Guatemala

MACVEAN, R. B., and NIEVES, F. C. Educational re-organisation in Guatemala. Vol. 1, No. 3, Feb. 1958, pp. 18–24.

NATIONAL AREA STUDIES

Guatemala (continued)

WILLIAMS, T. D. Wastage rates and teacher quality in Guatemala primary schools. Vol. 9, No. 1, Feb. 1965, pp. 46–52.

Guinea, Republic of

STERN, T. N. Political aspects of Guinean education. Vol. 8, No. 1, June 1964, pp. 98–103.

Hong Kong

CRAMER, J. F. The Chinese colleges in Hong Kong. Vol. 3, No. 1, June 1959, pp. 26–29.

India

LUX, D. G. Technical education in India. Vol. 7, No. 3, Feb. 1964. pp. 301–306.
SCHLESINGER, B. Student unrest in Indian universities. Vol. 6, No. 3, Feb. 1963, pp. 218–223.

Indonesia

FISCHER, J. Education and political modernisation in Burma and Indonesia. Vol. 9, No. 3, Oct. 1965, pp. 282–287.
SARUMPAET, J. P. New era in Indonesian education. Vol. 7, No. 1, June 1963, pp. 66–73.
VAN DER KROEF, J. M. Social dysfunctions of Indonesian education. Vol. 2, No. 2, Oct. 1958, pp. 15–20.
WILLIAMS, L. E. Nationalistic indoctrination in the Chinese minority schools of Indonesia. Vol. 1, No. 3, Feb. 1958, pp. 12–17.

Iran

AFZAL, M. Problems of secondary education in Iran. Vol. 6, No. 2, Oct. 1962, pp. 86–92.
ARASTEH, R. Growth of modern education in Iran. Vol. 3, No. 3, Feb. 1960, pp. 33–40.

Ireland: Eire

ATKINSON, N. The school structure in the Republic of Ireland. Vol. 8, No. 3, Dec. 1964, pp. 276–281.

Israel

BELSKY, F. Religion and education in Israel. Vol. 2, No. 1, June 1958, pp. 22–27.
ROBINSOHN, S. B. Problems of education in Israel. Vol. 7, No. 2, Oct. 1963, pp. 125–141.

INDEXES TO IMPORTANT PERIODICALS

Italy

BORGHI, L., and SCARANGELLO, A. Italy's ten-year education plan. Vol. 4, No. 1, June 1960, pp. 26–30.
HANS, N. State and church in education in Italy and France. Vol. 1, No. 3, Feb. 1958, pp. 10–12.
SCANLON, D. G. Some comparative reflections on German and Italian school reforms. Vol. 4, No. 1, June 1960. pp. 31–34.
SCARANGELLO, A. Church and state in Italian education. Vol. 5, No. 3, Feb. 1962, pp. 199–207.
SCARANGELLO, A. Italian universities today. Vol. 1, No. 1, June 1957, pp. 10–12.

Japan

ADAMS, D. Rebirth of moral education in Japan. Vol. 4, No. 1, June 1960, pp. 61–64.
ALTBACH, P. G. Japanese students and Japanese politics. Vol. 7, No. 2, Oct. 1963, pp. 181–188.
DUKE, B. C. The irony of Japanese postwar education. Vol. 6, No. 3, Feb. 1963, pp. 212–217.
DUKE, B. C. The new guide for teaching moral education in Japan. Vol. 8, No. 2, Oct. 1964, pp. 186–190.
KOBAYASHI, T. How to visit Japanese schools. Vol. 8, No. 1, June 1964, pp. 65–72.
KOBAYASHI, T. Tokugawa education as a foundation of modern education in Japan. Vol. 9, No. 3, Oct. 1965, pp. 288–302.
MITSUHASHI, S. Conceptions and images of the physical world: a comparison of Japanese and American pupils. Vol. 6, No. 2, Oct. 1962, pp. 142–147.
PASSIN, H. Japanese education; guide to a bibliography of materials in the English language. Vol. 9, No. 1, Feb. 1965, pp. 81–101.
SHIMBORI, M. A historical and social note on moral education in Japan. Vol. 4, No. 2, Oct. 1960, pp. 97–101.

Kenya

ANDERSON, J. E. The Kenya education commission report: an African view of educational planning. Vol. 9, No. 2, June 1965, pp. 201–207.

Korea

ADAMS, D. Problems of reconstruction in Korean education. Vol. 3, No. 3, Feb. 1960, pp. 27–32.

Latin America

BURNS, H. W. Social class and education in Latin America. Vol. 6, No. 3, Feb. 1963, pp. 230–237.
DAVIS, R. G. Prototypes and stereotypes in Latin American universities. Vol. 9, No. 3, Oct. 1965, pp. 275–281.

NATIONAL AREA STUDIES

Latin America (continued)

FITZGERALD, D. T. The significance of American schools in Latin America. Vol. 1, No. 2, Oct. 1957, pp. 19–22.
HANS, N. Comparative study of Latin America. Vol. 5, No. 1, June 1961, pp. 17–26.
HAVIGHURST, J. R. Latin America and North American higher education. Vol. 4, No. 3, Feb. 1961, pp. 174–182.
HAVIGHURST, R. J., and ABREU, J. The problem of secondary education in Latin America. Vol. 5, No. 3, Feb. 1962, pp. 167–174.
LARREA, J. Random thoughts on economic basis of education in Latin America. Vol. 7, No. 2, Oct. 1963, pp. 163–165.
NITSCH, M. Fundamental integral education: radio schools in Latin America. Vol. 8, No. 3, Dec. 1964, pp. 340–343.

Malaya

KOH, E. K. American educational policy in the Philippines and the British policy in Malaya, 1898–1935. Vol. 9, No. 2, June 1965, pp. 139–146.

Middle East

ABDUL-HADI, Mohammed. The new trends in Arab education. Vol. 1, No. 3, Feb. 1958, pp. 24–31.

Mongolian People's Republic

KRUEGER, J. R. Education in the Mongolian People's Republic. Vol. 4, No. 3, Feb. 1961, pp. 183–187.

Netherlands

MAAS, J. Van Lutsenburg. The 'Mammoth Law' reforms in Dutch education. Vol. 7, No. 3, Feb. 1964, pp. 279–285.
SEIF, N. S. The teaching of modern languages in Belgium, England, Holland and Germany. Vol. 9, No. 2, June 1965, pp. 163–169.
WILSON, N. H. Dutch schools and religious segmentation. Vol. 3, No. 2, Oct. 1959, pp. 19–24.
VELEMA, E. Primary and post-primary education in the Netherlands. Vol. 7, No. 2, Oct. 1963, pp. 119–124.

New Zealand

BEEBY, C. E. Stages in the growth of a primary education system. Vol. 6, No. 1, June 1962, pp. 2–11.
DUNCAN, E. R. Teaching arithmetic in the United States and New Zealand. Vol. 5, No. 1, June 1961, pp. 59–62.
MITCHELL, F. W. Religious instruction and observances in the public schools of New Zealand. Vol. 7, No. 3, Feb. 1964, pp. 297–300.
SMALL, J. J. Religion and the schools in New Zealand 1877–1963. Vol. 9, No. 1, Feb. 1965, pp 53–62
WATSON, J. E. The social position of teachers in New Zealand. Vol. 8, No. 3, Dec. 1964, pp. 327–333.

INDEXES TO IMPORTANT PERIODICALS

Norway
HANSEN, L. S. Ends and means in Norwegian educational reform. Vol. 8, No. 3, Dec. 1964, pp. 269–275.

Pakistan
PESHKIN, A. Education of the Muslim elite and the creation of Pakistan. Vol. 6, No. 2, Oct. 1962, pp. 152–159.

Philippines
HUNT, C. L., and MCHALE, T. R. Education and Philippine economic development. Vol. 9, No. 1, Feb. 1965, pp. 63–73.
KOH, E. K. American educational policy in the Philippines and the British policy in Malaya, 1898–1935. Vol. 9, No. 2, June 1965, pp. 139–146.
SAMONTE, Q. S. Land tenure and public school enrolment in the Philippines. Vol. 5, No. 2, Oct. 1961, pp. 136–141.

Puerto Rico
HEIFETZ, R. Manpower planning: a case study from Puerto Rico. Vol. 8, No. 1, June 1964, pp. 28–36.

Samoa, Western
BEEBY, C. E. Stages in the growth of a primary education system. Vol. 6, No. 1, June 1962, pp. 2–11.

Somalia
DAWSON, G. G. Education in Somalia. Vol. 8, No. 2, Oct. 1964, pp. 199–214.

South Africa, Republic of
HEY, P. D. African aspirations for education in rural Natal. Vol. 5, No. 2, Oct. 1961, pp. 112–117.
HEY, P. D. The rural Zulu teacher in Natal. Vol. 5, No. 1, June 1961, pp. 54–58.
LOW, V. N. Education for the Bantu: a South African dilemma. Vol. 2, No. 2, Oct. 1958, pp. 21–27.
MACMILLAN, R. G. Education and legislation in South Africa. Vol. 6, No. 1, June 1962, pp. 58–62.
MUIR, R. K., and TUNMER, R. The Africans' drive for education in South Africa. Vol. 9, No. 3, Oct. 1965, pp. 303–322.
MUNROE, D. The education of Europeans in South Africa. Vol. 5, No. 2, Oct. 1961, pp. 105–111.
ROSE, B. W. Bantu education as a facet of South African policy. Vol. 9, No. 2, June 1965, pp. 208–212.
SCANLON, D. G. Education and communism in Africa south of the Sahara. Vol. 2, No. 3, Feb. 1959, pp. 4–8.

Southern Rhodesia
PARKER, F. Education of Africans in Southern Rhodesia. Vol. 3, No. 2, Oct. 1959, pp. 27–32.

Spain
CLARK, A. J. The reform of secondary education in Spain. Vol. 9, No. 1, Feb. 1965, pp. 25–32.

NATIONAL AREA STUDIES

Spain (continued)
ESTARELLAS, J. The education of Don Quixote. Vol. 6, No. 1, June 1962, pp. 25–33.

Sudan
BESHIR, M. O. Some problems of university education in the Sudan. Vol. 5, No. 1, June 1961, pp. 50–53.
GANNON, E. J. Education in the Sudan. Vol. 9, No. 3, Oct. 1965, pp. 323–330.

Sweden
CANFIELD, A. T. Folk high schools in Denmark and Sweden: a comparative analysis. Vol. 9, No. 1, Feb. 1965, pp. 18–24.
HUSEN, T. Loss of talent in selective school systems: the case of Sweden. Vol. 4, No. 2, Oct. 1960, pp. 70–74.

Switzerland
JOLLY, R. Elementary schools in Geneva, Switzerland, and Oakland, California. Vol. 5, No. 1, June 1961, pp. 67–68.

Syria
POTTER, W. N. Modern education in Syria. Vol. 5, No. 1, June 1961, pp. 35–38.

Tanganyika
HORNSBY, G. Church and education in the Lake Nyasa region of Tanganyika. Vol. 6, No. 1, June 1962, pp. 63–68.

Thailand
SMYTHE, H. H., and SASIDHORN, N. Educational planning in Thailand. Vol. 8, No. 1, June 1964, pp. 37–40.

Turkey
VEXILARD, A., and AYTAC, K. The 'village institutes' in Turkey. Vol. 8, No. 1, June 1964, pp. 41–47.

Uganda
ELKAN, S. Primary school leavers in Uganda. Vol. 4, No. 2, Oct. 1960, pp. 102–109

Union of Soviet Socialist Republics
BEREDAY, G. Z. F. Japanese studies on Soviet education. Vol. 8, No. 2, Oct. 1964, pp. 176–185.
BEREDAY, G. Z. F. Recent developments in the Soviet schools. Vol. 1, No. 1, June 1957, pp. 4–7 and Vol. 1, No. 2, Oct. 1957, pp. 10–18.
BEREDAY, G. Z. F., and SCHLESINGER, I. Teacher salaries in the Soviet Union. Vol. 6, No. 3, Feb. 1963, pp. 200–208.
BEREDAY, G. Z. F., and STRETCH, B. B. Political education in the USA and USSR. Vol. 7, No. 1, June 1963, pp. 9–16
BIGELOW, K. W. Some comparative reflections on Soviet and Chinese higher education. Vol. 4, No. 3, Feb. 1961, pp. 169–173.
BILINSKY, Y. Education of Non-Russian peoples in the Soviet Union. Vol. 8, No. 1, June 1964, pp. 78–89.

INDEXES TO IMPORTANT PERIODICALS

Union of Soviet Socialist Republics (continued)

BOITER, A. The Khruschev school reform. Vol. 2, No. 3, Feb. 1959, pp. 8–14.

COUNTS, G. S. A word about the Soviet teacher. Vol. 5, No. 1, June 1961, pp. 13–16.

CHAUNCEY, H. Some comparative checkpoints between American and Soviet secondary education. Vol. 2, No. 3, Feb. 1959, pp. 18–20.

DEWITT, N. Basic comparative data on Soviet and American education. Vol. 2, No. 1, June 1958, pp. 9–11.

DEWITT, N. Soviet economic education. Vol. 7, No. 3, Feb. 1964, pp. 262–266.

DEWITT, N. Strategic problems of educational policy in the Soviet Union and the United States. Vol. 7, No. 1, June 1963, pp. 4–8.

DRYLAND, A. R. Polytechnical education in the USA and the USSR. Vol. 9, No. 2, June 1965, pp. 132–138.

HANS, N., K. D. Ushinsky, Russian pioneer of comparative education. Vol. 5, No. 3, Feb. 1962, pp. 162–166.

HANS, N. The Soviet approach to comparative education. Vol. 8, No. 1, June 1964, pp. 90–93.

HARRIS, D. L. Education of linguistic minorities in the USA and the USSR. Vol. 6, No. 3, Feb. 1963, pp. 191–199.

HIGGINSON, J. H. English education—between the USA and the USSR. Vol. 2, No. 1, June 1958, pp. 16–19.

JUVILER, P. H. Current reform trends in Soviet higher education, 1959–1960. Vol. 4, No. 3, Feb. 1961, pp. 149–158.

KAHAN, A. The economics of vocational training in the USSR. Vol. 4, No. 2, Oct. 1960, pp. 75–83.

MARCHIONY, J. A. The rise of Soviet athletics. Vol. 7, No. 1, June 1963, pp. 17–27.

MEDLIN, W. K., and CAVE, W. M. Social change and education in developing areas; Uzbekistan. Vol. 8, No. 2, Oct. 1964, pp. 166–175.

MEDLIN, W. K. Soviet pedagogical academy and the new school plans. Vol. 2, No. 2, Oct. 1958, pp. 12–14.

MOOS, E. The changes in Soviet schools in September 1964. Vol. 8, No. 3, Dec. 1964, pp. 264–268.

PENNAR, J. Five years after Krushchev's school reform. Vol. 8, No. 1, June 1964, pp. 73–77.

ROSEN, S. M. Problems in evaluating Soviet education. Vol. 8, No. 2, Oct. 1964, pp. 153–165.

ROUCEK, J. S. Juvenile delinquency and crime in the Soviet bloc. Vol. 3, No. 3, Feb. 1960, pp. 40–47.

RUDMAN, H. C. Moscow symposium on higher education, 1962. Vol. 7, No. 3, Feb. 1964, pp. 315–323.

RYWKIN, M. S. Incentives in the Soviet schools. Vol. 2, No. 1, June 1958, pp. 19–21.

VOGEL, A. W. Indoctrination of teachers of English in the Soviet Pedagogical Institute. Vol. 3, No. 2, Oct. 1959, pp. 32–35.

NATIONAL AREA STUDIES

Union of Soviet Socialist Republics (continued)

WILOCH, J. T. New models in Soviet education. Vol. 3, No. 2, Oct. 1959, pp. 5–13.

ZEPPER, J. T. Educational research in the USSR. Vol. 7, No. 3, Feb. 1964, pp. 267–272.

ZEPPER, J. T., N. K. Krupskaya on complex themes in Soviet education. Vol. 9, No. 1, Feb. 1965, pp. 33–37.

United Arab Republic

ABDUL-HADI, Mohammed. The new trends in Arab education. Vol. 1, No. 3, Feb. 1958, pp. 24–31.

United Nations Trust Territories

MILLER, R. I. Educational priorities in the United Nations Trust territories. Vol. 2, No. 3, Feb. 1959, pp. 20–24.

United States of America

BEREDAY, G. Z. F., and STRETCH, B. B. Political education in the USA and USSR. Vol. 7, No. 1, June 1963, pp. 9–16.

BIDWELL, C. E., and KAZAMIAS, A. M. Religion, politics and popular education: an historical comparison of England and America. Vol. 6, No. 2, Oct. 1962, pp. 97–110.

CHAUNCY, H. Some comparative checkpoints between American and Soviet secondary education. Vol. 2, No. 3, Feb. 1959, pp. 18–20.

DEWITT, N. Basic comparative data on Soviet and American education. Vol. 2, No. 1, June 1958, pp. 9–11.

DEWITT, N. Strategic problems of educational policy in the Soviet Union and the United States. Vol. 7, No. 1, June 1963, pp. 4–8.

DOWNEY, L. W. The task of the public school in the United States and Canada. Vol. 4, No. 2, Oct. 1960, pp. 118–120.

DRYLAND, A. R. Polytechnical education in the USA and the USSR. Vol. 9, No. 2, June 1965, pp. 132–138.

DUNCAN, E. R. Teaching arithmetic in the United States and New Zealand. Vol. 5, No. 1, June 1961, pp. 59–62.

HARRIS, D. L. Education of linguistic minorities in the U.S. and the USSR. Vol. 6, No. 3, Feb. 1963, pp. 191–199.

HAVIGHURST, R. J. Latin American and North American higher education. Vol. 4, No. 3, Feb. 1961, pp. 174–182.

HIGGINSON, J. H. English education—between the U.S. and the USSR. Vol. 2, No. 1, June 1958, pp. 16–19.

JOLLY, R. Elementary schools in Geneva, Switzerland and Oakland, California. Vol. 5, No. 1, June 1961, pp. 67–68.

KETTELKAMP, G. C. Foreign language teaching in Western Europe and central United States. Vol. 5, No. 1, June 1961, pp. 63–66.

LLOYD, J. W. British and American education in cultural perspective. Vol. 6, No. 1, June 1962, pp. 16–24.

MITSUHASHI, S. Conceptions and images of the physical world: a comparison of Japanese and American pupils. Vol. 6, No. 2, Oct. 1962, pp. 142–147.

INDEXES TO IMPORTANT PERIODICALS

United States of America (continued)

NOEL, E. W. Sponsored and contest mobility in America and England; a rejoinder to Ralph H. Turner. Vol. 6, No. 2, Oct. 1962, pp. 148–151.
PRESTON, R. C. Issues raised by the Wiesbaden-Philadelphia reading study. Vol. 7, No. 1, June 1963, pp. 61–65.
SHAPIRO, S. Some socioeconomic determinants of expenditures for education. Vol. 6, No. 2, Oct. 1962, pp. 160–166
WESLEY, E. B. American studies in British universities. Vol. 5, No. 3, Feb. 1962, pp. 182–188.

Uruguay

PELAEZ, L. C. Autonomy and student co-government in the University of Uruguay. Vol. 7, No. 2, Oct. 1963, pp. 166–172.

Yugoslavia

GEORGEOFF, J. Yugoslav youth and student organisation. Vol. 8, No. 1, June 1964, pp. 104–111.

COUNTRY INDEX to *COMPARATIVE EDUCATION*. Issued three times a year, Oxford and New York, Pergamon Press. Vol. 1, 1964 to Vol. 2, March 1966.

Africa

ASHBY, Sir Eric. Some problems of universities in new countries of the British Commonwealth. Vol. 2, No. 1, Nov. 1965, pp. 1–10.
RIMMINGTON, G. T. The development of universities in Africa. Vol. 1, No. 2, March 1965, pp. 105–112.
ROSE, B. Educational policy and problems in the former High Commission Territories of Africa. Vol. 1, No. 2, March 1965, pp. 113–118.

Australia

FRENCH, E. L. The Australian tradition in secondary education, 1814-1900. Vol. 1, No. 2, March 1965, pp. 89–103.
PARTRIDGE, P. H. Universities in Australia. Vol. 2, No. 1, Nov. 1965, pp. 19–30.

Canada

KATZ, J. Bilingualism and biculturalism in Canada. Vol. 2, No. 2, March 1966, pp. 113–118.
KATZ, J. Canada and the International Co-operation Year in education. Vol. 1, No. 2, March 1965, pp. 79–88.

NATIONAL AREA STUDIES

France
CAPELLE, J. The observation and guidance phase in French secondary education. Vol. 1, No. 3, June 1965, pp. 171–179.
HALLS, W. Educational planning in an industrial society: the French experience. Vol. 1, No. 1, Oct. 1964, pp. 19–28.

Germany
ROBINSOHN, S. B. The newly founded Institute for Educational Research (Institut für Bildungsforschung) within the Max-Planck-Gesellschaft. Vol. 2, No. 1, Nov. 1965, pp. 31–35.

Great Britain. England and Wales
PETERSON, A. D. C. Secondary re-organisation in England and Wales. Vol. 1, No. 3, June 1965, pp. 161–169.
TAYLOR, W. The university teacher of education in England. Vol. 1, No. 3, June 1965, pp. 193–201.
VENABLES, Sir P. Confusion, concentration and clarification in higher education. Vol. 2, No. 1, Nov. 1965, pp. 11–18.

Hungary
RICHMOND, W. K. Educational planning in Hungary. Vol. 2, No. 2, March, 1966, pp. 93–105.

Japan
KING, E. J. Educational progress and social problems in Japan. Vol. 1, No. 2, March 1965, pp. 63–77.

Nepal
WOOD, H. B. Mobile normal school in Nepal. Vol. 1, No. 2, March 1965, pp. 119–124.

New Zealand
MINOGUE, W. J. D. Education in a dependent culture—New Zealand: some problems relating to British influence in New Zealand education. Vol. 1, No. 3, June 1965, pp. 203–209.

Norway
STENHOUSE, L. Comprehensive education in Norway: a developing system. Vol. 2, No. 1, Nov. 1965, pp. 37–41.

Sweden
DAHLLOF, U. Recent reforms of secondary education in Sweden. Vol. 2, No. 2, March 1966, pp. 71–92.
HUSEN, T. Educational change in Sweden. Vol. 1, No. 3, June 1965, pp. 181–191.

United States of America
CHAUSOW, H. M., and ZIGERELL, J. J. Instructional television: the recruiting and training of teachers. Vol. 2, No. 2, March 1966, pp. 107–112.
HOKE, G. A. Custodial obligations: comprehensive secondary schools in England and the United States. Vol. 2, No. 2, March 1966, pp. 119–124.

4

CROSS-CULTURAL AND CASE STUDIES

Truly comparative or cross-national studies demand for their success knowledge of at least two national systems of education. Teachers of comparative education will find that the knowledge students have of their own system of education offers a good starting point from which to develop two-country comparisons. Indeed careful comparative studies based on recognizable problems in the students' own system should help them to understand these issues better and therefore should contribute to their general professional education. The danger of comparing data acquired through experience of living and working in one system with data about another drawn from statistics and literature should be apparent.

The literature listed in the previous chapter was intended to make it possible to students to acquire information about a national system of education in relation to its general sociological background. In this chapter a selection is made from the growing number of books in which a comparative study of one aspect or level of education is made. Some explicitly comparative studies take as their starting point relationships between education and an aspect of the socio-economic or political context. Other investigations start from a very explicit analysis of a common problem.

The placing of this material after the chapter dealing with area studies or national systems of education implies no hard and fast teaching rule. Several of the general textbooks listed in Chapter 1 would lead students more directly to cross-cultural or cross-national than to area studies. Both the 'factors' and 'problems' approaches may appeal to some teachers and even to some beginning students as the most satisfactory way into the study of comparative education. These approaches should help to show how similar influences have helped to fashion different national systems of education and how common educational problems find unique manifestation and promote unique solutions in different countries.

The constant need, whatever the starting point, to strengthen and deepen one's knowledge of a particular country or countries and to seek more rigorous methods of comparison should be apparent to comparative educationists whatever basic methodology they adopt.

CROSS-CULTURAL AND CASE STUDIES

George BEREDAY's *Comparative Method in Education* (q.v.) lays down carefully identified and described steps in an approach to truly comparative studies. Each of these steps is illustrated in a case study. Nicholas HANS' *Comparative Education* (q.v.) is based on a 'factors' approach and the influence—surveyed historically—of such factors as language, geography, race, political ideology and social class is illustrated by reference to a number of different countries. In *Problems in Education: A Comparative Approach*, Brian HOLMES (q.v.) applies the problem approach of Dewey to comparative education and suggests how common problems may be analysed. He illustrates his methodology in case studies.

Case Studies (restricted in this chapter to single countries) may in fact be taken as an integral part of *Cross-Cultural* and *Cross-National Studies*. They are designed to throw very considerable light either on one aspect of or one problem associated with education in a selected country. For example, W. R. FRASER in *Education and Society in Modern France* (q.v.) concentrates his attention largely on the politics of French educational reform since 1945. Philip J. FOSTER in *Education and Social Change in Ghana*, London, Routledge & Kegan Paul, 1965, is principally concerned with the relationship between the provision of secondary education and the development of the economy of a country such as Ghana. Neither of these books, nor similar ones, set out to give a comprehensive picture of the educational system in the country. They do throw light on particular problems and should provoke further reading. In doing these things they are valuable aids to a deeper understanding of the system as a whole.

Cross-Cultural and *Cross-National* comparative studies presuppose the existence of some basis for comparison. World-wide investigations assume either that the influence of a selected factor can be examined in practically every country in the world, or that some problems are sufficiently similar to make world-wide comparisons of their unique features justifiable. It should not be supposed that beginning students will be able to distinguish clearly between the various methodologies presently being proposed and developed. Further refinements in the techniques of comparative education research have, as the literature shows, encouraged the careful analysis of selected issues or problems within a region in which the nation states quite evidently share certain comparable difficulties in planning the growth of education.

In this chapter three main and by no means entirely exclusive types of study have been identified, namely; (i) *World Cross-Cultural Studies;* (ii) *Regional Cross-National Studies* and (iii) *Case*

WORLD CROSS-CULTURAL STUDIES

Studies. Within each group the coverage varies greatly according to the volume. This organization, nevertheless, should enable readers to build on the literature listed in Chapter 3, *Area Studies*, without difficulty.

As in the case of the latter, *Cross-Cultural* and *Cross-National Studies* are prepared by various agencies. Some of these are *World Organizations*, others are *Regional Organizations* and many are *University Centres of Comparative Education*. Very often the authorship of these large international enquiries is ascribed to one person, but frequently they are the outcome of some kind of collective effort—a conference, a seminar or a sponsored enquiry.

SECTION I. WORLD CROSS-CULTURAL STUDIES

1. International Organizations

The United Nations and its special agencies publish many cross-cultural comparative studies of value to comparative educationists. The former's *Demographic Yearbook* provides world coverage and includes a special topic in each volume but generally speaking UN publications deal with regions and topics rather than with the world as a whole. The WORLD HEALTH ORGANISATION (WHO) publishes many epidemiological and vital statistics on a world basis. A selected list of publications is given in HMSO *International Organisations Publications*, annual, London, HMSO as a supplement to *Government Publications*, annual, London, HMSO (q.v.).

Unesco, of course, is the special agency whose publications are of particular interest to educationists. In its *World Survey of Education* (q.v.) are found comparative articles drawing together data from member states about the developments in selected stages of education. Its series *Educational Studies and Documents* include many titles useful in comparative education courses. One of the most valuable is No. 43 *The Organisation of the School Year, a Comparative Study* because it gives basic information about the length of a school year, vacations, times of attendance and so on. Another series, *Education Abstracts*, has been discontinued but among its useful annotated bibliographies are *Teaching Comparative Education*, *Education Abstracts*, Vol. XV, No. 4, 1963 and *Educational Planning; a Preliminary Listing*, *Education Abstracts*, Vol. XIV, No. 2, 1962. There are volumes on health education, primary education, history teaching, rural education and second language teaching.

At least two special Unesco institutes should be mentioned. Since its establishment in 1951 the Unesco Institute for Education in

Hamburg has undertaken comparative and international studies in education. It has done this through the planning and holding of international conferences and seminars and the publication of reports based on them. It publishes the *International Review of Education* and has collaborated very closely with the International Project for the Evaluation of Educational Achievement (IEA) whose first report was published in two volumes in 1967 as the *International Study of Achievement in Mathematics, A Comparison of Twelve Countries*, edited by T. Husén, 2 vols., Stockholm, Almqvist and Wiksell, and New York, Wiley, 1967.

In 'Institute Notes' in *International Review of Education* Vol. XII, No. 3, 1966, pp. 388–99 as director of the Hamburg Institute G. ÖGREN outlined the changes in the constitution and the new horizons in the work of Unesco and the Institute. The constitution states that one of the purposes of the Institute is to prepare and carry out a study programme in the field of comparative education and of broad international scope along the lines laid down by the General Conference of Unesco.

A bibliography of publications of the Institute is provided in *Education Abstracts*, Paris, Unesco, Vol. XII, No. 10, Dec. 1960. Several series have been established, namely: *Teaching for International Understanding: Comparative Study of the evolution and forms and needs of leisure; Intellectual Processes: an International Study of Intellectual Ability; Achievements and Functioning in Children* (distribution restricted) and *Parent Education: an International Survey* by H. H. STERN, published jointly by the University of Hull and the Unesco Institute for Education, 1960.

For comparative educationists *Relevant Data in Comparative Education*, Hamburg, Unesco Institute for Education, 1963, presented by Brian HOLMES and S. B. ROBINSOHN offers a scheme on which descriptive accounts of national educational systems can be based. The framework presented by the second of the working groups of the expert meeting on which the report is founded may be particularly valuable from this viewpoint.

The planned development of education has also received increasing attention from Unesco. The Unesco International Institute for Educational Planning was founded in 1963 to promote and conduct advanced training and research for educational planning. Its aim is to help all member states of Unesco to develop their educational systems as an integral part of their over-all national, economic and social development. In 1964 a *Directory of Training and Research Institutions* was published by Unesco International Institute for Educational Planning. Information about the Institute can be found in *International Review of Education*, Hamburg, Unesco, Vol. XII, No. 3, 1966, pp. 333-45. The publications of the Institute include both regional and case studies by named authors. Much of the work deals with Africa. Several titles are listed.

A number of international studies bearing on education and development have been produced by international agencies. Volumes prepared by the United Nations and OECD may be used to illustrate a growing volume of important literature.

UNITED NATIONS, *Science and Technology for Development*, Vol. VI, *Education and Training*, New York, 1963 is part of an eight-volume report of the United Nations Conference on the application of science and technology to the less developed areas of the world. The argument presented is that in the organization of education and training of people as primary factors in the growth of these countries piecemeal attempts cannot succeed. The first chapter analyses the gap between educational provision in the wealthy countries and that in the poorer regions of the world. The next chapter deals with the principles of educational planning; Chapter 3 with some basic educational problems related to the stages of education (primary, secondary and higher) and research. In the next chapter the subject of training personnel in the skills and techniques of industry are discussed while Chapter 5 deals with new forms of adult education in countries where a large percentage of the population is illiterate. Chapter 6 is concerned with some new media of communication through which education can be effectively provided for the mass of people and the last chapter brings together under the heading 'International Co-operation' some of the general ideas, trends and patterns of international co-operation which have resulted from the growth of science and technology. Africa, Latin America, India, the Philippines, the United Arab Republic, the USSR and Yugoslavia are among the countries which receive most attention either because of the problems they face or because their successes provide interesting lessons.

ORGANISATION FOR ECONOMIC CO-OPERATION AND DEVELOPMENT, *Policy Conference on Economic Growth and Investment in Education*, Washington, 16th-20th October 1961, OECD 1965, 2nd printing is the report of a conference which took place at the Brookings Institution, Washington. This volume is a collection of five short reports published in the first instance as separate volumes as follows:

I   Summary Report and Conclusions and Keynote Speeches.
II   'Targets for Education in Europe in 1970', a paper by I. SVENNILSON in association with F. EDDING and H. L. ELVIN.

III 'The Challenge of Aid to Newly Developing Countries', papers by A. LEWIS, F. HARBISON, J. TINBERGEN in association with H. C. BOS and J. VAIZEY.
IV 'The Planning of Education in Relation to Economic Growth', papers by R. POIGNANT, S. MOBERG and M. ELAZAR.
V 'International Flows of Students', paper by J. R. GASS and R. F. LYONS.

The whole conference was based on the need for Governments to plan the spending of increasing amounts of money on education. The strategies to be developed need to be based on a recognition that poverty need no longer exist and that the aspirations of democratic peoples need to be met. A second factor influencing strategy is the explosion of scientific and technological knowledge. These new forces constitute part of modern life and culture and cannot with safety be ignored if new levels of culture are to be reached. The success of Government policies to raise economic standards and cultural levels depends as much on trained people as on money. Consequently one of the challenges is the education of personnel who can at one and the same time contribute to economic growth and to human betterment. Keynote speeches were made by distinguished U.S. government and OECD officials. Many countries were represented as were many international organizations interested in economic development and education. All the papers are closely reasoned and contain a wealth of statistical data in tabular form. Many of the issues are those which have been of central concern to comparative educationists for some time but the emphasis of the conference is economic.

A number of enquiries sponsored by Unesco in collaboration with other organizations add to the material of this chapter. A series of volumes with the International Association of Universities has been established. *Access to Higher Education, International Study of University Admission* in two volumes by Frank BOWLES (q.v.) is an example of this collaboration. The study covers countries from all parts of the world.

2. University Centres

It is not easy for individuals or even departments of comparative education to carry through world international enquiries. Several important centres, however, produce them. The University of London Institute of Education and King's College have a tradition going back to the 1920s. Teacher's College, Columbia University, has been a centre of comparative education studies for a somewhat longer period of time. More recently the International Education

WORLD CROSS-CULTURAL STUDIES

Institute in Frankfurt-am-Main, the Comparative Education Center at Chicago University, the Departments of Education at Michigan and Pittsburgh Universities have all published extensively in the field.

Information about the work of some of these centres can be found in journals. For example the reasons for the founding of the Max Planck Institut für Bildungsforschung in Berlin are described by S. B. ROBINSOHN in *Comparative Education*, Vol. 2, No. 1, Nov. 1965, pp. 31–35. The *Comparative Education Review* carries several articles on the work in various centres. George Z. F. BEREDAY wrote on 'Comparative Education at Columbia University' in Vol. 4, No. 1, June 1960, pp. 15–17; J. A. LAUWERYS on 'Comparative Education at the University of London' in Vol. 3, No. 2, 1962, pp. 3–4; C. A. ANDERSON on 'University of Chicago program in Comparative Education', Vol. 12, No. 1, 1966, pp. 80–91; an account was given by V. A. VEIKSHAN of the Moscow centre in comparative education (The Department of Contemporary Education and Schools Abroad) in Vol. 3, No. 1, June 1959, pp. 4–5; F. HILKER'S account of the Documentation and Information Centre in Bonn appeared in Vol. 3, No. 3, Feb. 1960, pp. 13–15; and the work of the comparative education centre at the Pädagogische Hochschule in Bremen under the director Horst E. WITTIG is given in Vol. 8, No. 3, Dec. 1964, pp. 359. The aims and purposes of the Hochschule für Internationale pädagogische Forschung in Frankfurt-am-Main were stated in a pamphlet issued by this institute for research in international education in 1953.

Before the second world war there were two well-known major reference works prepared from comparative viewpoints. The *Educational Yearbook* published between 1924 and 1944 was edited for the International Institute of Teacher's College, Columbia University, New York, by I. L. KANDEL, Professor of Comparative Education at Teacher's College. The information in these volumes is largely of historical value but they do represent an early attempt to organize comparative material round problems, themes or levels of education. BEREDAY in *Comparative Method in Education* (q.v.) has listed the problems and countries treated throughout the whole period of publication. Of particular interest are the volumes which deal with selected socio-economic or political problems in relation to education such as: education in colonial dependencies (1931), church and state relations (1932), political philosophies in school systems (1934) and post-war reconstruction (1944). Other volumes deal with levels of education; elementary school curricula (1925), secondary school expansion (1930), and higher education (1943).

CROSS-CULTURAL AND CASE STUDIES

Theories of education are compared in philosophy of national systems (1929) and liberal education (1939). Special attention was given to rural education (1938) and to adult education (1940). Teaching methods (1924), teacher training (1927) and teacher associations (1935) were studied in volumes which throw light on teaching generally. Europe, the USA and the British Commonwealth countries are most frequently treated in case studies but one volume is devoted to Latin America (1942).

The other *Year Book of Education* was published before the war (from 1932) on behalf of the University of London Institute of Education. It provided statistical data from many countries throughout the world and special articles, often written by Nicholas HANS, on selected problems or themes. Particular attention was given in these pre-war articles to British Commonwealth countries. An attempt was made to keep readers up to date so that again the historical value of these volumes is considerable and they may be consulted in libraries. It is hoped that an over-all index to these volumes may be published in the near future.

During and immediately after the second world war the *Year Book of Education* was not published. When publication was resumed there was a change of policy. Agencies such as Unesco and the IBE were able to collect data from all over the world. Editorial policy, under an editorial board and the joint editors Nicholas HANS and J. A. LAUWERYS, was to organize each volume round a theme or problem. The first post-war volumes were devoted to the problems created for education by the war. Subsequently major problems arising either in the socio-economic or political spheres of society or within the educational sector have been treated comparatively on a world-wide basis. This policy continued after 1953 when the first volume to be published on behalf of the University of London Institute of Education and Teacher's College, Columbia University, New York, appeared under the joint editorship of Robert King HALL, Nicholas HANS, and J. A. LAUWERYS. It was continued when George Z. F. BEREDAY became American joint editor with LAUWERYS in 1957 and when David SCANLON succeeded him in the 1968 volume. In 1965 the title of the volume was changed to *The World Year Book of Education* published in London by Evans Brothers and in New York by Harcourt Brace & World.

Each year a theme or problem is taken and examined on a world-wide basis. About a third of the articles come from England and the British Commonwealth, a third from USA and a third from the rest of the world. Brief titles since 1948 are:

WORLD CROSS-CULTURAL STUDIES

1948 The Effects of the War on Education.
1949 The Effects of the War on Education.
1950 The Effects of the War on Education.
1951 Occupational Selection and Differentiation through Education.
1952 The Reform of Education
1953 The Social Position of Teachers.
1954 Education and the Transformation of Societies.
1955 Guidance and Counselling.
1956 Education and Economics.
1957 Education and Philosophy.
1958 The Secondary School Curriculum.
1959 Higher Education.
1960 Communication Media and the School.
1961 Concepts of Excellence in Education.
1962 The Gifted Child.
1963 The Education and Training of Teachers.
1964 Education and International Life.
1965 The Education Explosion.
1966 Church and State in Education.
1967 Education and Planning.
1968 Education in Industry.

These year books are the outcome of the research and experience of individual writers invited by the editors to analyse issues on the basis of a carefully prepared outline but with freedom to interpret and comment in a way that might not be possible for members of a ministry of education. The volumes can be used in a variety of ways.

The long editorial essays, written by several collaborating persons offer in themselves comparative essays in which important problems are analysed and illustrated by reference to conditions in a number of countries. They throw useful light on issues in English and American education. The themes are further analysed in long theoretical articles within each of the volumes. Case studies from most of the major countries of the world illustrate the general issues. Thus cross-cultural studies on selected issues are available and over the years the same or a similar question has been treated in more than one volume. Trends can therefore be discerned. Since by intention an attempt is made to include in each volume about a third of the articles from England and the British Commonwealth, another third from the USA and the remainder from the rest of the world it is possible to use the year books to complement *National Area Studies* with *National Case Studies*. Over the last twenty years most aspects of education in the USA and in England have been dealt with in an interpretative manner.

The following grouping of volumes may help students to build up educational theory and develop deeper insights into the educational systems of selected national systems.

Moral and Philosophical Aspects of Education—1951, 1957, 1964 and 1966.
Selection and Gifted Children—1952, 1961 and 1962.
The Curriculum and New Media in Education—1958 and 1960.
Higher Education and Teacher Training—1953, 1959 and 1963.
The Problems of Reconstruction and Expansion—1948, 1949 and 1965.
Economic and Planning Aspects of Education—1954, 1956 and 1967.

None of the volumes attempts to describe for every major country of the world the main features of the educational system or even of the topic under consideration. Nevertheless articles on England and Wales, the USA, the USSR, France and India will be found in virtually every volume. Case studies from Germany, Scandinavia, the Netherlands, Belgium, countries in Latin America, Japan, and former British Commonwealth countries are less frequent but often included. As reference books they provide (*a*) analyses of important problems, (*b*) depth studies of particular systems, and (*c*) comparative interpretations of stages of education—primary, secondary, tertiary.

In every volume since 1948 the analysis provided has placed education in its social, economic and political contexts. The interpretations are by experts in the field and in some instances represent an official line.

3. Individual Authors

Several individual authors have prepared books on educational topics which, if they do not touch on every country of the world, certainly have a world-wide flavour. Eric ASHBY *Universities: British, Indian, African* (q.v.) is an analysis of the transplantation of British prototype universities into the British Commonwealth. *Educational Policy and the Mission Schools* edited by Brian HOLMES (q.v.) examines the difficulties encountered in several territories by the early missionaries. *Ministries of Education, their Function and Organisation* by Kathryn HEATH (q.v.) and *Educational Systems of the World* by M. T. SASNETT (q.v.) provide surveys of selected aspects of education. These and a growing number of other books often present interpretative analyses on which may be based more intensive and extensive cross-national investigations.

Several books deal with socio-economic and political problems in the context of education. *Education and Political Development*, Princeton, Princeton University Press, 1965 edited by James S. COLEMAN is an example of a cross-cultural study based on the relationship between education and the formation of new political elites. Case studies written by several authors are introduced in a long article by the editor. Another example is *Government Policy and International Education*, New York, Wiley, 1965 edited by Stewart FRASER. Although the emphasis is on U.S. policy, articles by Canadian, French and German authors are included.

Selected Bibliography by Author

Eric ASHBY, *Universities, British, Indian, African—a Study in the Ecology of Higher Education*, London, Weidenfeld & Nicholson, 1966 is based on the work of the author over a period of twelve years as adviser on the development of African universities. Most of his visits were concerned with finance, building programmes, expansion, administration and the spectrum of studies. A Carnegie Corporation grant enabled the author to work with a professional historian in interpreting his experiences. The book is an outcome of this partnership. It provides a historical setting by discussing the European university models of medieval times and the nineteenth century and how aspects of these models were transplanted in other parts of the world. Part II deals with the universities of India from a historical viewpoint dealing with the launching of the university system about 100 years ago, and the reforms introduced under Lord Curzon and as a result of the Calcutta University Commission. The African studies start from the author's assessment that African universities have their roots entirely in a system brought from the West and that aspirations for higher education grew up in the absence of any official policy for it in any of the British dependencies in tropical Africa until after the first world war. Subsequent chapters deal with the reports on which policy has been evolved, the influences of British and American practices on higher education in Africa, and the concepts and constitutional arrangements relating to autonomy and academic freedom in the universities. The final chapter consists of case studies of higher education in South Africa, Ethiopia, the Congolese Republic and French policy in her colonial territories. The volume is backed by extensive documentation, summaries of important reports and a long bibliography.

CROSS-CULTURAL AND CASE STUDIES

Robert E. ASHER et al., *Development of the Emerging Countries: an Agenda for Research*, Washington, The Brookings Institution, 1962 consists of seven chapters by named authors dealing with planning and development in emerging countries. Many of the topics are of central concern to comparative educationists; they include a discussion on ways of analysing economic and political change, research on rural problems, technological change, foreign assistance and (by Mary Jean BOWMAN and C. Arnold ANDERSON) the role of education in development. Analytical and theoretical, the book provides a basis for further study of actual cases.

Frank BOWLES, *Access to Higher Education, International Study of University Admissions*, Paris, Unesco; New York, Columbia University Press, 1963, Vols. I and II is the report of the Director of an international study sponsored by Unesco and the International Association of Universities and supported by a grant from the Carnegie Corporation. In Volume I the author analyses the problem of admission to universities in the post-war era and classifies the solutions in terms of expanding systems, steady and contracting systems. The effects of the changes in structure of the secondary stage of education are also discussed. Tables and diagrammatic representations provide clear comparative information on England and Wales, the USA, the UAR, Ghana, Brazil, Chile, India, France and Japan, USSR, New Zealand, South Africa and Senegal. Volume II includes careful studies of the educational systems in these countries designed to show how the structure of the school system, the content of the curriculum and the examination system influences the admission procedures. The magnitude of the problem and the methods of solving the excess of candidates over university places are described. A very good example of a cross-national comparative study of a problem created by educational and socio-economic factors.

Adam CURLE, *Educational Strategy for Developing Countries, a Study of Educational and Social Factors in Relation to Economic Growth*, London, Tavistock Publications, 1963 is largely concerned with the practice of education in underdeveloped countries. The author's suggestion that men are more important than money in economic development is of general interest since it gives education high priority.

John W. HANSON and Cole S. BREMBECK (eds), *Education and the Development of Nations*, New York, Holt, Rinehart & Winston, 1966 deals with the capacity of education to assist in the development of nations. It is primarily concerned with the developing countries of the world in Africa and Asia. Several articles are of general value because the analysis is relevant over a wider field than that covered by case studies and there are references to Europe and the Americas. The book is made up of forty-seven essays selected from a wide range of social science literature and bridged by editorial introductions. Each chapter is followed by a lengthy further reading list and there is a bibliography at the end. The volume raises many issues of interest to comparative educationists whose area of concern is the developing nations and the application of economic theories and techniques to the study of educational practice.

Brian HOLMES (ed.), *Educational Policy and the Mission Schools, Case Studies from the British Empire*, London, Routledge & Kegan Paul, 1967 is a collection of chapters written by former students of the Comparative Education Department in the Institute of Education, University of London. Attention is focused on the difficulties the early British missionaries faced when they attempted to set up schools in various parts of the world. The authors show how particular circumstances at the time of arrival helped or hindered the missionaries in their work. Some assessment is also made of the outcome of missionary educational activity, e.g. the extent to which they helped to establish an economic and political elite and the degree to which they were a divisive force in multicultural societies. The territories included in the study are the Bahamas, Ceylon, Kerala, Kashmir, Egypt, Cyprus and Eastern Nigeria. Most of the material is historical but the comparative approach throws light on present problems in these countries.

E. J. KING, *World Perspectives in Education*, London, Methuen, 1965 reviews the principles of and persistent problems in education from a comparative viewpoint. Many of the topics included have been treated more fully in various *World Year Books of Education* (q.v.) but the book provides the author's own assessment and interpretation of the issues.

Martena Tenney SASNETT, *Educational Systems of the World*, Los Angeles, University of Southern California Press, 1952 is now rather old but in giving details of some eighty countries throughout the world in order to reveal salient features and to evaluate foreign credentials in the USA much clearly organized data are given. The following stages of education are outlined: pre-school, primary, secondary, technical and vocational and higher. The focus of attention is, however, entrance requirements to institutions of higher learning throughout the world.

SECTION II. REGIONAL CROSS-NATIONAL STUDIES

1. International Organizations

Unesco has been responsible for the establishment of several regional agencies and regional studies. The Regional Fundamental Education Centre in Latin America (CREFAL) was set up in Mexico; the Arab States Fundamental Education Centre (ASFEC) in Egypt. The reports of these and other centres and the regional conferences and seminars arranged by Unesco are listed in *Unesco General Catalogue of Publications 1946–1959*, Paris, Unesco, 1962 and later *Supplements*, e.g. *General Catalogue of Unesco Publications and Unesco-sponsored Publications, Supplement 1960–1963*, Paris, Unesco, 1964.

2. Regional Organizations

Since the second world war there have developed agencies whose special task it has been to study aspects of a particular region and to encourage within it various forms of co-operation. Many of these agencies have carried out cross-national studies which are of value to the comparative educationist. Many of the reports published bear directly on educational policy and developments but there are also a great many which provide information about the social, economic and political backgrounds to education.

For example, THE COUNCIL OF EUROPE was established by ten nations in 1949 since when its membership has grown to some eighteen countries. As its aim it has the achievement of greater unity of the members and the furthering of their economic and social progress. The COUNCIL FOR CULTURAL CO-OPERATION was set up in 1962 and is assisted by committees on selected aspects of education. A series of publications records the findings of expert studies and inter-governmental reports in four main sections, namely:

I   Higher Education and Research.
II General and Technical Education.
III Out-of-School Education.
IV General Activities not included above.

A selection of these reports appears in the annotated bibliography at the end of this chapter.

The ORGANISATION FOR ECONOMIC CO-OPERATION AND DEVELOPMENT (OECD) was established in 1961 as a successor to the ORGANISATION FOR EUROPEAN ECONOMIC CO-OPERATION (OEEC) which was established in 1948 to allocate Marshall Plan aid and help post-war recovery. The scope of OECD has broadened and is

REGIONAL CROSS-NATIONAL STUDIES

designed to serve the twenty-one member states as an instrument of disseminating information on which policy can be based and as a forum for the discussion of polity and for the sharing of ideas. The OECD 1966 *Catalogue of Publications*, Paris, 2 rue André-Pascal, 75 Paris, OECD, 1966 lists the various publications under various headings, e.g. Economy, Manpower and Social Affairs, and Education and Science. A catalogue is due in 1968. The work of OECD is carried out through committees. Those concerned with education are the Committee for Science Policy, the Committee for Research Co-operation and the Committee for Scientific and Technical Personnel. Science policy, long-term educational planning, the improvement of school science teaching and the pooling of resources for scientific research are among the major interests of these committees. Some publications result from regional conferences, others from articles written by a number of experts. Some of the titles of considerable relevance in comparative education are annotated at the end of the chapter. ORGANISATION FOR ECONOMIC CO-OPERATION AND DEVELOPMENT, *Curriculum Improvement and Educational Development*, Modernizing Our Schools, Paris, OECD, 1966 is the report prepared at the invitation of the Committee for Scientific and Technical Personnel and draws heavily on work undertaken in other areas by this committee. It is in two parts; the first deals with basic concepts and considerations, the second with an analysis of problems and developments. In the first part a number of principles of policy are stated, they include the affirmation that every person should be provided (as far as possible) with an education according to his needs and abilities; that the curricula at all levels of education must be adjusted to the needs of an expanded school population; that curricula must provide for a satisfactory general education and for the rapid incorporation of new knowledge; that science and the arts should be regarded as complementary; and that research in learning is essential in every country to improve the curriculum and quality of instruction.

Neither the EUROPEAN COMMUNITY nor the EUROPEAN FREE TRADE ASSOCIATION (EFTA) list publications of direct value to students of education. The WESTERN EUROPEAN UNION, however, has a Working Party on Educational Films of the countries belonging to it.

Selected Bibliography by Organization and Author

Volumes sponsored by world or regional organizations are listed either under the appropriate agency and where it seemed proper under the author responsible for the publication. The order followed

CROSS-CULTURAL AND CASE STUDIES

is EUROPE, THE AMERICAS, ASIA, AFRICA and THE MIDDLE AND NEAR EAST. Unesco and IBE (q.v.) issue many publications which may be regarded as cross-national comparative studies. They are listed elsewhere and discussed in Chapter 3, Area Studies. Some of those published under the authorship of an individual have been listed in the bibliographies (by author).

Europe

COUNCIL OF EUROPE, COUNCIL FOR CULTURAL CO-OPERATION, *Civics and European Education at the Primary and Secondary Level*, Education in Europe, Section II, General and Technical Education, No. 2, Strasbourg, 1963 is in two parts. The first reviews the work in civics education done by inter-governmental and non-governmental organizations since 1949; the second part gives the position in 1963 of civics teaching in Europe based on an enquiry carried out by the Secretariat of the European Cultural Centre in Geneva. In the first part brief reports of courses held, civics as a specific school subject and the contribution the traditional subjects can make to civics are given. The enquiry on which the second part is based was carried out on the basis of a questionnaire drawn up by the Secretariat. The questions were designed to discover the ways in which civics was taught in the schools, the courses, syllabuses and methods used, the staff employed, the teaching aids provided, the related educational activities and the results of the teaching. Brief accounts from each of the countries appear under the appropriate groups of questions. The results and conclusions provide a basis for comparative analysis.

COUNCIL OF EUROPE, *Leisure-time Facilities for Young People from 13–25 Years of Age*, Strasbourg, Council for Cultural Cooperation, Education in Europe, Series III, No. 4, 1965 is the outcome of a survey carried out with the assistance of Unesco by the Space for Youth Foundation, Rotterdam. The coverage is by no means complete; not all the countries of Europe which adhere to the Cultural Convention of the Council of Europe are represented. Topics such as comprehensive planning, types of facilities including homes and hostels, youth clubs and centres, general leisure time facilities and outdoor provisions are dealt with and contain relevant information from six selected countries. The final chapter presents accounts of recent experimental projects in France, the Federal German Republic, the Netherlands, Switzerland and England. Plans of these centres are given in diagrammatic and pictorial form.

COUNCIL OF EUROPE, Joseph MAJAULT, *Teacher Training*, Education in Europe, Section II, General and Technical Education, No. 4,

REGIONAL CROSS-NATIONAL STUDIES

Strasbourg, Council of Europe, Council for Cultural Co-operation, 1965 provides a cross-national comparison for seventeen European countries and Iceland. Some of the general problems of making comparisons are described by the author, who then goes on to outline under each country the system of training of primary school teachers. The age of entry, period of attendance and course of general studies are mentioned. Accounts of systems of secondary school teacher training are then given, and finally for teachers in vocational and technical schools. Some general conclusions about the problems and solutions complete the volume. Clear comparative tables, diagrams and recapitulations of material add to the value of the study.

COUNCIL OF EUROPE, Council for Cultural Co-operation, *Training the Trainer*, Strasbourg, Education in Europe, Series III, No. 3, 1964 provides a suggested programme for general leaders of physical recreation and sport. It arose from a meeting in 1962 near Bonn at which governmental experts recommended the need for a short course to train general leaders of physical education and sport. An agreed programme was drawn up at a subsequent meeting of experts covering 100 hours of instruction. The programme included aspects of teacher training, biology, physical education and movement training, games and other outdoor pursuits. This is a very practical study and provides clear directives for the training of leaders in physical education and sport.

COUNCIL OF EUROPE, Council for Cultural Co-operation, *Research and Techniques for the Benefit of Modern Language Teaching*, Strasbourg, Education in Europe, Section IV, No. 3, 1964 is the report of a refresher course held at Strasbourg in 1963 by the Regional Branch of the Association of Modern Language Teachers and the Council of Europe. The starting point is a recognition of the fact that in recent years a large number of widely differing commercial methods for language teaching have been put forward many with exaggerated claims. Against this the writer of the preface claims that the best method is direct acquisition of a language through living in the country under conditions which will enable the learner to forget as much as possible of his mother tongue. Articles on new research, new methods and techniques (including language laboratory, tape recorder, new audio-visual presentation) are by named authors. Co-operation and co-ordination problems are discussed by personnel from the University of Strasbourg and the Council of Europe in chapters in Part III. A list of recommendations of general aims and principles is given in Part IV of the volume.

CROSS-CULTURAL AND CASE STUDIES

The Americas

The creation in 1948 of the ORGANISATION OF AMERICAN STATES was designed to give new strength to the alliance of the Americas. At the same time the DEPARTMENT OF CULTURE OF THE PAN-AMERICAN UNION came into being, it followed the example of Unesco in covering three aspects of life—education, science and culture. Its Department of Educational Affairs tackles problems under a number of specialized sections—fundamental education, secondary education, technical and vocational education, and aspects of higher education. Inter-American seminars are convened for specialists who direct their attention to practical tasks of improving education in the territories concerned. The findings and recommendations of the seminars are published.

PAN-AMERICAN UNION, DEPARTMENT OF EDUCATIONAL AFFAIRS, *Challenges and Achievements of Education in Latin America*, Washington, Organization of American States, 1964 is a report of the Eastern Regional Conference of the Comparative Education Society in 1964 sponsored by the Pan-American Union and prepared by the co-ordinator of the conference, Mrs Estellita HART. It comprises a number of chapters written by named authors. Topics include: procedures and machinery for evaluating educational development in the Americas; the role of comparative education in international co-operation; a comparative historical review of education in the Americas; the contemporary educational scene in Latin America; educational planning; university education; science education and the ten-year plan under the alliance of progress. There is also a case study on Peru. The summary draws together points made by individual speakers and offers general proposals for the future.

UNESCO INTERNATIONAL INSTITUTE FOR EDUCATIONAL PLANNING, *Problems and Strategies of Educational Planning*, Paris, Unesco, 1965 is the report of a seminar which brought together over eighty participants from national governments and international agencies. The seminar was held in Paris and lasted for five weeks. One focus of attention were the socio-economic, political and educational conditions in Latin America which affect educational planning. The second theme was how educational planning can be effectively linked with social and economic development. Another was how educational planning could help to co-ordinate and make more efficient external aid. Finally the organizational and administrative arrangements needed to ensure the success of planning was taken as another theme. The chapter by the Director of the International Institute for Educational Planning, Philip H. COOMBS, sets the stage

REGIONAL CROSS-NATIONAL STUDIES

by presenting some general reflections on planning in Latin America. Subsequent chapters by named authors sketch in the economic background, the social and political problems and the educational background of Latin America. Chapter III reviews the achievements so far of planning, Chapter IV some major challenges and Chapter V reviews some of the highlights of the seminar.

Asia

The COLOMBO PLAN FOR CO-OPERATIVE ECONOMIC DEVELOPMENT IN SOUTH AND SOUTH-EAST ASIA originated as a British Commonwealth organization in 1950. It draws in countries in the great Asian arc from Pakistan, India through Burma, Cambodia, Viet-Nam, Indonesia, Malaysia, Borneo and countries like Australia, New Zealand. The plan aimed at the economic development of the area as a whole but education has always been central to its concern through the training of young men and women, and the establishment of training institutes, schools and colleges. The ANNUAL REPORT OF THE CONSULTATIVE COMMITTEE published by Her Majesty's Stationery Office gives an account of the work in this part of the world. It includes some aspects of education. The Karachi plan represents an attempt by governments of Asia to establish educational priorities. Its findings are reported in (q.v.) p. 45.

UNESCO SCIENCE POLICY STUDIES AND DOCUMENTS No. 3, *National Science Policies in Countries of South and South-East Asia* is a comparative study based on the proceedings of the Third Regional Meeting of Representatives of National Scientific Research Organizations of South and South-East Asia, Canberra, Australia, Feb. 17–21, 1964.

UNESCO and INTERNATIONAL ASSOCIATION OF UNIVERSITIES, Howard HAYDEN, *Higher Education and Development in South-East Asia*, Paris, Unesco and the International Association of Universities, Vol. 1, 1967 is the director's report of a study set up in co-operation with and the support of the Ford Foundation. The work began in 1961 and from then until 1965 extensive enquiries were made into the actual and potential contributions of higher education in the countries of South-East Asia to the achievements of the goals of cultural and social development. The first of three volumes is the director's synthetic analysis of the complex data assembled by the study. He deals first with the geographical, historical and social backgrounds of Burma, Thailand, Malaysia (Malaya and Singapore), Laos, Cambodia, Viet-Nam, Indonesia and the Philippines. Differences of language, ethnic background and political ideologies are described against a growing concept of regional needs and problems. Patterns of education are outlined with relevant quantitative data. Against the economic position of the countries, high-level manpower needs are reviewed in the light of economic development plans. In subsequent chapters special issues are taken up such as the expansion of higher education and social mobility; language policy for higher education; teacher education and the quality of educational and cultural developments; the growth of post-secondary institutions; and regional co-operation in higher education. The final chapter identifies major issues and conclusions. It is followed by appendices. Figures and tables are used extensively throughout the volume to support the analysis made.

Volume II, *Country Profiles* is by Howard HAYDEN and THE OFFICE OF THE STUDY IN KUALA LUMPUR.

Volume III, Part I, *High-level Manpower for Development*, is by Guy HUNTER; and Part II, *Language Policy and Higher Education*, is by Richard Noss.

Africa

Great interest has been shown in the political developments in the African continent. The diversities of culture, language, religion, race and levels of economic development have perhaps prevented the establishment of organizations devoted to cultural and educational research and co-operation for all the countries, or even some of them, of Africa. The Addis Ababa Conference was an important landmark. Its findings are recorded in UNITED NATIONS, Economic Commission for Africa, and UNESCO, *Conference of African States on the Development of Education in Africa, Addis Ababa, May 15-25, 1961, final report.*

UNESCO: DEVELOPMENT OF HIGHER EDUCATION, *The Teaching of Sciences in African Universities* is a report of the Seminar on the Teaching of Basic Sciences in African Universities, Rabat, Dec. 13–22, 1962.

SECTION III. CASE STUDIES

1. International Organizations

Several publications of the Unesco International Institute for Educational Planning are case studies in that they deal with selected problems in a particular country. The number of such accounts is likely to grow. A few are annotated here as a guide to further publications. Generally speaking, however, world organizations are committed by their terms of reference to initiate and support international enquiries. Unesco's own pilot projects in the field of

CASE STUDIES

fundamental education, e.g. in Patzcuaro, Mexico, are in a very real sense case studies from which much general theory may be learned. One example of a Unesco case study is S. G. SHAPOVALENKO (ed.), *Polytechnical Education in the USSR* (Unesco Monographs on Education), Paris, Unesco, 1963.

2. Regional Organizations

Again these organizations are primarily interested in issues of concern to all their members. Rather few case studies are therefore to be expected. The organization for Economic Co-operation and Development (OECD), however, has made economic surveys of various European countries and the United States. In its *Education and Development* series as part of *The Mediterranean Regional Project: An Experiment in Planning by Six Countries* there are country reports on Greece, Spain, Turkey and Yugoslavia.

The Pan-American Union, Washington, D.C. is responsible for a few case studies. For example, its Division of Labor and Social Affairs published in 1957 in its *Workers' Education Series* an account of an experiment in workers' education in El Salvador entitled *Labor Institutes in El Salvador*. The Institute of Inter-American Affairs, Division of Education has also been responsible for studies of aspects of education in selected Latin American countries. Comparative educationists with a special interest in these countries would do well to consult a comprehensive bibliography of publications by these agencies.

3. Individual Authors

The number of books dealing with aspects of education in a selected country is too great to make it possible to give anything like a comprehensive list in this chapter. Some guide lines may be given to help those who wish to build up a depth knowledge of a particular country.

FRASER's (q.v.) volume on France and FOSTER's (q.v.) book on Ghana have already been mentioned. They are both in Routledge & Kegan Paul's well-known series The International Library of Sociology and Social Reconstruction. Other volumes in this series are: R. H. SAMUEL and R. H. THOMAS, *Education and Society in Modern Germany*, 1949, J. BENTWICH, *Education in Israel*, 1965, R. P. DORE, *Education in Tokugawa Japan*, and Brian and Joan SIMON (eds), *Educational Psychology in the USSR*, 1963.

Case studies on education in China are rather rare. CHANG-TU HU has analysed the reforms in Chinese education over the last decade and provided translations of articles by prominent Chinese leaders in *Chinese Education under Communism*, New York Bureau of Publications, Teacher's College, Columbia University, 1962 (Classics in Education, No. 7). Stewart FRASER has compiled in translation a great many speeches, articles and documents on education from Communist China in *Chinese Communist Education*, New York, Wiley, 1965.

Vernon MALLINSON is well-known for his interest in and knowledge of Belgian affairs. His *Power and Politics in Belgian Education*, London, Heinemann was published in 1963. His *Modern Belgian Literature*, London, Heinemann was published in 1967 (q.v.).

If the Gown Fits is an illuminating case study in Australian university politics by A. P. ROWE published by the Melbourne University Press in 1960.

These random samples are mentioned here to indicate the range in case studies both in terms of topic and method of investigation. Those listed and annotated in this chapter have, for the most part, been written by comparative educationists and therefore reflect the interests and methodology of scholars working in this field. Many of them should provide a foundation on which further research in depth can be initiated. Others are the outcome of research, some features of which will be reviewed in the next chapter.

4. Selected Bibliography by Author

Harold R. W. BENJAMIN, *Higher Education in the American Republics*, New York, McGraw-Hill, 1965 is a report of one of the first projects of the Council on Higher Education in the American Republics (CHEAR). A number of consultants helped the author who also made use of special field studies and research reports. More than a hundred Latin American universities were visited in various countries. The introduction to the volume comprises a brief comparative study of higher education followed by a very brief account of the European prototypes on which the early institutions of higher education in Spanish America were based during the period 1538–1850. In this section the traditional and more recent aims of higher education in Spanish America (and Brazil) are compared by implication with those of the USA. Part 2 deals with the institutions and personnel of the universities in the Southern Spanish American region, the Caribbean Countries, Central America and Mexico, Brazil and the United States of America. In the conclusion the present provision and future trends in higher education are discussed. The author is of the opinion that if higher education can in the future provide the driving spirit of effective

CASE STUDIES

action the countries of Latin America will be ensured of a splendid age.

J. D. CHESSWAS, *Educational Planning and Development in Uganda* (African research monographs), Unesco: International Institute for Educational Planning, 1966 is one of the series which includes monographs dealing with the aspects of planning in selected countries, e.g. Nigeria, Tanzania and Senegal. This volume is by an officer who was formerly in charge of educational planning in Uganda. He stresses the need for co-ordination and the creation of a planning unit within the Ministry of Education. Techniques in the formulation and implementation of educational plans are described. Statistics of the educational system of Uganda are given and ways of planning the structure and content of education are discussed. Appendices in tabular form provide a great deal of information about the school system.

Adam CURLE, *Planning for Education in Pakistan*, London, Tavistock Publications, 1966 is a personal case study of the problems of educational planning in Pakistan. The author deals with his work as a short-term consultant to the planning commission of the Pakistan government. He admits that the book is written both for the person seriously interested in planning and for those who are interested in a gossipy account of a foreign adviser. Over twenty tables provide the reader with considerable factual data. Much of the narrative is impressionistic and succeeds in giving the reader a sense of the problems facing educationists in the country. The author can do little more than predict that whatever happens Pakistan is bound to pass through a period of disturbing social, political and psychological changes. As an introduction to the problems of this and other similar countries this book is of value.

Robert King HALL, *Education for a New Japan*, New Haven, Yale University Press, 1949 is a case study in the impact of foreign (largely American) educational thought and practice on Japan. It is carefully documented and should not now be regarded as providing an accurate picture of education in Japan but it reveals the successes and failures of a policy to democratize a defeated nation through the reform of its educational system.

Harold J. NOAH, *Financing Soviet Schools*, Studies of the Russian Institute, Columbia University, New York, Teacher's College Press, Columbia University, 1966 is a revised version of a dissertation presented at Columbia University. The author first describes the system of formal education in the Soviet Union under the 1958 reforms. He then goes on to deal with the various sources of funds made available for education before discussing the state budget, fiscal management and education. Teachers' Salaries in the light of wages policies, urban-rural differentials and wage costs per pupil are examined. There is a long bibliography of Soviet and other sources and several important Soviet documents as appendices.

H. H. STERN, *Parent Education—An International Study*, University of Hull and The Unesco Institute for Education, Hamburg, 1960 is the outcome of a five-year period of collaboration between the two institutions responsible for its publication. The starting points of the enquiry were (*a*) the recognition that a large proportion of the world's children live under pitiable conditions, (*b*) that hostility, prejudice, nationalism create group conflicts and international tension, and (*c*) that mental and physical disabilities frequently have their origin in the years of growth when the child is dependent on his parents. Parent education is seen as one aspect of social policy which might help to alleviate some of these problems. Part I deals with the medical and pyschological, the educational and the social arguments in favour of parent education. Part II describes the developments in this field through advisory services, mass media, the relationship between the home and schools and specialized services. Part III takes up the pattern of parent education in four different countries: USA, France, the Federal Republic of Germany, and the U.K. The final part concerns itself with remaining doubts and difficulties. There are a number of appendices and a very extensive bibliography.

J. F. THORNLEY, *The Planning of Primary Education in Northern Nigeria* (African research monographs), Paris, Unesco: International Institute for Educational Planning, 1966 is in a series devoted to aspects of educational studies (q.v.). Important reports such as the Ashby Commission, the Archer Report, the Government Plan, and the Oldman Report on the Education Authorities are reviewed in the first section. In the second section the plan is elaborated for primary education. External assistance is briefly discussed and the achievements and failures of the plan are assessed.

SECTION IV. USEFUL BIBLIOGRAPHIES

HMSO, *International Organisations Publications*, Supplement to Government Publications, 19—, London, HMSO, is a catalogue of international organizations' publications for the year prior to publication. Organizations include international agencies, such as United Nations, and its agencies, the International Atomic Energy

USEFUL BIBLIOGRAPHIES

Agency, the International Monetary Fund, etc., and regional organizations such as the Council of Europe, the Western European Union, the Organisation for Economic Co-operation and Development and the Organisation of American States. Reports, titles in series, yearbooks and periodicals are listed.

Organisation for Economic Co-operation and Development, *Catalogue of Publications* 19—, Paris, OECD, 19— contains an alphabetical index of titles and authors as well as titles classified for easy reference on the main general activities of the Organisation. These include Economics, Statistics, Manpower and Social Affairs, and Education and Science. Areas of particular concern to OECD in education are Science Policy, Long-term Education Planning, the Improvement of School Science Teaching, and the Pooling of Resources for Scientific Research. Titles of conference reports, trends in reform, and reviews of national policy indicate the range of interest of OECD in education. Some of them are annotated in this section.

5
LIBRARY TOOLS AND RESEARCH IN COMPARATIVE EDUCATION

This chapter endeavours to link up the tools for research with the centres for research, and describes publications coming from these centres and societies in comparative education.

Section 1. Research Trends

The scope of comparative education has widened since the second world war no doubt because of the renewed interest in cultural borrowing as a means of educational reform. Studies of foreign systems of education have often been undertaken with the intention of improving the investigator's own system. Government reports such as CROWTHER (15 to 18) and ROBBINS on *Higher Education* in England, have increasingly included comparative data. Much of the work of Unesco has been based on the requests made by member governments for information on which to establish reform policies.

At the same time students should perhaps be warned that caution is needed when they read books urging upon their own or other governments reforms based on eulogies of foreign schools. Many comparative arguments have been built on rather little evidence and somewhat naïve interpretations. Pejorative accounts may be as misleading as eulogies. There is in the USA, for example, a great deal of literature dealing with the so-called defects of the American schools. Glowing accounts of education in Europe and particularly in the USSR have been used by American critics of their own system to urge reform. In England the comprehensive school debates have drawn heavily on American and Swedish experience and research.

Research is of course constantly in progress. Much careful planning and many research data go into the preparation of the major reference works already mentioned such as Unesco's *World Survey of Education* (q.v.) the IBE's *Yearbooks* (q.v.) and the *World Year Book of Education* (q.v.). Regional organizations such as the Council of Europe and the Organisation for Economic

Co-operation and Development, to whose publications reference has already been made, are also engaged in what might be termed applied research. Readers will be able to find references to these studies either in previous chapters or in the bibliographies.

Inevitably, at another level, much of the research in comparative education is carried out in University Departments and Research Institutes. Traditionally, perhaps, the orientation of the work was historical. Pioneers in the English-speaking world like KANDEL (q.v.) and HANS (q.v.) based their interpretations on historical analysis. This tradition continues to flourish and many research theses are still basically historical and most of them take some account of the historical antecedents of present policies. Indeed it is not possible to understand the present without some knowledge of the past. Research theses devoted to the historical development of education in selected countries add greatly to knowledge of present problems and provide invaluable data for national case studies. One example of the cumulative value of this kind of research are the theses largely supervised by the late Sophia WEITZMAN at the University of London Institute of Education which were concerned with the history of education in India and Pakistan. Ceylon, too, has been the focus of attention more recently. This tradition continues so that the antecedents of many present-day educational systems, particularly in the British Commonwealth, may be known.

The present trend in comparative education research takes its impetus, perhaps, from the views of Sir Michael SADLER who pointed out that education could only be correctly understood when seen in relation to other aspects of society. There can be no doubt that the use of techniques adapted from sociology, psychology and political science is growing. Many scholars claim that research in comparative education is necessarily interdisciplinary in character and must depend for its success on the use it can make of these social science techniques. At the same time it is recognized that the subject has methodologies of its own which must be applied with rigour. Moreover the direct and uncritical application of a technique drawn from one of the social sciences may lead to unfortunate results.

The object of much recent research has been practical. Comparative education has been seen as an instrument of reform and the planned development of education. Certainly much attention has been given to this aim and to the role of the social sciences by the Comparative Education Society in Europe. The findings of the Conference, held every other year, have been published in the

Proceedings of the Society: *Comparative Education Research and the Determinants of Educational Policy*, Amsterdam Meeting, 1963 and *General Education in a Changing World*, Berlin, 1965. In both volumes the contribution made by comparative education research to the formulation of policy is stressed. At the same time great attention is paid to the part the social sciences—statistics, economics, sociology and political science—should play in the development of comparative education.

The list of members of the Comparative Education Society in Europe is published in the Amsterdam Conference Proceedings (q.v.). It shows how wide is the interest in comparative education throughout Europe. Reference has already been made to the work of some of the centres in Hamburg, Berlin and Bonn, and articles about them are listed in a previous chapter. Readers will, however, note from this list, that most of the universities of the Netherlands and Belgium have persons initiating and conducting comparative education research and teaching. Many distinguished pioneers work in Germany. In and near Paris are several centres at which work is done. Austrian members are at Innsbruck and Vienna. In Spain work is carried on in Madrid and at a new centre in Barcelona. The centre in Geneva has already been mentioned. In Italy members come from Florence and Rome. The Scandinavian universities are well represented. Among the founder members are scholars from Yugoslavia and Poland. More recently the interest in comparative education research has become more pronounced in the German Democratic Republic, Czechoslovakia and the USSR. Some of these centres publish important journals but since few of them are in English they have not been annotated in this bibliography. Nevertheless research workers in the field should be familiar with foreign literature and some titles of periodicals are listed later in the chapter.

In the English-speaking world the University of London and Teacher's College, Columbia University, New York have long been centres of research and teaching. The *World Year Book* for which editorially they are jointly responsible has already been described in some detail. Since the second world war several departments in England and the USA have strengthened their interest in and promoted teaching and research in comparative education. The Department of Education at Reading prepares many students for research degrees in this field, and has an extensive teaching programme. The Department of Education at Oxford University too has done a considerable amount of similar work. Most of the other English universities include on their teaching staff persons whose interest and research in comparative education qualify them for membership of the Comparative Education Society in Europe. The Scottish Universities are also represented by individual members. The names of these scholars can be found in the Amsterdam *Proceedings of the Society* (q.v.).

In the USA a number of factors, including that country's new post-war international role, have helped to promote interest in comparative education. This resulted in a Government bill in 1966 designed to aid the establishment throughout the country of international centres. A number of universities along with Columbia engage in comparative education research. The Comparative Education Center in Chicago was established in 1958 and has produced a number of studies, particularly in the economics of education. The Department of Education at Michigan University has many students preparing research theses in the field. Other university centres are George Peabody College, Nashville; Pittsburgh University; Syracuse University; Stanford; Wisconsin; University of California at Los Angeles; New York University; Boston University; and the University of Pennsylvannia. Many other institutions are developing programmes in comparative education and the Comparative Education Society, USA draws together interested professors and research workers.

There has been a growth of interest in Canada (Alberta, McGill and Vancouver), in Australia (Sydney and Melbourne), New Zealand, India, Ceylon and Japan. Several Latin American scholars work in the field. In most of these countries the possibilities of establishing comparative education societies have been discussed. There is little doubt that through such organizations collaboration in research will be strengthened.

Before considering in more detail the aims and organization of the societies which already exist; it is appropriate to point out to intending research students some of the basic aids. The development of libraries, documentation centres, bibliographies, abstracting services and other aids are essential to the progress of research. Teachers of comparative education and students would be well advised before embarking on their own research, however modest, to familiarize themselves with these basic aids. They should then consult some of the many theses and research reports listed in the third section of this chapter. The work done by members of the various comparative education societies should be consulted by any student engaged on postgraduate enquiries since this will give a comprehensive picture of the range, scope and type of investigation being promoted by leaders in the field.

LIBRARY TOOLS AND RESEARCH

Section 2. Library Tools

The sources intended for investigation in this section are the 'tools' or aids that assist in amassing information and publications other than those described in an earlier chapter. Bibliographies of particular countries were included in the chapter on area studies since they seemed most useful in that context. Those described here are the tools that lecturers might advise their students to use in compiling a bibliography for a special essay or a thesis, as well as being the tools that a librarian would use both for assistance in building up and maintaining the stock of a comparative library of education, or the comparative section of an education library, and for finding material in answer to a particular enquiry. The material is arranged according to the classification tenets of beginning with the general and going on to the specific and then back to the general, having covered specific areas of the world as well as subject areas relative to the teaching of comparative education.

A librarian begins a search for information by looking at an encyclopedia in order to get a general over-all view on a subject as well as a short bibliography. Almost every Education Library will have:

W. S. MONROE, *Encyclopedia of Educational Research*, 3rd edn, edited by C. W. Harris with the assistance of M. R. Liba, New York, Macmillan, 1960. There he will find an article by G. F. KNELLER, 'Comparative education', pp. 316–323. This article gives the aims and values, nature and content, method, present status and problems of comparative education. The bibliography contains references that are mainly to journals and conference reports.

An over-all review of the literature of comparative education appears every three years in the *Review of Educational Research*. This is the official publication of the American Education Research Association. The review which appeared in Vol. XXXIV, No. 1, 1964 was written by William BRICKMAN. It surveys the literature in comparative education since 1960. Reports are given of the material on the history, theory, methodology, general works, textbooks, reference works, statistics, yearbooks. Studies of educational systems of one country are not reported unless they are of a comparative nature. The previous review in 1961 contained few entries compared with that of 1964, demonstrating the rapid growth in the literature of the subject in the last few years. The comparative education journals might then be searched for general articles on comparative education. The simplest way of tracking down articles is to use the published periodical subject indexes. For the *Compara-*

LIBRARY TOOLS

tive Education Review and other American journals which from time to time contain an article of interest on Comparative Education use the American index published by H. W. Wilson: *Education Index* published monthly except during June and August. There are various cumulations culminating in a bound two-yearly issue. Volume 1 covers 1929–32 and thereafter to date. This is a subject and author index in one sequence.

The International Review of Education is also indexed in this American index but also appears in:

The British Education Index, compiled by the librarians of the Institutes of Education since 1954 and published four times a year and cumulated every two years approximately. The English journal *Comparative Education* will also be indexed in this. This index is arranged in alphabetical order of subject headings based on educational terminology with a second section arranged in alphabetical order of authors' names. Another source useful both for the beginner and the advanced reader in comparative education is the annual *Year Book of Education* now the *World Year Book of Education* published since 1932 by Evans Brothers, London and New York (q.v.). This is indexed in the *British Education Index* since 1954, and in *The Education Index*. A cumulative index for 1932–62 can be found on cards at the Institute of Education Comparative Education Library, London, and may eventually be published.

The librarian or student beginning to study comparative education now has some idea of the nature of comparative education and wishes to collect some information on a particular country. He would do well to turn to the *Unesco World Surveys of Education*. In reading through the introduction to these and seeking to see how they are arranged he would find both a definition of comparative education and a method of investigation. These volumes have been described in detail in a previous chapter. They make a very good starting point for information on a particular country and the bibliography at the end of each country description leads on to further material. The diagrams of the education system and the glossary of educational terms in the language of the country concerned are a help, too, in understanding publication in languages other than one's own. These volumes are kept up to date by the annual *International Yearbook of Education*. This is a joint publication of Unesco and the International Bureau of Education, Geneva. This was published 1933–39, and 1946 to date. It is valuable for current information and statistics. It gives a survey of educational progress during the previous year and national reports of education. It includes, too, a list of leading officials in the Ministries of Education.

Another Unesco volume that is a companion volume to the *Surveys* is the *International Guide to Educational Documentation 1955–1960*, Paris, 1963. This book is a guide to sources of documentation. Under each country there is a list of the principal sources for obtaining material and names of reference books where further information may be found. It is not intended to be a bibliography itself, though bibliographies are listed where other information is lacking. Lists of books in English put out by the Ministry or information service of a country can often be obtained through this source.

Two other extremely useful Unesco tool publications which have now ceased appearing are the series:

(1) *Educational Studies and Documents* 1953–65. These came out five times a year and the subjects treated were usually national case studies or reports on Unesco projects. Examples are:

An *International Directory of Education Associations*, 1959, No. 34.

An *International List of Educational Periodicals*, 1957, No. 23.

(2) *Education Abstracts*, 1949–64. These contained an introductory article on a particular aspect of education followed by abstracts of books and documents relating to the topic from various countries. *Teaching Comparative Education*, 1963, No. 4 (q.v.) came out in this series. This is an annotated bibliography listing the main texts with an introduction on the teaching of the subject.

Another international publication that offers a constant service in keeping the reader up to date in publications of other countries is the *Bulletin of the International Bureau of Education*, 1926 to date, Geneva, IBE, quarterly. This contains a section of news items and an annotated bibliography of recent books arranged in classified order. This is cumulated annually and is also available in a card index service. It is in fact the acquisitions list of the education library of the International Bureau of Education; it therefore covers a wide area of publications. Since the annotations are supplied in English as well as in French this is a very useful source for tracking down recent publications both for the librarian and the teacher.

A similar publication from the United States is the *Foreign Education Digest*, Berkeley, California, 1936 to date, mimeographed, quarterly. It is divided into two parts. Part 1 contains digests classified into distinct groups. Part 2 is an annotated bibliography of education from all over the world. Approximately half the entries are digests of articles from journals and the rest reports and books.

LIBRARY TOOLS

This would be particularly useful to a College of Education Library since it gives an over-all picture of what is happening in education in many parts of the world in a fairly direct and straightforward way.

The *United States Office of Education* brings out a variety of publications including bibliographies on education in other countries. These have often been quoted in the areas studies section under the countries concerned.

A recent publication that deals with education in Europe is: COUNCIL OF EUROPE, Documentation Centre for Education in Europe, *Compendium of Basic Bibliographies by Country*, Strasbourg, Council of Europe, 1966 onwards. These bibliographies give a list of the most important periodicals and basic works on education and the organization of teaching in each of the member states of the Council for Cultural Co-operation and have been compiled with the help of national correspondents. It is intended to publish a revised edition at the beginning of each year.

Another service from this Centre is:

COUNCIL OF EUROPE, Documentation Centre for Education in Europe, *Abstracts*, Strasbourg, Council of Europe, 1965 onwards. These are abstracts of the legal aspects of education in Europe (laws, decrees, acts, reports) passed since 1965. These are issued in the form of a loose-leaf binder so that it can be kept up to date. It is arranged by country in the first instance and pages may be filed either chronologically or according to the school system—primary, secondary, etc., as preferred.

Embassies and Information Offices are often very useful sources of information and sometimes issue publications particularly concerned with education. Such publications are:

Education in France. Published four times a year by the Cultural Services of the French Embassy, New York, 1957 to date. This covers developments in French education at all levels including abstracts of theses, the creation of new schools and universities, book reviews and often includes illustrations. The various reforms in French education are well covered.

Education in Germany, 1963 to date. Obtainable through the German Embassy in London. Published by Inter Nationes, Bonn, Germany. This is a mimeographed bulletin. It includes articles, news in brief, interviews with educationists, guide to new developments and reports.

Another source for material on Europe are the jointly compiled lists of stocks in the libraries of the Institutes of Education in England.

LIBRARY TOOLS AND RESEARCH

Education in France; Education in Germany: These lists give the location of the books in the U.K. Institute Libraries. The lists may be obtained from University of Southampton, Institute of Education.

Another valuable abstracting service emanating from Europe is *CIRF Abstracts*, 1961 to date issued every two months by the Geneva International Labour Office. This International Vocational Training Information Centre has an extensive programme for information and research on training workers, supervisors and technicians including teachers in training in these fields and these abstracts are programmes and experiences described in periodicals, books, reports, etc. These abstracts cover countries in East Europe as well as the West and other countries as well. Eastern Europe has several abstracting services that are in English. Among these are:

Abstracts of Bulgarian Scientific Literature, Philosophy and Pedagogics, Sofia, Bulgarian Academy of Sciences, Centre for Scientific Information and Documentation. Published twice a year, 1958 to date. This gives fairly detailed summaries of the article or book so that the abstracts act as an information service.

Quarterly Review of Scientific Publications, Warsaw, Polish Academy of Sciences, Documentation and Scientific Information Centre. The purpose of this review is to give, in English, information on publications brought out by various centres of the Polish Academy of Sciences, Schools of academic standard, Research institutes, and Scientific Societies.

Soviet Education, New York, International Arts and Sciences Press, 1958 to date, quarterly, contains complete translations of important scholarly articles appearing in leading Soviet journals.

Education in the USSR is a collection of readings from Soviet journals. Edited by F. ABLIN, 2 Vols, International Arts and Sciences Press, 1963. This is arranged under broad subject areas and enables the reader to take a quick look at the literature that has been appearing in the Soviet journals for the previous few years.

Selected Bibliography of Yugoslav Educational Materials, Belgrade, Nolit Publishing House, 1965 to date. This is prepared, translated and published for the Office of Education of the Department of Health, Education and Welfare. This gives annotations in English of educational materials—articles, documents and reports.

India has an abstracting service for education journals: *Indian Education Abstracts*, New Delhi, Ministry of Education, 1955 to date, quarterly, confined to books and periodicals on education published in India or on Indian education in English. Over fifty Indian journals are indexed. Each entry includes bibliographical details and gives a synopsis of the article showing the author's intention and his conclusions. A location guide to Indian material in London Libraries has been compiled by M. A. GREAVES, *Education in British India* 1698–1947: A bibliography and comprehensive guide to sources of information in London (F.L.A. thesis 1966).

The United States Office of Education has recently begun a type of abstracts for Burma: *Burma Education Abstracts*, occasional publication, Vol. 1, 1961–62. Vol. 2, 1962–63, Vol. 3, 1963–64. Compiled for the Division of International Studies and Services, Bureau of International Education, U.S. Department of Health, Education and Welfare, Office of Education. This is published as a research document for institutions having an active research interest in education in Burma. These volumes contain photocopy abstracted material, articles, comments, all taken from a larger survey.

THE AUSTRALIAN COUNCIL FOR EDUCATIONAL RESEARCH publishes: *Australian Education Index* 1958 to date. This is a quarterly index to books, pamphlets and periodical articles on education and psychology published in Australia, works on Australian education and works by Australian authors published in other countries.

African publications have been well organized and information about them is disseminated by the STANDING CONFERENCE ON LIBRARY MATERIALS ON AFRICA (SCOLMA). Scolma was established in 1962 in order to improve the coverage of publications needed for African studies, by co-ordinating their acquisition and facilitating their use through bibliographic aids. The Conference has published a guide to special collections on Africa and a list of these on Africa. The *Scolma Directory of Libraries and Special Collections on Africa* lists all the libraries and societies concerned with acquiring material information on Africa. The second edition was published in 1967 and may be obtained from Crosby Lockwood & Sons Ltd., London. The UNIVERSITY OF LONDON, INSTITUTE OF EDUCATION, DEPARTMENT OF EDUCATION IN TROPICAL AREAS, puts out a typed information bulletin: *African Education Abstracts* to date. This is not an abstracting service in the accepted sense but information is given on developments concerned with African education, books and articles in journals. This would be useful to a College library beginning to build up a stock of books on Africa.

African Abstracts, London, International African Institute with the assistance of Unesco, quarterly, 1950 to date. This is a quarterly review of ethnological, social (including education) and linguistic studies appearing in current journals and has a rather more specialized and research approach.

LIBRARY TOOLS AND RESEARCH

The Commonwealth has a useful location and source guide in: *Guide to Resources for Commonwealth Studies* by A. R. HEWITT, University of London, Institute of Commonwealth Studies, 1957. This guide is intended for advanced research workers, particularly those who have come from overseas, since it locates material in London, Oxford and Cambridge. Bibliographies and works of reference are listed under countries or areas. This makes it valuable also to anyone building up a library or students compiling bibliographies for theses. A. R. HEWITT has also compiled *A Union List of Commonwealth Newspapers in London, Oxford and Cambridge*, London, Athlone Press, 1960.

There are other guides, source books, bibliographies, and abstracting services which may be mentioned in relation to subject areas, for example:

P. HEPWORTH, *How to Find Out in History:* a guide to sources of information for all (Commonwealth and International Library) Oxford, Pergamon Press, 1966. This bibliography is useful for tracing sources for historical material on other countries as well as Great Britain. It lists also contemporary bibliographies on other countries. It is a concise book, perhaps of more use to the young student rather than the advanced research student.

THE BRITISH COUNCIL has formed a language centre known as ETIC, the English Teaching Information Centre. This publishes in a mimeographed form an *English Teaching Bibliography* which began in 1961 and covered works then in print; supplements are issued at intervals. There is also *English Teaching Abstracts* 1961 to date. This is a quarterly review of articles on linguistic studies and the teaching of English as a second language. Fairly concise summaries are given. This would be of use to the language teachers teaching comparative education and wanting material on such problems as 'bilingualism'.

Another CENTRE FOR INFORMATION ON LANGUAGE TEACHING (CILT) was established in 1967. It is housed in the same place as ETIC, State House, High Holborn, London W.C.1, and was set up by the Secretary of State for Education and Science and the Secretary of State for Scotland. The work of the new Centre will include the provision of information about research findings in linguistics, language studies, psychology and teaching methodology which are relevant to the improvement of language teaching at all levels. CILT will aim to deal with those languages including English as a second language, which are most widely taught in Britain. There will be a library and a documentation centre.

The sociologist teaching comparative education would find

LIBRARY TOOLS

helpful: *Sociology of Education Abstracts*, Liverpool, 1965 to date. This new quarterly arose out of a partnership between the University of Liverpool School of Education, and Departments of Social Science and Adult Education, and the Department of Sociology, Edge Hill College of Education. It provides a comprehensive summary of sociology research and writing relevant to the study of education. Some 150 journals from all over the world are abstracted by sociologists. It is intended to help the reader organize his professional reading. *Sociological Abstracts*, New York, Sociology Abstracts, quarterly, 1953 to date. These abstracts are international in scope and cover about 100 journals and also Ph.D. dissertations.

International Bibliography of Sociology, Vol. X—London, Stevens and Sons, Chicago, Aldine Publishing Co., 1962 to date. This is prepared by the International Committee for Social Science Documentation. Vols. I-IX, 1952-61 were published by Unesco. Economics, politics and anthropology are all covered in this series. The sociology volumes are particularly useful for comparative material on social change. Books as well as articles in journals are included.

Social Sciences and Humanities Index, New York, Wilson, 1965 to date. This was formerly the International Index 1907-65. It is a quarterly with an annual cumulation. It is a subject and author index to articles in the social sciences and humanities. It lists, too, comparative articles on economic and manpower developments.

The economics of education is fast developing as a subject for study. Teachers, students and librarians are all well provided for in: M. BLAUG, *Economics of Education:* a selected annotated bibliography. London, New York, Pergamon Press, 1966. The annotations are of sufficient length to provide information in themselves as well as being a guide to help the reader decide if he wants to see the work concerned. It also makes it possible for students of different levels of study to use it.

Technical education has been provided by two services in England as well as the CIRF international service already described. *Technical Educational Abstracts*, London, National Foundation for Educational Research, 1961 to date. Publication has been irregular but after 1966 will be quarterly with subject, author and title indexes, the fourth number of each volume will contain a cumulated subject index to the volume. The articles abstracted are concerned with technical and further education including education and training for industry, commerce and agriculture.

Bacie Bibliography, London, British Association for Commercial and Industrial Education, Vol. 1960-62. The *Bacie Journal* includes a bibliographical supplement to each number. This has been cumulated to make this bibliography, with the addition of a subject index. The bibliography lists a selection of the most important publications published in the field of education and training in industry and commerce.

The period immediately after the second world war when technological development was gathering momentum was covered by: B. BOARD, compiler, *The Effect of Technological Progress on Education*, a classified bibliography from British sources 1945–57, London, Institute of Production Engineers, 1959.

Many teachers of comparative education will probably begin by teaching about international understanding. There is now so much material in this field particularly in pamphlet form that it is difficult to describe it. Perhaps it is sufficient to give the names of three associations that bring out publications other than the obvious ones such as Unesco and the Unesco Institute of Education at Hamburg.

COUNCIL FOR EDUCATION IN WORLD CITIZENSHIP, London. Among other things it published *Education for International Understanding*, CEWC, 1965. This is a comprehensive guide to the organizations in Britain concerned with international education and describes the services provided by each.

THE PARLIAMENTARY GROUP FOR WORLD GOVERNMENT, London is another organization that concerns itself with the world perspective. It has published:

History Syllabuses and a World Perspective, a comparative survey of examination syllabuses in use in Britain and overseas. A new edition was published in 1967, in conjunction with Longmans, Green & Co.

THE ATLANTIC INFORMATION CENTRE FOR TEACHERS, London. This exists to assist teachers of current international affairs in the secondary schools of Europe and America. Each term it publishes *The World and the School*, a review containing material for current affairs lessons and discussion.

The Year Book of Education (q.v.) for 1964 was called *Education and International Life* and contained a great deal of comparative information on international understanding.

History teachers might find interesting:

Towards World Understanding by S. A. SMITH, London, Library Association.

Another bibliography prepared with the subject in mind is:

Readings on International Understanding: a selected list for curriculum workers. Prepared by J. KATZ for the Phi Delta Kappa

Commission on International Relations in Education, 1964. This is intended to assist teachers in specific fields to find material which will be helpful in showing the international aspect of their knowledge.

The teaching of immigrant children is another area where there is a link with comparative education and where material and research is increasing. A review of the literature was published in:

Educational Research, Journal of the National Foundation for Educational Research, Vol. VIII, No. 3, 1966, pp.163–181. 'Coloured immigrant children: a survey of research, studies and literature on their educational problems and potential in Britain', by R. J. GOLDMAN and F. M. TAYLOR.

There are a number of publications that may be obtained free and are useful both for teachers and librarians. The two following booklets are a guide to these.

M. O. M. MORRIS (ed) *Treasure Chest for Teachers*, London, The Schoolmaster Publishing Co., Revised edn, 1963. This lists the bodies from which teachers can obtain information or instructional material, such as foreign embassies, commercial firms, societies and so on.

L. S. KENWORTHY, *Free and Inexpensive Materials on World Affairs*, 5th edn, New York, Columbia University, Teacher's College, Bureau of Publications, 1963. Most of the items included in this list have been published since 1960. They come from a wide variety of institutions representing different points of view. A list of addresses of the institutions supplying material is given at the end of the booklet.

For research students and those who want to build up a vast amount of references to material on other countries there are of course the catalogues of the large libraries and some of the small libraries have printed catalogues also. Among these are:

BRITISH MUSEUM *General Catalogue of Printed Books*, photolithographic edition to 1955, London, British Museum, 1965–66, 263 vols. with additions 1963, 5 vols.

Royal Commonwealth Society Catalogue, Vols. 1–3, subject catalogue 1930–37, Vol. 4, biography catalogue 1961. This last volume lists all biographical material concerning persons connected with the Commonwealth found in this library. Periodical articles are frequently included.

West India Library Catalogue. This is a list of books arranged by subject which were in the West India Committee Library in 1940. This list is especially rich in pamphlets dealing with slavery and emancipation.

PUBLIC RECORD OFFICE, *Guide to the Contents of the Public Record Office*, London, HMSO, 1963.

Most countries now produce national bibliographies which are made up of all the publications published in the country concerned in a weekly, monthly, quarterly, yearly and cumulated form. For Great Britain there is the:

British National Bibliography published by the Council of the British National Bibliography, 1950 to date. This is a subject list of the new books published in Great Britain classified according to the Dewey decimal classification with an author and title index. Thus all the books on education are brought together and also all the books on each country.

Journals naturally contain the most up-to-date material. The most important ones in comparative education have already been mentioned in this chapter; others that contain comparative articles are:

British Journal of Educational Studies, London, Faber, 1952. Published twice a year. This contains scholarly articles often of the source type. For example: 'Some sources for French educational history to 1789' by H. C. BARNARD, Vol. 11, No. 2, May 1954, pp. 166–169. Vernon MALLINSON has written on sources for Belgium education, J. L. HENDERSON for German education, A. C. F. BEALES for Spanish education, etc.

Comparative Studies in Society and History: an international quarterly, The Hague, Mouton, 1958 to date. This journal is concerned more with comparative method than comparative education.

Educational Sciences: an international journal, Vol. 1, 1966 onwards. London, Pergamon Press, three times a year. This is a new international journal on education and therefore any country may be used as an example to illustrate the subject chosen for investigation.

International Journal of Adult and Youth Education, Paris, Unesco, 1949 to date, quarterly. This was previously called Fundamental and Adult Education. This journal is mainly concerned with adult education, social education, international understanding and problems of education in developing countries.

Trends in Education, London, Department of Education and Science, quarterly, 1966 onwards. This is a new journal intended for teachers in order to keep them up to date with trends in education and therefore has articles on education in other countries and on such matters as world history teaching.

This section on tools should perhaps conclude with a reference to the 'Foskett' and 'Kimmance' publications since they are both particularly concerned with the tools of education and the writer has referred to these in writing this section.

D. J. FOSKETT, *How to Find Out:* educational research (Commonwealth and International Library), London, Pergamon Press, 1965. Chapter 8 deals with comparative education as one of the specific fields of research.

S. K. KIMMANCE, *A Guide to the Literature of Education*, University of London Institute of Education, Education Libraries Bulletin, Supplement No. 1, Revised edition, 1961. This is a guide to the literature of education and is not intended to be a comprehensive bibliography. It should form the basis of an education library and is therefore of particular interest to any education librarian.

Section 3. Preparing for Research

Compared with many subjects taught at the university Comparative Education is relatively new. Its methods and content have not been defined very exactly. Many methodologies are being developed often through debates and discussions and many techniques taken from the social sciences are being experimented with. The number of persons throughout the world whose professional position makes it possible for them to devote their time exclusively to Comparative Education is small but growing.

At the same time many more institutions of higher learning are introducing courses in Comparative Education and the amount of research completed and in progress is considerable.

Students and teachers preparing to embark on a piece of research would do well, if they are not already familiar with it, to review the literature in comparative education which is concerned with methodology and which gives some indication of the topics which are of interest to scholars in the field. Mention has already been made of the societies established fairly recently to promote comparative and international studies. Their formation, aims, organization and activities throw light on the general state of affairs at the moment.

In the United States of America the COMPARATIVE EDUCATION SOCIETY was organized at the third Annual Conference on Comparative Education sponsored and held at the School of Education, New York University in 1956. *Proceedings* of the first two meetings have been published—the first dealt with the role of comparative education in the education of teachers, the second was concerned with the teaching of comparative education. The *Proceedings* of the third meeting devoted to comparative education in theory and practice have been reprinted from the *Journal of Educational*

Sociology (New York), Vol. 30, No. 3, 1956, pp. 113–160. A report of this conference by W. W. BRICKMAN was published in the *International Review of Education* (Hamburg), Vol. III, No. 1, 1957, pp. 111–2. Subsequent conferences in New York dealt with comparative education and foreign educational service (4th Conference) and teaching about Soviet education (5th Conference) the *Proceedings* of which were published as a supplement to *School and Society*, New York, Vol. LXXXVI, No. 2140, 1958, pp.2–23 and reported by BRICKMAN in *International Review of Education*, Hamburg. Vol. V, No. 1, 1959, pp. 84–5. The sixth annual conference was on research and was also reported in the *International Review of Education*, Vol. VI, No. 1, 1960.

The Constitution of the Society was agreed in 1959 and a revised version was presented at the general meeting in 1967. Among the purposes of the Society are the promotion of teaching and research, the facilitation of publication and distribution of cross-cultural and inter-disciplinary studies and the encouragement of exchanges and other visits abroad by educators. Membership is open to teachers of comparative or international education, those engaged in these studies in international and other non-university organizations and to professional educationists who have shown interest in the field. Student membership is restricted to those who are spending at least half time in graduate study, and such membership can last for no longer than five years.

The Comparative Education Society holds general meetings and regional meetings each year, the reports of which are either published as separate documents or in the Society's official journal the *Comparative Education Review* edited until 1967 by George BEREDAY of Columbia University and since then by Harold J. NOAH from the same institution. Publications sponsored by the Society include *The Changing Soviet School*, London, Constable, 1961, edited by G. Z. F. BEREDAY, W. W. BRICKMAN and G. H. READ (q.v.). Collaboration with the COMPARATIVE EDUCATION SOCIETY IN EUROPE has been initiated and it is hoped that joint research projects will result from it in future.

The Comparative Education Society in Europe was formed in London in 1961 under the joint sponsorship of the University of London, Institute of Education and the Unesco Institute for Education in Hamburg. It was established to meet needs which had been expressed at an informal meeting of many pioneers of comparative education in London in 1951 (reported by W. W. BRICKMAN in *School and Society*, New York, Vol. LXXIII, No. 1902, pp. 334–5) and at a meeting held at the Unesco Institute in Hamburg in 1955.

PREPARING FOR RESEARCH

The *Proceedings* of this meeting were published by the Institute and a report of it by E. J. KING appeared in the *International Review of Education*, Vol. 1, No. 3, 1955, pp. 375–8. A report of the 1961 London conference by Brian HOLMES may be found in Vol. VII, No. 3, 1961, pp. 354–6 in the *Review*. Notices and the major papers read at subsequent conferences of the Society have appeared in the *International Review of Education*, in particular Vol. 9, No. 2, 1963, pp. 129–225 and Vol. II, No. 4, 1965, pp. 385–484.

The Constitution of the Comparative Education Society in Europe was drafted at a Meeting at the International Centre at Sèvres in 1962 and presented and accepted at the first general meeting of the Society held in Amsterdam in 1963. In preparation for this conference an expert meeting was arranged by the Unesco Institute for Education in Hamburg in March 1963 the report of which *Relevant Data in Comparative Education* (q.v.) was presented by Brian HOLMES and S. B. ROBINSOHN at the conference and published by the Institute. The full conference report has been published by the Society under the title *Comparative Education Research and the Determinants of Educational Policy*. It includes articles by L. FERNIG of Unesco and P. ROSSELLO of IBE, the names of members and the Constitution. The theme at the Berlin conference in 1965 was *General Education in a Changing World* which was published by Nijhoff, The Hague in 1967. It includes articles by J. A. LAUWERYS, E. SIMON, A. BANOVITCH, G. de LANDSHEERE, F. EDDING, Ph. J. IDENBURG, F. BOWLES, and B. HOLMES as well as papers and discussions presented at symposia on teaching and research in comparative education. These papers indicate the range of work going on in Europe. The 1967 conference was held in Ghent. The theme was *The University in the Education System* and papers were read on the new functions of the universities, teaching and faculty-student relations in them, and university reforms in various countries.

The stated aims of the Society are to promote and improve teaching of comparative education, to stimulate research, to facilitate the publication and distribution of comparative studies, to interest professors in other disciplines in the international dimensions of their work, to encourage exchanges, collaboration with other societies and to co-operate with workers in other disciplines. Membership is not restricted on the basis of country or region but it is restricted to teachers and research workers in comparative and international education and to those persons actively engaged in this kind of work in international agencies and other institutions of higher learning. Among its members are persons from most countries of Europe, from USA, Canada, Australia, New Zealand and Japan. Co-operation with other societies has been developed and national sections of the Society have been established.

In the Federal German Republic active regional meetings take place. At the University of Reading a conference was held in September 1965 at which a proposal to establish a British section of the Comparative Education Society in Europe was made and accepted. Papers were read which were published under the title *The Place of Comparative Education in the Training of Teachers*, edited by P. J. MERCIER.

A second conference was held in Reading in September 1966 at which the Constitution was adopted and papers dealing with various aspects of the teaching of comparative education were read. The aims of the U.K. Section of the Society are broadly in line with those of the parent body. Membership is not, however, restricted and student or associate members are accepted. Vernon MALLINSON of the Department of Education, University of Reading, Reading, was appointed Secretary and Paul MERCIER of the Reading Institute as Information Officer. The intention of the section is to promote in the British Isles comparative and international studies, provide bibliographical material, organize conferences and study groups and encourage study tours abroad.

As well as articles of interest to comparative educationists the *International Review of Education*, Hamburg, and the *Comparative Education Review*, New York, contain notes, references, bibliographies and reports of meetings and conferences. These two journals make it possible for interested persons to keep in touch with activities in comparative and international education.

Many of the articles deal with methodology; these and others have been listed in *Teaching Comparative Education* (q.v.) in the Unesco *Education Abstracts* series. An *Analytical Bibliography on Comparative Education* of items available in Unesco has been prepared in mimeographed form by the Unesco Department of School and Higher Education (Reference WS/0664.20-Ed, 1964). The main parts are: Part I, Attempts at Definition of Comparative Education; Part II, History, Development and Status of a Discipline of Comparative Education; Part III, Aims and Scope of Studies in the Field of Comparative Education; Part IV, Discussions on Methodology in Comparative Education; Part V, Teaching of Comparative Education; Part VI, Proceedings, Reports on Meetings on Comparative Education; Part VII, Library tools, Bibliographies and Glossaries for Comparative Education Studies. The arrangement in each part is by author. Most of the entries are periodical articles in English, French, German and Spanish.

Information on research centres in general can be obtained from publications such as that published by THE ORGANISATION FOR ECONOMIC CO-OPERATION AND DEVELOPMENT CENTRE, which was established in 1962, to bring together the knowledge and experience of member countries regarding economic policies and aid. It has three divisions, *External Relations-Documentation*, *Research* and *Training and Co-operation*. The *Catalogue of Social and Economic Development Institutes and Programme Research* published in Paris in 1966 provides particulars about 100 institutes in 35 countries. Many of them have been set up since 1950 and the publishers hope that they will foster greater co-operation. The contents are by country arranged alphabetically, they include developed and developing countries from Europe, the Americas, Africa and Asia and international organizations. Each organization is described under the following heads: General, which includes the name of the director, the aims and staffing; Training activities; Research activities; and Publications and documents. The information is concise and gives a clear picture of the kind of work carried out.

Another line of approach is through individual researchers rather than organizations.

The NATIONAL REGISTER OF EDUCATIONAL RESEARCHERS published by Phi Delta Kappa in Bloomington, Indiana, and compiled by the Bureau of Educational Research, College of Education, Ohio State University, was published in 1966. The biographies are arranged alphabetically. They include personal vita, educational background, professional position and research activities. The list runs to some 6,000 American researchers.

Several reports place comparative education research within the context of educational research in general. THE ORGANIZING COMMITTEE, INTERNATIONAL CONFERENCE ON EDUCATIONAL RESEARCH in Japan published in 1961 *Proceedings of the International Conference on Educational Research*. The conference was held in Tokyo during the first week of September 1959 and was attended by participants from Austria, Belgium, Canada, the Republic of China, England, France, Germany, India, Philippines, Saudia Arabia, the USA, as well as many scholars from Japan. It was organized by the Japan Society for the Study of Education. The main topics considered were: Problems and Methodology of Comparative Education; Eastern and Western Understanding, and Education; and Industry and Education. Part I contains addresses of welcome and opening remarks. Part II is made up of articles on the status of educational research in the countries from which participants came. Part III contains a number of articles on comparative education of general and historical interest including one by J. A. LAUWERYS on 'Problems and Methodology of Comparative Education'. Part IV is concerned with East-West understanding and the role education can play in fostering it. Part V is devoted to papers on industry and education and Part VI includes summaries, concluding remarks and so on. A supplement to this volume *Present Status of Educational Research in Japan* was published by the same committee in 1961. It covers a broad spectrum of educational research.

Another congress devoted to educational research was held in Oslo in May 1961. Papers presented there were published by the International Association for the Advancement of Educational Research under the title *The Role of Educational Research in Social Education*, Oslo, 1961. Among the papers were several read by comparative educationists and in particular one by N. HANS on 'Sociological Aspects of Comparative Education'.

Even more wide ranging were the research topics discussed at a meeting held in Cambridge in 1965. The report is in two volumes. M. J. LANGEVELD et al. *Paedagogica Europaea*: *The European Yearbook of Educational Research*, Edinburgh and London, Chambers, Vol. 1, 1965, and Vol. II, 1966 is in two volumes and was intended to provide a European forum for the discussion of educational questions. An editorial board of educationists assisted by other specialists drew together papers on various aspects of education read at the Congress of the International Association for the Advancement of Educational Research at Cambridge in August 1965. The first volume contains thirteen articles, two international reports (Council of Europe and Conferences of European Ministers of Education), three national reports from Sweden, Switzerland and the United Kingdom. LANGEVELD's article is entitled 'In Search of Research'; the others deal with a variety of topics including psychology in the USSR, the statistical aspects of the Robbins report, and the success of selection procedures in the German schools. In the second volume there are reports from OECD and Holland. Topics covered include educating a whole world, moral education, behaviour problems among adolescent boys and the contribution of research to education. Valuable interpretative articles are among this potpourri and could well be used as the basis of extended cross-national studies.

In the USA a volume edited by Keith GOLDHAMMER and Stanley ELAM *Dissemination and Implementation*, Third annual Phi Delta Kappa Symposium on Educational Research, Bloomington, Indiana,

PREPARING FOR RESEARCH

Phi Delta Kappa, 1962 is the report of a meeting held at the University of Oregon in July 1961. It was intended to follow this volume with one in 1962 devoted to operations research and systems analysis in education. Papers were read and discussed and included topics such as electronic methods of storing research data, the role of private philanthropy in disseminating information, the functions of various local and national agencies in this task and the problems of using communication media in the dissemination and implementation of educational research. A stimulating analytical volume concerned more with problems than with accomplished fact.

In Canada THE ONTARIO INSTITUTE FOR STUDIES IN EDUCATION published *Emerging Strategies and Structures for Educational Change*, Proceedings of the Anniversary invitational Conference in June 1966, Ontario, Publication Series No. 2 in 1966. It is the report of a conference called to celebrate the first anniversary of the establishment of the Ontario Institute for Studies in Education. Its purpose is to undertake a far-reaching programme of educational planning and basic research into aspects of education. As the title suggests, the theme was the possibility of developing strategies for change in the light of the need for educational change. The plans for change which have emerged in the USA, Britain, Quebec and Ontario are examined in a collection of articles by named authors. One report is by Philip TAYLOR, Director of the Schools Council in England—a useful review of research possibilities in educational planning.

These publications should enable the student to see the possibilities of research in comparative education in relation to educational investigations generally. The next step is to draw up a bibliography of published work which may bear on the topic chosen for study. The library tools referred to in Section II of this chapter should make this possible.

Some attempt should also be made to discover the unpublished material relating to the selected topic. This will be for the most part in the form of completed or in-progress theses. A number of bibliographies make it possible to ensure that the subject has not been treated before or is not at the moment a topic of research.

Paedogogica Historica edited by R. L. PLANCKE of Ghent gives a list of these relevant to comparative education which are either complete or in progress. The cover is wide and is a useful starting point when attempting to discover on-going research. A complementary periodical *Scientia Paedagogica Experimentalis* edited by R. VERBIST also lists some on-going research which may be of interest to comparative educationists.

Several publications in the USA are useful guides to theses. The U.S. DEPARTMENT OF STATE, OFFICE OF EXTERNAL RESEARCH prepares lists of current research by private scholars and academic centres. Some of these lists are of studies currently in progress, others contain recently completed studies and some list both in-progress and completed theses. The areas covered by the *External Research* Lists in this series are, (*i*) USSR and Eastern Europe, (*ii*) Asia, (*iii*) Western Europe, Great Britain and Canada, (*iv*) Middle East, (*v*) Africa, (*vi*) American Republics and (*vii*) International Affairs. The subjects covered in one series are the social sciences. The first part deals with general theses about the area as a whole. This is followed by titles relating to each of the countries in the region. Among the topics in the general section and the area study section is education. A typical publication is U.S. DEPARTMENT OF STATE, OFFICE OF EXTERNAL RESEARCH, *External Research Asia*. A list of current social science research by private scholars and academic centres No. 225, 1966. Some, but not all, of the items have brief annotations.

Similar in kind is the publication of THE ATLANTIC INSTITUTE *Atlantic Studies*, Vol. III, No. 2, XII, 1966 with the intention of keeping research workers informed and better able through co-operation to economize effort. Many of the titles concern political and economic relations among the Atlantic countries but there are sections on social and cultural relations. Titles such as history teaching at university level; technical and vocational education in Europe; and the Research Development Seminar in Comparative Education: Changing European Secondary Schools under the project Director Gerald H. READ will be of interest to comparative educationists. This bibliography includes only studies planned or in progress.

UNIVERSITY MICROFILMS Inc. make a monthly compilation *Dissertation Abstracts* of doctoral dissertations submitted to the firm. Each dissertation is listed under one or more subject heading. The main classification is by academic subject, e.g. agriculture, botany, etc., and the scope is comprehensive. One category is education which is sub-divided into General Administration, History, Physical, Pyschology, Religion, Teacher Training, Theory and Practice. Within each sub-section the arrangement is alphabetical by author, the title, however, being placed at the head of the entry. The annotations are long and detailed. A useful reference periodical though few titles may in any volume be of interest to comparative educationists.

It is naturally rather easier to draw up comprehensive lists of complete theses. In England two publications cover education.

PREPARING FOR RESEARCH

ASLIB. *Index to Theses*. Index to theses accepted for higher degrees in the universities of Great Britain and Ireland, Vol. 1, 1950–51, edited by P. D. Record, London, ASLIB, 1953; Vol. XV, 1964–5 edited by G. M. Paterson appeared in 1967. This is arranged by subject with an author index and index for subject headings. Comparative education appears as a separate subject heading.

National Foundation for Educational Research in England and Wales. A list of researches in education and educational psychology presented for higher degrees in the universities of the United Kingdom, Northern Ireland and the Irish Republic from 1918 to 1948, London, Newnes Educational Publishing Co., 1950. It was classified according to a modified Dewey decimal system by A. M. BLACKWELL. This was continued in supplements until *Current Researches in Education and Educational Psychology*, 1959–60 began. The last volume of these, 1961–63 published in 1965 by The National Foundation for Educational Research, is alphabetical by topic. Comparative education theses appear under the specific regions, countries and subjects.

There has recently been established the SOCIETY FOR RESEARCH INTO HIGHER EDUCATION LTD., London, which publishes a *Register of Research Projects in Higher Education* and *Abstracts*, both in a loose-leaf form, and these include some material on Comparative studies.

Research in the United States is well covered and has already been indicated but research on other countries is listed in Walter Crosby EELLS *American Dissertations on Foreign Education*, Washington, National Educational Association of the United States Committee on International Relations, 1959; this has as its criterion of inclusion of dissertations and theses the fact that they deal significantly with education or educators in a foreign country or with education of groups of foreign birth or ancestry in the United States. There are included some 1,690 doctors' dissertations and 4,026 masters'. A summary of the dissertations by continents and countries is given. Great Britain is credited with the most titles, followed by China, Germany and France. It also gives a list of the institutions in the USA regarded as the principal graduate schools and the number of doctors' dissertations accepted. Columbia leads the way, followed by New York University. Sources and related publications are given at the end of the introduction. The classification of actual dissertations is General, Composite, and then by continents—Africa, North America, South America, Asia, Europe, Oceania and the USA. Within each region there are general and composite studies followed by individual country entries. Within each country the classification is according to whether it is a doctor's or master's study and the list is within each sub-section alphabetical by author. The items are not annotated but are an extremely comprehensive cover of American studies in comparative and international education.

Finally many universities hold lists of theses and sometimes abstracts of them. The University of London publishes regularly the titles and authors of research theses accepted by the university. They are classified by subject. Comparative education topics are to be found under Education; Historical and Comparative Studies. The University library also has abstracts of theses from other universities in Britain and other countries.

Reports from individual departments frequently list the theses presented by students from the department and accepted by the university. An example of such a service are the *Notes and Abstracts in the Social Foundations of American and International Education* published by the School of Education, The University of Michigan at regular intervals. The *Reports* from the Comparative Education Center, School of Education, Chicago University list theses and publications by members of the department. These are published regularly.

At the University of London Institute of Education two lists of theses submitted by students have been prepared in mimeograph form. The first is by author, the second by subject and places comparative studies under the appropriate country heading.

A review of the literature in cognate fields is a prerequisite to research. It is hoped that this chapter will enable teachers and students of comparative education to check without difficulty the extent and in what manner the topic of their choice has been handled by other researchers. Most topics are capable of a variety of treatments and it should not be supposed that a review of theses titles in progress or completed provides enough evidence to enable a student to proceed with or abandon a particular research topic. It should warn him. Where titles seem to bear very closely on his own proposals it would be wise to consult the thesis itself. Comparative education as an academic study depends for its growth on research which is both varied and related. There is tremendous scope and much original work to be done in the three fields we have defined as *Area Studies, Cross-Cultural and Cross-National Studies* and *Case Studies*.

INDEXES

In both indexes, *Person and Title* and *Subject*, certain abbreviations have been adopted and entries are listed in accordance with them rather than with the full name of the organization, etc.; they include:

ASLIB	Association of Special Libraries and Information Bureaux
HMSO	Her Majesty's Stationery Office
OECD	Organization for Economic Co-operation and Development
UAR	United Arab Republic
UNESCO	United Nations Educational, Scientific and Cultural Organization
USA	United States of America
USSR	Union of Soviet Socialist Republics

PERSON AND TITLE INDEX

This index includes all publications and persons mentioned in the text. Publications have been entered under the name of the author, but in the case of those prepared by organizations, societies, agencies, etc., entries are under the title of the publication as well as under the name of the appropriate sponsoring body. If the latter is not clear in the title its official title is given in brackets.

Joint authorship is cross referenced. The title appears only under the first named author, is not repeated, but pagination is given in each case.

Articles from periodicals are in quotes. The titles of the periodicals listed on pages 73–86 are not given in this index. An 'a' after the page number following the author's name indicates one of these articles.

ABDUL-HADI, Mohammed, 80a, 84a
ABLIN, F., *Education in the USSR*, 120
ABRAHAMS, Peter, *The Blacks*, 20
Abstracts of Bulgarian Scientific Literature, Philosophy and Pedagogics. (Bulgaria Academy of Sciences), 120
ACHEBE, Chinua
— *Arrow of God*, 20, 21
— *No Longer at Ease*, 20, 21
— *Things Fall Apart*, 20, 21
Achievements and functioning in children. (UNESCO), 90
ADAMS, Don, 79a
—*See* I. N. THUT and Don ADAMS, 7, 24
African Abstracts. (International African Institute), 121
African Education Abstracts. (London University), 121
African Writers' Series, 20
AFZAL, M., 78a
AKRAWI, M., *See* R. D. MATTHEWS and M. AKRAWI, 70
ALEXANDER, T. and PARKER, B., *The New Education in the German Republic*, 60
ALEXANDER, W., *Education in England: the National System. How it works*, 56
ALTBACH, P. G. 79a
Analytical bibliography on comparative education of items available in Unesco, 130
ANDERSON, C. Arnold, 98
— *University of Chicago program in comparative education*, 93
ANDERSON, D., 75a
ANDERSON, G. E. 79a
Annual bibliography of the International Bureau of education, 28
ANWEILER, O., 76a
APANASEWICZ, N. and ROSEN, S. M. *Eastern Europe: a bibliography of English-language materials*, 67
ARASTEH, R., 78a
— *Education and social awakening in Iran*, 71
Archer Report, 110
ARCHIBALD, J. F., 16
ARMYTAGE, W. H. G., 77a
ARNOLD, Matthew, *The popular education in France*, 2
ARRICALE, F. C., 74a
ASHBY, Eric, 85a
— *Universities: British, Indian, African—a study in the ecology of higher education*, 96, 97
Ashby Commission Report, 36, 110

PERSON AND TITLE INDEX

ASHER, Robert E. *et al.*, *Development of the emerging countries: an agenda for research*, 98
Asia and Africa. A select bibliography for schools. (School of Oriental and African Studies), 37
ASLIB, *Index to theses*, 135
ATKINSON, N., 78a
ATLANTIC INFORMATION CENTRE FOR TEACHERS (THE), *The world and the school*, 124
ATLANTIC INSTITUTE (THE),
Atlantic Studies, 124
AUSTIN, Sarah, (Translator), 3
AUSTRALIAN COUNCIL FOR EDUCATIONAL RESEARCH, *Australian Education Index*, 121
Australian Journal, 15
Australian Journal of Education, 52
AYTAC, K., 82a

BACIE *bibliography*, (British Association for Commercial and Industrial Education), 123
BACIE *Journal*, 123
BANOVITCH, A., 129
BARCAN, A., *A short history of education in New South Wales*, 51
BARNARD, Henry
— *Institutions and statistics of public instruction in different countries*, 3
— *National education*, 3
— *Systems*, 3
BARNARD, H. C., '*Some sources for French educational history to 1789*', 126
BARON, George
— *A bibliographical guide to the English educational system*, 58
— *Society, schools and progress in England*, 57
BATT, J., 77a
BEEBY, C. E., 80a, 81a
BELL, I. F., *See* F. E. WATTERS and I. F. BELL, 18–19
BELSKY, F., 78a
BENJAMIN, H. R. W., *Higher education in the American republics*, 41, 108
BENTLEY, A., 77a
BENTWICH, J. S., *Education in Israel*, 71, 107
BEREDAY, George Z. F., 49, 82a, 84a, 94, 128
— BRICKMAN, W. W. and READ, G.H. (eds). *The changing Soviet schools: the comparative education society field study in the USSR*, 65, 128
— '*Comparative education at Columbia university*', 93
— *Comparative method in education*, 4, 88, 93
— and VOLPICELLI, L. (eds). *Public education in America: a new interpretation of purpose and practice*, 39
BESHIR, M. O., 82a
BIDWELL, C. E., 77a, 84a
BIGELOW, K. W., 74a, 82a
BILINSKY, Y., 82a
Blackboard Jungle, 11
BLACKWELL, A. M., 135
BLAUG, M., *Economics of education*, 123
BOARD, B., (compiler). *The effect of technological progress on education, a classified bibliography from British sources 1945–57*, 124
BOARD OF EDUCATION *Special reports on educational subjects* (Vol. 9, Germany), 3
BOITER, A., 83a
BOKTOR, A., *The development and expansion of education in the United Arab Republic*, 72
BOLDREWOOD, Rolf, *Robbery under arms*, 16
Bookbird (Journal), 50
BORGHI, L., 79a

PERSON AND TITLE INDEX

Bos, H. C., *See* A. Lewis, F. Harbison (and others), 92
Bowles, F., 129
Bowles, Frank, *Access to higher education, international study of university admission*, 92, 98
Bowman, Mary Jean, 98
Boyd, Martin
— *Brent of Bin Bin*, 17
— *The Monteforts*, 17
— *Ten creeks run*, 17
— *Back to Bool Bool*, 17
— *Up the country*, 17
Boyd, William, *The history of Western education*, 8
Brahman, R. L., *Education in the Rumanian People's Republic*, 65
Brembeck, Cole S., 73a
— and Weidner, E. W., *Education and development in India and Pakistan, a select and annotated bibliography*, 51
— *See* John W. Hanson and Cole S. Brembeck, 98
Brickman, William W., 76a, 116, 128
— *See* George Z. F. Bereday, W. W. Brickman and G. H. Read (eds), 65, 128
Bristow, Thelma, 11
British Association for Commercial and Industrial Education
— *Bacie bibliography*, 123
— *Bacie Journal*, 123
British Council, English Teaching Information Centre
— *English teaching abstracts*, 122
— *English teaching bibliography*, 122
British Education Index, 33, 73, 117
British Journal of Educational Studies, 126
British Museum, *General catalogue of printed books*, 125
British National Bibliography, 12, 126
Broughton, G. 22
— *A critical study of the development of V. S. Naipaul as a novelist in his four West Indian novels*, 22n
Browne, G. S. *See* J. F. Cramer and G. S. Browne, 5, 24
Brubacher, J. S., *A history of the problems of education*, 8
Bulgaria, Academy of Sciences, Centre for Scientific Information and Documentation, *Abstracts of Bulgarian Scientific Literature, Philosophy and Pedagogics*, 120
Bulletin of the International Bureau of Education, 28, 118
Bunn, R. F., 76a
Burma Education Abstracts, (USA, Dept. of Health, Education and Welfare), 121
Burns, D. G., *African education, an introductory survey of education in Commonwealth Countries*, 38
Burns, H. W., 79a

Canada Year Book, 37
Canfield, A. T., 75a, 82a
Capelle, J., 86a
Carter, James J., 11
Cave, W. M., 83a
Chabe, A. M., 74a
Challenges and achievements of education in Latin America. (Pan-American Union), 42, 104
Chamier, George, *A South Sea siren*, 13
Chang-tu Hu, 74a, 107
— (ed), *Chinese education under Communism*, 46, 108
Chauncey, H. 83a, 84a
Chausow, H. M., 86a
Cheal, J. E., 74a
Chen, T. H. E., *See* J. S. Roucek and K. V. Lottich, 63

PERSON AND TITLE INDEX

CHESSWAS, J. D., *Educational planning and development in Uganda*, 109
CHICAGO UNIVERSITY, SCHOOL OF EDUCATION, COMPARATIVE EDUCATION CENTRE. *Reports*, 136
CIRF, *Abstracts*, 120, 123
Civics and European education at the primary and secondary level. (Council of Europe), 102
CLARK, A. J., 77a, 81a
CLARKE, Marcus, *For the term of his natural life*, 15
CLIGNET, R. P., 73a
COLEMAN, James S., *Education and political development*, 77
COLLINS, Tom. *See* Joseph FURPHY, 17
COLOMBO PLAN, *Annual report of the consultative committee*, 105
COLUMBIA UNIVERSITY TEACHERS' COLLEGE AND UNIVERSITY OF LONDON INSTITUTE OF EDUCATION, *World Year Book of Education*, 94, 99, 112, 114, 117
COMENIUS, Jan, 64
Comparative Education (Journal), 33, 93, 117
— (Country Index), 85–86
Comparative education research and the determinants of educational policy. (Comparative Education Society in Europe), 114, 115, 129
Comparative Education Review (Journal), 33, 37, 93, 116–7, 128, 130
— (Country Index), 73–85
COMPARATIVE EDUCATION SOCIETY IN EUROPE. *Amsterdam proceedings of the society.* (i.e., *Comparative education research and the determinants of educational policy*), 114, 115, 129
— *Berlin proceedings of the society.* (i.e., *General education in a changing world*), 114, 129
— *Ghent proceedings.* (i.e., *The university in the education system*). 129
COMPARATIVE EDUCATION SOCIETY IN EUROPE, BRITISH SECTION, *The place of Comparative education in the training of teachers*, 130
COMPARATIVE EDUCATION SOCIETY, USA, *Proceedings*, 127, 128
Comparative Studies in Society and History: an international quarterly, 126
Compendium of basic bibliographies by country, (Council of Europe), 119
Compulsory education in New Zealand, (UNESCO), 53
Confluence, (Journal), 10
CONTON, William, *The African*, 20
COOMBS, Philip H., 104
COSTER, S. De, 74a
COTTLE, T., *Frank Melton's Luck*, 13
COUCH, Margaret (compiler), *Education in Africa: a select bibliography*, 36
COUNCIL FOR EDUCATION IN WORLD CITIZENSHIP, *Education for international understanding*, 124
COUNCIL OF EUROPE, *Leisure-time facilities for young people from 13–25 years of age*, 102
— COUNCIL FOR CULTURAL CO-OPERATION, *Civics and European education at the primary and secondary level*, 102
— — *Research and techniques for the benefit of modern language teaching*, 103
— — *School Systems: a guide*, 54
— — *Training the trainer*, 103
— DOCUMENTATION CENTRE FOR EDUCATION IN EUROPE, *Abstracts*, 119
— — *Compendium of basic bibliographies by country*, 119
COUNTS, G. S. A., 83a
COUSIN, Victor
— *On the state of education in Holland as regards schools for working classes and for the poor*, 3
— *Report on the state of public instruction in Prussia*, 3
COWAN, L. G., O'CONNELL, J. and SCANLON, D. G. (eds), *Education and nation-building in Africa*, 33
COWAN, R. W. T. (ed), *Education for Australians: a symposium*, 52

PERSON AND TITLE INDEX

CRAMER, J. F., 78a
— and BROWNE, G. S., *Contemporary education*, 5, 24
CREMIN, Lawrence A.
— *The transformation of the school*, 10
— *The genius of American education*, 10
Crowther Report, 77, 112
CUBBERLEY, E. P., *The History of education*, 10
CURLE, Adam
— *Educational strategy for developing countries, a study of educational and social factors in relation to economic growth*, 98
— *Planning for education in Pakistan*, 109
Current Researches in education and educational psychology, 1959–60, 135
Curriculum improvement and educational development, modernizing our schools, (OECD), 101
CURRIE, George (Chairman), *Report of the Commission on education in New Zealand*, 53
CURTIS, S. J., *History of education in Great Britain*, 57
CURZON, Lord, 97

DAHLLOF, Urban, 86a
— ZETTERLUND, Sven and OBERG, Henning, *Secondary education in Sweden*, 69
DALVI, M. A., 77a
DAMAS, Leon, *Somehow we survive*, 21
DAVIES, A. F. and ENCEL, S., *Australian society*, 15
DAVIS, R. G., 79a
DAWSON, G. G., 81a
DE COSTER, S., 74a
DE LANDSHEERE, G., 129
DE MADARIAGA, S., *Englishmen, Frenchmen, Spaniards*, 10
DERRETT, M. E., *The modern Indian novel in English, a comparative approach*, 22
DESCARTES, Renée, 10
DEWEY, John, 10, 40, 88
DE WITT, N., 83a, 84a
DE YOUNG, C. A. and WYNN, R., *American education*, 39
Directory of training and research institutions, (UNESCO), 90
Dissemination and implementation, third annual Phi Delta Kappa Symposium on educational research, 132
Dissertation Abstracts, (University Microfilms), 134
DIXON, C. W., 32
— *Society, Schools and progress in Scandinavia*, 68
DOBINSON, C. H., 75a
DOMINION BUREAU OF STATISTICS, EDUCATION DIVISION, RESEARCH SECTION
— *A bibliographical guide to Canadian education*, 38
— *The organization and administration of public schools*, 38
DON QUIXOTE, 82
DORE, R. P., *Education in Tokugawa, Japan*, 48, 107
DOWNEY, L. W., 74a, 84a
DRYLAND, A. R., 83a, 84a
DUDLEY, L. P., 73a
DUIJKER, H. C. J. and FRIDA, N. H., 'National character and national stereotypes', 9–10
DUKE, B. C., 79a
DUNCAN, E. R., 80a, 84a
DUTTON, G.P.H. (ed), *The literature of Australia*, 15

ECKSTEIN, M., 77a
EDDING, F., 76a, 129
— *See* I. SVENNILSON, F. EDDING and H. L. ELVIN, 54, 91
Education Abstracts, (UNESCO), 89, 118, 130
Education and development series, (OECD), 107

PERSON AND TITLE INDEX

Education and international life, (The Year Book of Education 1964), 124
Education for international understandings, (Council for Education in World Citizenship), 124
Education in Asia, (Japan, Ministry of Education), 45
Education in Europe, a report on education in the countries of Europe, (National Association of Schoolmasters), 54
Education in France, (France, Embassy New York), 119
Education in Germany, (West Germany, Embassy London), 119
Education in the German Democratic Republic, 64
Education Index, 117
Educational data: Republic of Portugal, (USA, Dept. of Health, Education and Welfare), 63
Educational planning: a preliminary listing, (UNESCO), 89
Educational Sciences: an international journal, 126
Educational Studies and Documents Series, (UNESCO), 89, 118
Educational Yearbook, 93
EELLS, Walter C., *American dissertations on foreign education*, 135
ELAZAR, M., *See* R. POIGNANT, S. MOBERG and M. ELAZAR, 92
ELAM, Stanley, *See* Keith GOLDHAMMER and Stanley ELAM (eds), 132
ELKAN, S., 82a
ELVIN, H. L., *See* I. SVENNILSON, F. EDDING and H. L. ELVIN, 54, 91
Emerging strategies and structures for educational change, Proceedings of the anniversary invitational conference in June 1966, (The Ontario Institute for Studies in Education), 133
ENCEL, S., *See* A. F. DAVIES and S. ENCEL, 15
ENDERWITZ, H., 76a
English Teaching Abstracts, (British Council), 122
English Teaching Bibliography, (British Council), 122
ENRIGHT, D. J., *The world of dew*, 10
ERCOLE, Velia, *No Escape*, 16
ESTARELLAS, J., 82a
EVANS, P. C. C., 73a
External research Asia, (USA, Dept. of State), 134
EXTERNAL RESEARCH LISTS, (USA, Dept. of State), 134

FAHMY, M. S., 75a
FERNIG, L., 129
FINLAYSON, Roderick, 14
FISCHER, J., 74a, 78a
— *Universities in Southeast Asia: an essay on comparison and development*, 45
FITZGERALD, D. T., 80a
FLETCHER, Basil, 28
FODOR, Michael (compiler), *Books in the East*, 50
Foreign Education Digest, 118
FOSKETT, D. J., *How to find out: educational research*, 126, 127
FOSTER, A., 73a
FOSTER, Philip J., 73a, 76a
— *Education and Social change in Ghana*, 35, 88, 107
FRANCE, EMBASSY NEW YORK, *Education in France*, 119
FRASER, Stewart E. 73a, 74a
— (compiler and ed.), *Chinese communist education, Records of the first decade*, 46, 108
— *Government policy and international education*, 97
—(Translator), *Jullien's plan for comparative education*, 24
FRASER, W. R., 75a
— *Education and society in modern France*, 59, 88, 107
FREEBURGER, A. R. and HAUCH, C. C., *Education in Peru*, 43
FRENCH, E. L., 85a

PERSON AND TITLE INDEX

FRIDA, N. H. *See* H. C. J. DUIJKER and N. H. FRIDA, 9–10
FROESE, L., 4
Fundamental and adult education (Journal), 126
FURPHY, Joseph, *Such is life*, 17

GANDHI, Mahatma, 47
GANNON, E. J., 82a
GASS, J. R. and LYONS, R. F., *International flows of students*, 92
General catalogue of publications 1946–1959, (UNESCO), 100
General catalogue of Unesco publications and Unesco sponsored publications, 100
General education in a changing world, (Comparative Education Society in Europe), 114, 129
GEORGEFF, J., 85a
GILL, C. C., *Education and social change in Chile*, 43
GILLET, M., 75a
GOLDHAMMER, Keith and ELAM, Stanley (eds), *Dissemination and implementation, third annual Phi Delta Kappa Symposium on educational research*, 132
GOLDMAN, R. J. and TAYLOR, F. M., 'Coloured immigrant children: a survey of research, studies and literature on their educative problems and potential in Britain', 125
GOOD, H. G., *A history of American education*, 39
GORDON, S. C. (Compiler), *A century of West Indian education: a source book*, 44
GORER, G., *The American people—a study in national character*, 10
GRANT, Nigel, *Soviet education*, 66
GREAVES, M. A., *Education in British India 1698–1947*, 121
GREENE, Maxime, *The public school and the private vision—a search for America in education and literature*, 10
GROSSMAN, Edith, *The heart of the bush*, 13
GUGGISBERG, Gordon, 76
Guide to the contents of the Public Record Office, 126
GUNN, Mrs Aeneas, *The little black princess of the never never*, 17
GUTERMAN, S. L., 75a, 77a

HAHN, W., 76a
HALL, Robert King, 94
— *Education for a new Japan*, 109
HALLS, W. D., 86a
— *Society, schools and progress in France*, 59
HANS, Nicholas, 75a, 79a, 80a, 83a, 94, 113
— *Comparative education*, 5, 88
— 'Sociological Aspects of comparative education', 132
HANSEN, G. B., 77a
HANSEN, L. S., 81a
HANSON, John W. and BREMBECK, Cole S. (eds), *Education and development of nations*, 98
HARBISON, F., *See* A. LEWIS, F. HARBISON (and others), 92
HARRIS, C. W., (ed), *See* W. S. MONROE, *Encyclopedia*, 116
HARRIS, D. L., 83a, 84a
HARRIS, William Torrey, 11
— *Annual report of the commissioner of education for the year 1888–89*, 3
HART, Estellita, 104
HARTFORD, E. F., *Education in the United States*, 40
HAUCH, C. C.
— *The current situation in Latin American education*, 41
— *See* A. R. FREEBURGER and C. C. HAUCH, 43
HAVIGHURST, R. J., 80a, 84a
— and MOREIRA, J. R., *Society and education in Brazil*, 42
HAWTHORNE, J. R., Nathaniel, 11
HAYDEN, Howard,
— *Higher education and development in South-East Asia*, Vol. 1, 105

PERSON AND TITLE INDEX

— *Higher education and development in South-East Asia*, Vol. II, *Country Profiles*, 106
HEATH, Kathryn, *Ministries of education, their function and organisation*, 96
HEGEL, G. W. F., 10
HEIFETZ, R., 81a
HENDERSON, J. L., 126
HENTY, G. A., *Maori and settler*, 13
HEPWORTH, P., *How to find out in history: a guide to sources of information for all*, 122
HERBERT, Xavier, *Capricornia*, 17
HEWITT, A. R.
— *Guide to resources of Commonwealth Studies*, 122
— *A union list of Commonwealth newspapers in London, Oxford and Cambridge*, 122
HEY, P. D., 81a
HIGGINSON, J. H., 83a, 84a
Higher Education and development in South-East Asia, Vol. I, 105
— Vol. II, *Country Profiles*, 106
— Vol. III, Part I, *High level manpower for development*, 106
— — Part II, *Language policy and higher education*, 106
HILKER, F., 4, 76a, 93
HILLIARD, Noel, *Maori girl*, 14
History syllabuses and a world perspective, (The Parliamentary Group for World Government), 124
HMSO
— *Government Publications*, 89
— *International organisations publications, Supplement to Government Publications*, 89, 110
HOFMANN, E., 75a
HOFMANN, H., 76a
HOKE, G. A., 86a
HOLMES, Brian,
— 30, 129
— (ed) *Educational Policy and the Mission Schools*, 90, 99
— *Problems in education: a comparative approach*, 6, 88
— 'Rational constructs in comparative education', 10
— and ROBINSOHN, S. B., *Relevant data in comparative education*, 90, 129
HORNE, David, *The lucky country, Australia in the sixties*, 15
HORNSBY, G., 82a
HUEBENER, T., 76a
— *The schools of West Germany: a study of German elementary and secondary schools*, 60
HUNT, C. L., 81a
HUNTER, Guy, *Higher Education and development in South-East Asia*, Vol. III, Part 1, *High level manpower for development*, 106
HUQ, Muhammed S.
— *Compulsory education in Pakistan*, 49
— *Education and development strategy in South and South-East Asia*, 44
HUSEN, Torsten, 82a, 86a
— *An International Study of achievement in mathematics, a comparison of twelve countries*, 90
HUUS, Helen, *The education of children and youth in Norway*, 32, 69
HYLLA, E., 76a

IDENBURG, Ph. J., 129
— *Education in the Netherlands*, 62
Imaginative Literature from the Commonwealth, (National Book League), 12
INDIA, MINISTRY OF EDUCATION, *Indian Education Abstracts*, 120
— NATIONAL COUNCIL OF EDUCATIONAL RESEARCH AND TRAINING, *Review of education in India 1947–61*, 48

PERSON AND TITLE INDEX

Indian Education Absracts, (India, Ministry of Education), 120
Index to theses, (ASLIB), 135
Intellectual processes: an international study of intellectual ability. (UNESCO), 90
INTERNATIONAL AFRICAN INSTITUTE, *African Abstracts*, 121
INTERNATIONAL ASSOCIATION FOR THE ADVANCEMENT OF EDUCATIONAL RESEARCH,
— *The role of educational research in social education*, 132
INTERNATIONAL ASSOCIATION OF UNIVERSITIES, See *Higher education and development in South-East Asia*, Vols. I-III, 105, 106
International Bibliography of Sociology, (International Committee for Social Science Documentation), 123
INTERNATIONAL BUREAU OF EDUCATION
— *Annual bibliography of the* . . . , 28
— *Bulletin of the*, 28, 118
— *International card index service*, 28
— AND UNESCO, *International Year Book of Education*, 28, 29, 112, 117
— — *Recommendations of the International Conference on Public Education*, 30
— — *Sessions of the International Conference on Public Education*, 28, 29, 30
INTERNATIONAL COMMITTEE FOR SOCIAL SCIENCE DOCUMENTATION, *International Bibliography of Sociology*, 123
INTERNATIONAL CONFERENCE ON EDUCATIONAL RESEARCH, ORGANIZING COMMITTEE
— *Present studies of educational research in Japan*, 132
— *Proceedings of the International Conference on Educational Research*, 131
International Directory of Education Associations, (UNESCO), 32, 118
International guide to educational documentation 1955-1960, (UNESCO), 118
International Index, 123
International Journal of Adult and Youth Education, 126
International Library of Sociology and Social Reconstruction, (Routledge & Kegan Paul), 107
International list of educational periodicals, An (UNESCO), 118
International Review of Education, (Journal), 10, 33, 73, 90, 91, 117, 128, 129, 130
International Year Book of Education, 28, 29, 112, 117
IYENGAR, K. R. S., *Indian writing in English*, 22

JACOBSON, E. S., 77a
JAPAN, MINISTRY OF EDUCATION, RESEARCH BUREAU IN CO-OPERATION WITH UNESCO, *Education in Asia*, 45
JOLLY, R., 75a, 82a, 84a
Journal of Commonwealth Literature, 12
Journal of Educational Sociology, 127-8
Journal of Educational Studies, 11
JULLIEN DE PARIS, Marc-Antoine, *Esquisse d'un ouvrage sur l'education comparée*, 24
JUSTMAN, J., *The Italian people and their schools*, 62
JUVILER, P. H., 83a

KAHAN, A., 83a
KANDEL, I. L., 93, 113
— *Comparative education*, 3
— *The new era in education—a comparative study*, 9
KATZ, J., 74a, 85a
— (ed), *Canadian education today: a symposium*, 38
— *Readings on international understanding*, 124
KAY, Joseph, *The social conditions of the people in England and Europe*, 3
KAYE, B., *Bringing up children in Ghana: an impressionistic survey*, 37
KAYE, Louis, *Tybal men*, 17
KAZAMIAS, A. M., 77a, 84a
— *Education and the quest for modernity in Turkey*, 72
— and MASSIALAS, G. B., *Tradition and change in education*, 6
—*See* P. NASH., A. M. KAZAMIAS and H. J. PERKINSON, 8

PERSON AND TITLE INDEX

KENWORTHY, L. S.
— *Free and inexpensive materials on world affairs*, 125
— *Studying South America in elementary and secondary schools*, 44
KERR, A. J. I., *Schools of Scotland*, 59
KETTELKAMP, G. C., 75a, 84a
KIMBALL, S. T., 74a
KIMMANCE, S. K., *A guide to the literature of education*, 126, 127
KING, Edmund J., 30, 77a, 86a, 129
— (ed.) *The history of western education*, 8
— *Other schools and ours*, 6, 24
— *Society, schools and progress in the USA*, 40
— *World perspectives in education*, 99
KINGSLEY, Henry, *The recollections of Geoffrey Hamlyn*, 16
KIRKPATRICK, J., 76a
KLEMPERER, L. VON, *Austria, A survey of Austrian education and guide to the academic placement of students from Austria in educational institutions in the United States of America*, 55
KLEPIKOV, V., 74a
KNELLER, G. F., 'Comparative education', 116
KOBAYASHI, T., 79a
KOH, E. K., 80a, 81a
KROEF, J. van der, 78a
KRUEGER, J. R., 80a
KRUPSKAYA, N. K., 66, 84
KRUSCHEV, Nikita, 83
KYÖSTIÖ, O. K., 75a

Labor institutes in El Salvador, (Pan-American Union), 107
Landfall (Journal), 14
LANDSHEERE, G. De, 129
LANGEVELD, M. J. et al. *Paedagogica Europaea: the European Year Book of Educational Research*, 132
LARREA, J., 80a
LAUWERYS, Joseph A., 74a, 94, 129
— 'Comparative education at the university of London', 93
— 'Problems on methodology of comparative education', 132
LAWSON, Henry, *While the Billy boils*, 17
LAWSON, R. F., 76a
Leisure-time facilities for young people from 13–25 years of age, (Council of Europe), 102
LERNER, D., and others, *The passing of traditional society: modernizing the Middle East*, 70
LESTER SMITH, W. O., *Government of education*, 57
LEVIN, D., *Soviet education today*, 66
LEWIS, A., HARBISON, F., TINBERGEN, J. with BOS, H. C. and VAIZEY, J. *The challenge of aid to newly developing countries*, 92
LEWIS, L. J., 73a
— *Education and political independence in Africa, and other essays*, 34
— *Society, schools and progress in Nigeria*, 35
— and LOVERIDGE, A. J., *The management of education*, 34
LIBA, M. R. *See* W. S. MONROE, *Encyclopedia*, 116
List of researches in education and educational psychology presented for higher degrees in the universities of the United Kingdom, Northern Ireland and the Irish Republic from 1918 to 1948, (National Foundation for Educational Research in England and Wales), 135
LLOYD, J. W., 77a, 84a
LOCKE, John, 10
LONDON UNIVERSITY INSTITUTE OF EDUCATION, DEPT. OF EDUCATION IN TROPICAL AREAS, *African Education Abstracts*, 121

PERSON AND TITLE INDEX

LONDON UNIVERSITY INSTITUTE OF EDUCATION AND COLUMBIA UNIVERSITY TEACHERS' COLLEGE, *World Year Book of Education*, 94, 99, 112, 114, 117
LOTTICH, K. V., 76a
— *See* J. S. ROUCEK and K. V. LOTTICH, 63
LOVERIDGE, A. J., *See* L. J. LEWIS and A. J. LOVERIDGE, 34
LOW, U. N., 81a
LUX, D. G., 78a
LYONS, R. F. (ed), *Problems and strategies of educational planning. Lessons from Latin America*, 41
LYONS, R. F., *See* J. R. GASS and R. F. LYONS, 92

MAAS, J. van Lutsenberg, 80a
MACAULEY, Lord, *Minute 1835*, 22, 47
MACDONALD, J., 74a
MCELLIGOT, T. J., *Education in Ireland*, 58
MCHALE, T. R., 81a
MCLAREN, Ian A., *See* M. TURNBULL and Ian A. MCLAREN, 13
MCLEOD, A. L. (ed), *The Commonwealth pen*, 12
MACMILLAN, R. G., 81a
MACVEAN, R. B., 77a
MADARIAGA, S. De, *Englishmen, Frenchmen, Spaniards*, 10
MAGNUSON, R. P., 74a
MAJAULT, Joseph
— *Teacher training*, 102
— *See* J. THOMAS and J. MAJAULT, 55
MAKARENKO, A. S., 66
MALE, G. A.
— *Education in France*, 60
— *See* M. L. MING and G. A. MALE, 70
MALLINSON, Vernon, 11, 74a, 126, 130
— *An introduction to the study of comparative education*, 7, 9
— *Modern Belgian literature*, 11, 108
— *Power and politics in Belgium education 1815 to 1961*, 56, 108
MANDER, Jane, *The story of a New Zealand river*, 13
MANN, Horace, 11
— *Seventh annual report of the Board of Education*, 3
MANSFIELD, Katherine, 13
MAO TSE-TUNG, *On the relation between knowledge and practice, between knowing and doing*, 47
MARAINI, F., *Meeting with Japan*, 10
MARCHIANY, J. A., 83a
MARTIN, L. H. (chairman). *Tertiary education in Australia: report of the Committee on the future of tertiary education in Australia to the Australian Universities Commission*, 52
MARX, Karl, 10
MASSIALAS, G. B., *See* A. M. KAZAMIAS and G. B. MASSIALAS, 6
MATTHEWS, R. D. and AKRAWI, M. *Education in Arab Countries of the Near East Egypt, Iraq, Palestine, Transjordan, Syria, Lebanon*, 70
MAYER, Martin, *The schools*, 8
Mediterannean regional project: an experiment in planning by six countries, (OECD), 107
Mediterranean regional project; Spain, (OECD), 63
MEDLIN, W. K., 83a
MELVILLE, Hermann, 11
MERCIER, Paul J, 130
— (ed), *The place of comparative education in the training of teachers*, 130
MEYER, A. E.
— *The development of education in the twentieth century*, 8
— *An educational history of the Western world*, 8

PERSON AND TITLE INDEX

MICHIGAN UNIVERSITY
— *Comparative education dissertation series*, 32
— SCHOOL OF EDUCATION, *Notes and abstracts in the social foundations of American and international education*, 136
MILLER, R. I., 84a
MING, M. L. and MALE, G. A. *Sweden: educational data*, 70
MINOGUE, W. J. D., 86a
MITCHELL, F. W., 80a
MITSUHASHI, S., 79a, 84a
MOBERG, S., *See* R. POIGNANT, S. MOBERG and M. ELAZAR, 92
MOEHLMAN, A. H. and ROUCEK, J. S. (eds), *Comparative education*, 7
MONROE, W. S., *Encyclopedia of educational research*, 116
MOOS, E., 83a
MOREIRA, J. R., 74a
— *See* R. J. HAVIGHURST and J. R. MOREIRA, 42
MORRIS, M. O. M. (ed), *Treasure chest for teachers*, 125
MUELDER, W. R., *Schools for a nation*, 46
MUIR, R. K., 81a
MULGAN, Alan, *Great days in New Zealand writing*, 13n
MULGAN, John, *Man alone*, 14
MUNROE, D., 81a
MYERS, C. N., *Education and national development in Mexico*, 43

NAIK, J. P., *See* S. NURULLAH and J. P. NAIK, 47
NAIPAUL, V. S., *A house for Mr. Biswas*, 22
NASH, P., 74a
— KAZAMIAS, A. M. and PERKINSON, H.J. *The educated man: studies in the history of educational thought*, 8
NATIONAL ASSOCIATION OF SCHOOLMASTERS, *Education in Europe, a report on education in the Countries of Europe*, 54
NATIONAL BOOK LEAGUE, *Imaginative Literature for the Commonwealth*, 12
NATIONAL FOUNDATION FOR EDUCATIONAL RESEARCH, IN ENGLAND AND WALES
— *Technical Educational Abstracts*, 123
— *A list of researches in education and educational psychology presented for higher degrees in the universities of the United Kingdom, Northern Ireland and the Irish Republic from 1918 to 1948*, 135
National register of educational researches, (Phi Delta Kappa), 131
National science policies in Countries of South and South-East Asia, (UNESCO), 105
NDUKA, D., *Western education and the Nigerian cultural background*, 36
NEFF, K. L.
— *Burma educational data*, 45
— *Selected bibliography of education in South East Asia*, 51
NELLEMANN, A., *Schools and education in Denmark*, 32, 68
NEW ZEALAND, *Official Yearbook*, 52
NIEVES, F. C., 77a
NITSCH, M., 80a
NOAH, Harold J., 128
— *Financing Soviet schools*, 109
NOEL, E. W., 77a, 85a
NOSS, Richard, *Higher education and development in South-East Asia*, Vol. III, Part II, *Language policy and higher education*, 116
Notes and abstracts in the social foundation of America and international education, (Michigan University), 136
NURULLAH, S. and NAIK, J. P. *A history of education in India*, 47

OBERG, Henning. *See* Urban DAHLLOF, Sven ZETTERLUND and Henning OBERG, 69
O'CONNEL, J., *See* L. G. COWAN, J. O'CONNELL and D. G. SCANLON (eds), 33

PERSON AND TITLE INDEX

OECD
— *Catalogue of Publications*, 101
— *The catalogue of social and economic development institutes and programmes research*, 131
— *Curriculum improvement and educational development, modernizing our schools*, 101
— *Education and development* (series), 107
— *Mediterranean regional project: an experiment in planning by six countries*, 107
— *Mediterranean regional project, Spain*, 63
— *Policy conference on economic growth and investment in education*, 54, 91
ÖGREN, G., 90
OITTINEN, R. H., *Education in Finland*, 69
Oldman Report, 110
ONTARIO INSTITUTE FOR STUDIES IN EDUCATION, *Emerging strategies and structures for educational change, Proceedings of the anniversary invitational Conference in June 1960*, 133
Organisation of the School Year, a comparative study, The (UNESCO), 89

Paedogogica Europaea: The European Yearbook of educational research, 132
Paedagogica Historica, 133
PAKISTAN QUARTERLY, *Education number 1966*, 49
PALMER, Vance, *The legend of the nineties*, 15
PAN-AMERICAN UNION
— DEPARTMENT OF EDUCATIONAL AFFAIRS, *Challenges and achievements of education in Latin America*, 42, 104
— DIVISION OF LABOR AND SOCIAL AFFAIRS
— — *Labor institues in El Salvador*, 107
— — *Workers' Education Series*, 107
PARKER, B., *See* T. ALEXANDER and B. PARKER, 60
PARKER, F., 81a
PARLIAMENTARY GROUP FOR WORLD GOVERNMENT (THE), *History Syllabuses and a world perspective*, 124
Parry Report 1959, 53
PARTRIDGE, P. H., 85a
PASSIN, H. J., 79a
— *'Japanese education: guide to a bibliography of materials in the English language'*, 51
— *Society and education in Japan*, 49
PASSOW, A. H., 77
PATERSON, G. M. (ed), *Index to theses accepted for higher degrees in the universities of Great Britain and Ireland*, Vol. XV, 135
PEARSON, J. D., *Oriental and Asian bibliography: an introduction with some reference to Africa*, 51
PEDLEY, F. H., *The educational system in England and Wales*, 58
PELAEZ, L. C., 85a
PENNAR, J., 83a
PERGAMON PRESS, *Society, Schools and Progress series*, 30
PERKINSON, H. J., *See* P. NASH, A. M. KAZAMIAS and H. J. PERKINSON, 8
PESHKIN, A., 81a
PETERSON, A. D. C., 86a
Phelps-Stokes Commission Report, 35, 36
PHI DELTA KAPPA, *National register of educational researchers*, 131
PHILLIPS, C. E., *The development of education in Canada*, 38
PITTSBURGH UNIVERSITY, *Studies in Comparative Education series*, 32
Place of comparative education in the training of teachers, (Comparative Education Society in Europe, British Section), 130
PLANCKE, R. L. (ed), *Paedagogica Historica*, 133
PLATO, *Republic*, 10
POIGNANT, R., MOBERG, S. and ELAZAR, M. *The Planning of education in relation to economic growth*, 92

PERSON AND TITLE INDEX

POLAND, ACADEMY OF SCIENCES, DOCUMENTATION AND SCIENTIFIC INFORMATION CENTRE, *Quarterly Review of Scientific Publication*, 120
Policy Conference on economic growth and investment in education, (OECD), 54, 91
POTTER, W. N., 82a
PRAED, Campbell, *The head station*, 16
Present status of educational research in Japan, (International Conference on Educational Research), 132
PRESS, J. (ed), *Commonwealth literature: unity and diversity in a common culture*, 12
PRESTON, R. C., 76a, 85a
PRITCHARD, Katherine, *Coonardoo*, 17
Problems and strategies of educational planning, (UNESCO), 104
Proceedings of the International Conference on Educational Research, 131
Public education in the Soviet Union, (USSR, Ministry of Education), 67
PUBLIC RECORD OFFICE, *Guide to the contents of the Public Record office*, 126

Quarterly Review of Scientific Publications, (Poland, Academy of Sciences), 120

RAHMAN, F., *New education in the making in Pakistan*, 50
RALEIGH, Dick, 13
RAMANATHAN, G., *Educational planning and national integration*, 47
READ, G. H., *See* George Z. F. BEREDAY, W. W. BRICKMAN and G. H. READ, 65, 128
READ, H., 134
Recommendations of the International Conferences on Public Education, 30
RECORD. P. D. (ed), *Index to theses accepted for higher degrees in the universities of Great Britain and Ireland*, Vol. 1, 135
REDL, H. B. (ed and trans), *Soviet educators on Soviet education*, 66
REE, H. A., 77a
REED, A. W., *Myths and legends of Australia*, 17
Register of research projects in higher education, The (Society for Research into Higher Education Ltd.), 135
Report of the Turkish national commission on education, (Turkey, Ministry of Education), 72
Report of meeting of ministers of education of Asian member states participating in the Karachi Plan, (UNESCO), 45, 105
Research and techniques for the benefit of modern language teaching, (Council of Europe), 103
Review of education in India 1947–61, (India, Ministry of Education), 48
Review of Educational Research, 52, 116, 125
RICHMOND, W. K., 86a
RIMMINGTON, G. T. 85a
RITCHIE, J. E., *The making of a Maori: a case study of a changing community*, 13
Robbins Report, 55, 112
ROBINSOHN, S. B., 78a, 86a, 93
— *See* Brian HOLMES and S. B. ROBINSOHN, 90, 129
RODERICK, Colin, *An introduction to Australian fiction*, 15
ROHNER, R. P., 74a
Role of educational research in social education, The (International Association for the Advancement of Educational Research), 132
ROSE, B., 85a
ROSE, B. W., 81a
ROSELLO, Pedro, 129
— *Les precurseurs du Bureau International d'Education*, 24
ROSEN, S. M., 83a
— *Significant aspects of Soviet education*, 67
ROTH, H., *A bibliography of New Zealand education*, 54
ROUCEK, J. S., 75a, 83a
— and LOTTICH, K. V. *Behind the iron curtain—the Soviet satellite states— East European nationalism and education*, 63
— *See* A. H. MOEHLMAN and J. S. ROUCEK (eds), 7

PERSON AND TITLE INDEX

ROUTLEDGE & KEGAN PAUL
— *The International Library of Sociology and Social Reconstruction*, 107
— *World Education Series*, 30
ROWE, A. P., *If the gown fits*, 108
ROYAL COMMONWEALTH SOCIETY, *Catalogue*, 125
RUDD, Steele, *On our selection*, 17
RUDMAN, H. C., 83a
RUGE, H., *Educational system in Scandinavia*, 68
RYAN, B., 74a
RYGA, George, *Ballad of a stone-picker*, 19
RYWKIN, M. S., 83a

SADLER, Michael E., 113
— *The unrest in secondary education in Germany and elsewhere*, 3.
SAMONTEI, Q. S., 81a
SAMUEL, R. H. and THOMAS, R. H. *Education and society in Modern Germany*, 60, 61, 107
SANDERS, C., *Educational writing and research in Australia 1960–1965, a bibliographical review*, 52
SARGESON, Frank
— *The making of a New Zealander*, 14
— *A man and his wife*, 14
SARUMPAET, J. P., 78a
SASIDHORN, H., 82a
SASNETT, Martena T., *Educational systems of the world*, 96, 99
SASSANI, A. H. K., *Education in Pakistan*, 50
SAVERY, Henry, *Quintus Servinton*, 15
SCANLAN, Nelle, *Pencarrow*, 14
SCANLON, David G., 76a, 81a, 94
— (ed), *Traditions of African education*, 34
— *See* L. G. COWAN, J. O'CONNELL and D. G. SCANLON (eds), 33
SCARANGELLO, A., 79a
SCARANGELLO, A. A., *Progress and trends in Italian education*, 62
SCHLESINGER, B., 78a
SCHNEIDER, F., 4
School and Society (Journal), 128
SCHOOL OF ORIENTAL AND AFRICAN STUDIES, *Asia and Africa. A select bibliography for schools*, 37
School systems: a guide, (Council of Europe), 54
Science and technology for development, Vol. VI, *Education and training*, (United Nations), 91
Science Policy Studies and Documents, (UNESCO), 105
Scientia Paedagogica Experimentalis, (Journal), 133
Scolma directory of libraries and special collections on Africa, 121
SEIF, N. S., 74a, 76a, 77a, 80a
Selected Bibliography of Yugoslav Educational Materials, (USA, Dept. of Health, Education and Welfare), 120
SENATOR FÜR VOLKSBILDUNG, *Schools in Berlin (West)*, 60
Sessions of the International Conference on Public Education, 28, 29, 30
SHAFER, S. M., 76a
SHAPIRO, S., 85a
SHAPOVALENKO, G. S. (ed), *Polytechnical education in the USSR*, 107
SHIMBORI, M., 79a
SHRIMALI, K. L., *Education in changing India*, 48
SIEGFRIED, A., *The character of peoples*, 10
SIMMONDS, E. H. S. (compiler), *Asia and Africa. A select bibliography for schools*, 37
SIMON, Brian and Joan (eds), *Educational psychology in the USSR*, 107
SIMON, E., 129
SINGER, G., *Teacher education in a communist state: Poland 1956–1961*, 64

PERSON AND TITLE INDEX

SMALL, J. J., 80a
SMITH, S. A., *Towards world understanding*, 124
SMYTHE, H. H., 82a
Social Sciences and Humanities Index, 123
SOCIETY FOR RESEARCH INTO HIGHER EDUCATION LTD.
— *Abstracts*, 135
— *Register of research projects in higher education*, 135
Society, schools and progress series, (Pergamon Press), 30, 59
Sociological Abstracts, 123
Sociology of Education Abstracts, 123
South and South-East Asia, (USA, Dept. of Health, Education and Welfare), 51
Soviet Education (Journal), 120
Spare the rod, 11
SPENCE, Catherine, *Clara Morison: a tale of South Australia during the gold fever*, 16
SPENCER, D. M., *Indian fiction in English, an annotated bibliography*, 21
SPOLTON, L., 11
SPRINGER, U. K., 76a
STANDING CONFERENCE ON LIBRARY MATERIALS ON AFRICA, *Scolma directory of libraries and special collections on Africa*, 121
STENHOUSE, L., 86a
STEPHENS, A. G., 7
STEPHENS, W. B., 77a
STERN, H. H.
— *Parent education—an international study*, 110
— *Parent education: an international survey*, 90
STERN, T. N., 78a
STEVENS, Joan, *The New Zealand novel*, 13
STONE, Louis, *Jonah*, 17
STOW, Randolph, *The merry-go-round in the sea*, 17
Studies in Comparative Education Series, (Pittsburgh University), 32
SVENNILSON, I. with F. EDDING and H. L. ELVIN. *Targets for education in Europe in 1970* (*Policy Conference on economic growth and investment in education*), 54, 91
Swiss Schools, 63
Sydney Bulletin, 16, 17

TAYLOR, F. M. *See* R. J. GOLDMAN and F. M. TAYLOR, 125
TAYLOR, Philip, 133
TAYLOR, W., 86a
Teaching Comparative Education (UNESCO), 89, 118, 130
Teaching for international understanding: Comparative study of the evolution and forms and deeds of leisure, (UNESCO), 90
Teaching of Sciences in African universities, The (UNESCO), 106
Technical Educational Abstracts, (National Foundation for Educational Research) 123
THAYER, V. T., *The role of the school in American society*, 40
THEOLOGIS, T. C., *Modern Greek education*, 61
THOMAS, J. and MAJAULT, Joseph, *Primary and secondary education: modern trends and common problems*, 55
THOMAS, R. H. *See* R. H. SAMUEL and R. H. THOMAS, 60, 61, 107
Thomas Report 1944, 53
THOREAU, Henry David, 11
THORNLEY, J. F., *The planning of primary education in Northern Nigeria*, 110
THUT, I. N., and ADAMS, Don, *Educational patterns in contemporary society*, 7, 24
TIBBLE, Anne, *African/English Literature*, 19
TINBERGEN, J. *See* A. LEWIS, F. HARBISON (and others), 92
TOMICH, V., *Education in Yugoslavia and the new reform*, 67
Training the trainer, (Council of Europe), 103
Trends in education (Journal), 126

PERSON AND TITLE INDEX

TURKEY, MINISTRY OF EDUCATION, *The report of the Turkish national commission on education*, 72
TURNBULL, M., *The changing land*, 13
TURNBULL, M. and MCLAREN, Ian A., *This land of New Zealand*, 13
TURNER, Ralph H., 77a, 84

UNESCO
— *Compulsory education in New Zealand*, 53
— *Education Abstracts*, 89, 118, 130
— *Educational planning: a preliminary listing*, 89
— *Educational Studies and Documents* (Series), 89, 118
— *General catalogue of publications 1946–1959*, 100
— *General catalogue of Unesco publications and Unesco-sponsored publications*, 100
— *An international directory of education associations*, 32, 118
— *An international list of educational periodicals*, 118
— *International guide to educational documentation 1955–1960*, 118
— *National Science Policies in countries of South and South-East Asia*, 105
— *The organisation of the school year, a comparative study*, 89
— *Report of meeting of ministers of education of Asian member states participating in the Karachi Plan*, 45, 105
— *Science Policy Studies and documents* (Series), 105
— *Teaching Comparative Education*, 89, 118, 130
— *Teaching international understanding: Comparative study of the evolution and forms and needs of leisure*, 90
— *The teaching of sciences in African universities*, 106
— *World handbook of educational organisations and statistics*, 25
— *World survey of education*, 25, 29, 89, 112, 117, 118
— *World survey of education, handbook of organisations and statistics*, 25
— *World survey of education*, Vol. II, *Primary education*, 26
— *World survey of education*, Vol. III, *Secondary Education*, 27
— *World survey of education*, Vol. IV, *Higher education*, 28
— DEPT. OF SCHOOL AND HIGHER EDUCATION. *Analytical bibliography on Comparative education of items available in Unesco*, 130
— INSTITUTE FOR EDUCATION, HAMBURG
— — *Achievements and functioning in children*, 90
— — *Intellectual processes: an international study of intellectual ability*, 90
— — *International Review of education*, 90
— — *Teaching for international understanding: Comparative study of the evolution and forms and needs of leisure*, 90
— INTERNATIONAL INSTITUTE FOR EDUCATIONAL PLANNING, *Directory of training and research institutions*, 90
— — *Problems and strategies of educational planning*, 104
— AND INTERNATIONAL BUREAU OF EDUCATION, *International Yearbook of education*, 28, 29, 112, 117
— *See also Higher education and development in South-East Asia*, Vols. I–III, 105, 106
— *See also* UNITED NATIONS, ECONOMIC COMMISSION FOR AFRICA AND UNESCO, 106

UNITED NATIONS
— *Demographic Yearbook*, 89
— *Science and technology for development*. Vol. VI, *Education and training*, 91
— ECONOMIC COMMISSION FOR AFRICA AND UNESCO, *Conference of African states on the development of education in Africa, Addis Ababa, May 15–25, 1961, final report*, 106

University in the education system, The (Comparative Education Society in Europe), 129
UNIVERSITY MICROFILMS INC, *Dissertation Abstracts*, 134

PERSON AND TITLE INDEX

USA
— DEPT OF HEALTH, EDUCATION AND WELFARE, EDUCATIONAL MATERIALS CENTER, DIVISION OF RESEARCH TRAINING AND DISSEMINATION, *South and South-East Asia*, 51
— DEPT. OF HEALTH, EDUCATION AND WELFARE, OFFICE OF EDUCATION
— — *Burma Education Abstracts*, 121
— — *Educational data: Republic of Portugal*, 63
— — *Selected bibliography of Yugoslav Educational materials*, 120

— DEPT. OF STATE, OFFICE OF EXTERNAL RESEARCH.
— — *External research Asia*, 134
— — *External research lists*, 134
USHINSKY, N. K. D., 83
USSR
— MINISTRY OF EDUCATION, RSFSR, *Public education in the Soviet union*, 67
— NOVOSTI PRESS AGENCY, *The birth of a vocation: creative technical work of children in the Soviet union*, 67

VAIZEY, J., *See* A. LEWIS, F. HARBISON (and others), 92
VAN DER KROEF, J., 78a
VAN LUTSENBERG MAAS, J., 80a
VEIKSHAN, V. A., 'The department of Contemporary education and schools abroad', 93
VELEMA, E., 80a
VENABLES, P., 86A
VERBIST, R. (ed), *Scientia Paedagogica Experimentalis*, 133
VEXILARD, A., 82a
VODINSKY, S., *Schools in Czechoslovakia*, 64
VOGEL, A. W., 83a
VOLPICELLI, Luigi, *See* George Z. F. BEREDAY, and L. VOLPICELLI, 39
VON KLEMPERER, L., *Austria. A survey of Austrian education and guide to the academic placement of students from Austria in educational institution in the United States of America*, 55

WARNER, Sylvia Ashton
— *Spinster*, 14
— *Teacher*, 14
WATSON, J. E., 80a
— *Intermediate schooling in New Zealand*, 53
WATTERS, R. E. and BELL, I. F. (compiler), *On Canadian literature 1806–1960, a check list of English-Canadian literature, its authors and language*, 18–19
WEI, C., 74a
WEIDNER, E. W. *See* C. S. BREMBECK and E. W. WEIDNER, 51
WEITZMAN, Sophia, 113
WESLEY, E. B., 85a
WEST GERMANY, EMBASSY LONDON, *Education in Germany*, 119
WEST INDIA LIBRARY, *Catalogue*, 125
WHITE, Patrick
— *The tree of man*, 18
— *Voss*, 18
WILLIAMS, L. E., 78a
WILLIAMS, T. D., 76a, 78a
WILCOCK, J. T., 84a
WILSON, N. H., 80a
WITTIG, Horst E., 93
WODAJO, M., 75a
WOOD, H. B., 86a
Wood's Despatch 1854, 47
Workers' Education Series, Pan-American Union, 107
World Affairs Guides, 44

PERSON AND TITLE INDEX

World and the School, The (Review), 124
World Education Series, (Routledge & Kegan Paul), 30
World Handbook of Educational organisations and statistics, (UNESCO), 25
World Survey of Education, (UNESCO), 25, 29, 89, 112, 117, 118
World Survey of Education, handbook of organisations and statistics, (UNESCO) 25
World Survey of Education, Vol. II, *Primary education*, (UNESCO), 26
World Survey of Education, Vol. III, *Secondary education*, (UNESCO), 27
World Survey of Education, Vol. IV, *Higher education*, (UNESCO), 28
World Year Book of Education, The, 94, 99, 112, 114, 117
World's classics series, 16
WYNN, R. *See* C. A. de YOUNG and R. WYNN, 39

YATES, B. A., 73a, 75a
— 'A bibliography on special problems in education in Tropical Africa', 37
— 'Educational policy and practice in tropical Africa: a general bibliography', 37
Year Book of Education, 24, 91, 117
YEAR BOOK OF EDUCATION 1964 (THE), *Education and international life*, 124
Yearbook of World Affairs, 12
YOUNG, C. A. de and WYNN, R. *American education*, 39
YU-KUANG CHU, 75a

ZEPPER, J. T., 84a
ZETTERLUND, Sven, *See* Urban DAHLLOF, Sven ZETTERLUND and Henning OBERG, 69
ZIGERELL, J. J., 86a

SUBJECT INDEX

Cross-references are restricted. Reference is made under the region to individual countries, e.g., Asia—see also under individual countries, but not *vice versa*.

Ability, 90
  Japan, 48
Aborigines, 17
Abstracting services, 119, 120, 122, 130, 135
  Africa, 121
  Bulgaria, 120
  Burma, 121
  English teaching, 122
  Europe, 120
  India, 120
  social factors and education, 123
Academic freedom
  Africa, 97
Achievement
  Japan, 48
Addis Ababa Conference, 106
Administration of education, 5, 6, 7, 26, 27, 28, 29, 134
  Africa, 33, 34, 97
  Australia, 52
  Austria, 54
  Belgium, 54
  bibliographies, 58
  Ceylon, 46
  Chile, 43
  Denmark, 54
  England, 56, 57, 58
  France, 54, 59, 60
  Germany, 61
  Greece, 62
  India, 47, 48
  Italy, 54, 62
  Latin America, 42
  Luxembourg, 54
  Netherlands, 54
  Norway, 54, 69
  Pakistan, 49
  Portugal, 54
  Scandinavia, 68
  Spain, 63
  Sweden, 54, 70
  UAR, 72
  USA, 39, 40
  West Germany, 54
  Yugoslavia, 67
Administration of schools
  Canada, 38

Adult education, 5, 7, 26, 91, 94, 126
  England, 123
  Peru, 43
  USA, 40
Africa, 1, 7, 31, 33–37, 56, 73, 85, 91, 99, 102, 106, 135
  abstracting services, 121
  academic freedom, 97
  administration of education, 33, 34, 97
  aid, 37
  annual reports, 35
  Belgian, 37, 56
  bibliographies, 33, 34, 36–37, 73, 97
  British, 37
  buildings, 97
  Communism, 81
  community development, 37
  control of education, 34
  curriculum, 97
  economics and education, 33–34
  finance, 34, 97
  French, 37
  further education, 33
  higher education, 33, 34, 85, 96, 97, 106
  history of education, 34
  language education, 37
  legislation, 34
  libraries, 51, 121
  literature, 19–21
  periodicals, 37, 121
  planning, 33, 34
  politics and education, 34, 73
  Portuguese, 37
  primary education, 33
  reports on education, 35, 37, 97
  research, 121, 134
  research centres, 131
  science teaching, 106
  secondary education, 33
  social change, 34
  social factors and education, 33
  Spanish, 37
  teacher training, 33, 37
  teachers, 37
  teaching methods, 37

SUBJECT INDEX

Africa—*contd.*
  technical education, 37
  vocational education, 37
  women's education, 37
  See also under areas (e.g. East Africa) and individual countries
African studies, 36, 121
Agricultural education
  England, 123
  Israel, 71
  Netherlands, 62
Agriculture, 134
  Belgium, 56
  Ghana, 35
  New Zealand, 53
Aid, 104
  Africa, 37
  Asia, 45
  Canada, 74
  Chile, 43
  developing countries, 92, 98
  Europe, 100
  Nigeria, 110
  Peru, 43
Aims of comparative education, 1, 8, 113, 116, 130
Aims of education, 7
  Asia, 44
  Ceylon, 46
  Scotland, 59
Albania, 64
Alberta, 115
Alliance for Progress, 42
American Council of Germany, 61
American Educational Research Association, 52, 116
American revolution, 39
American studies
  Great Britain, 85
  West Germany, 76
Americas, 31, 37–44, 99, 102, 104–105
  Fundamental education, 104
  higher education, 104
  history of education, 42, 104
  planning, 104
  research, 134
  research centres, 131
  science education, 104
  secondary education, 104, 124
  technical education, 104
  vocational education, 104
Amsterdam, 114, 115, 129
Anglicanism, 5
Annual reports, 3, 32, 33
  Africa, 35
Apprenticeship schools
  Czechoslovakia, 64
Arab education
  Israel, 71

Arab States Fundamental Education Centre, 100
Area studies, 2, 3–4, 5, 11, 24–86, 87, 89, 95, 102, 116, 132
Arithmetic teaching
  New Zealand, 80
  USA, 80, 84
Art education
  Sweden, 70
Asia, 1, 7, 31, 44–51, 73, 99, 102, 105–106, 135
  aims of education, 44
  aid, 45
  bibliographies, 37, 45, 50–51
  compulsory education, 45
  enrolment, 45
  educational theory, 44
  higher education 45, 105–106
  language problems, 106
  libraries, 51
  literature, 51
  manpower, 106
  planning, 44, 45
  primary education, 45
  research, 134
  research centres, 131
  social class, 45
  social factors and education, 105
  social mobility, 106
  socio-economic aspects, 45
  statistics, 45
  teacher training, 106
  teachers, 51
  See also under individual countries
Association of Modern Language Teachers, 103
Athletics
  USSR, 83
Atlantic Information Centre for Teachers, 124
Attitudes
  Brazil, 42
  Poland, 64
  USA, 40
Australasia, 31, 51–54
  bibliographies, 53
  See also under individual countries
Australia, 5, 31, 51–52, 73, 85, 105, 115, 130
  administration of education, 52
  bibliographies, 52
  church and education, 52
  curriculum, 52
  democracy and education, 52
  examinations, 52
  higher education, 52, 73, 85, 108
  history of education, 51
  indexing services, 121
  literature, 14–18, 19
  New South Wales, 51

SUBJECT INDEX

Australia—*contd.*
  periodicals, 121
  politics and education, 52
  private schools, 52
  psychology, 121
  Queensland, 51
  research, 51
  secondary education, 85
  social factors and education, 52
  Tasmania, 51
  teacher training, 52, 73
  teaching methods, 52
  technical education, 52
  tests and testing, 51
  Victoria, 51
Australian Council for Educational Research, 51, 121
Austria, 31, 54, 55, 73, 131
  administration of education, 54, 55
  bibliographies, 55
  curriculum, 55
  finance, 55
  glossaries, 54
  higher education, 55, 114
  history of education, 55
  international education, 73
  teacher salaries, 54

Bahamas
  Missionary education, 99
Baltic states, 64
Belgium, 5, 7, 31, 54, 56, 74, 96, 131
  administration of education, 54
  agriculture, 56
  bibliographies, 56
  church and education, 74
  colonies, 37, 56
  commercial education, 56
  economics and education, 56
  glossaries, 54
  higher education, 114
  history of education, 56, 126
  influence in Africa, 34, 56
  language teaching, 74, 76, 77, 80
  literature, 108
  politics and education, 56, 108
  schools pact 1959, 56
  state and education, 74
  teacher salaries, 54
  technical education, 56
Berlin, 60, 114, 129
Bibliographies, 5, 6, 7, 8, 25, 26, 107, 110–111, 116, 117, 118, 119, 121, 122, 123, 126, 127, 130, 133, 134
  administration of education, 58
  Africa, 33, 34, 36–37, 73, 97
  Asia, 37, 45, 50–51
  Australasia, 53
  Australia, 52

Bibliographies—*cont.*
  Austria, 55
  Belgium, 56
  Brazil, 42
  British Commonwealth, 53, 122
  Burma, 45
  Canada, 38
  Chile, 43
  China, 46
  control of education, 58
  Denmark, 69
  developing countries, 99
  Eastern Europe, 64, 67–68
  East Germany, 64
  economics and education, 123
  England, 58
  English teaching, 122
  Europe, 119
  Finland, 69
  France, 59, 60
  Germany, 60, 61
  Great Britain, 57, 97, 126
  higher education, 28
  immigrants, 125
  India, 47, 51, 97
  international understanding, 124
  Ireland, 59
  Italy, 62
  Japan, 49, 51, 79
  Latin America, 41, 44
  Middle East, 70
  Netherlands, 62
  New Zealand, 53, 54
  Nigeria, 36
  Norway, 69
  novels, 11, 12, 13, 15, 18, 19, 20, 21, 22
  Pakistan, 49, 50, 51
  parent education, 110
  Peru, 43
  Poland, 65
  primary education, 27
  Rumania, 65
  Scandinavia, 68
  Scotland, 59
  secondary education, 27
  social change, 123
  Sweden, 70
  Switzerland, 63
  technology, 124
  theses, 133–136
  Turkey, 72
  UAR, 72
  USA, 39, 40, 41
  USSR, 66, 110
  West Germany, 61
  Yugoslavia, 67, 120
Bilingualism, 122
Biology
  Europe, 103

SUBJECT INDEX

Boarding schools
  USSR, 66
Bonn, 103, 114
  Documentation and information centre, 93
Borneo, 105
Boston university, 115
Brazil, 31, 42, 74
  attitudes, 42
  bibliographies, 42
  church and education, 42
  curriculum, 42, 98
  economics and education, 42
  examinations, 98
  glossaries, 42
  higher education, 98, 108
  primary education, 24
  social factors and education, 42, 74
  socio-economic aspects, 42
  state and education, 42
  teaching, 42
Brazilian Government Centre for Educational Research, 42
Bremen, *Pädagogische Hochschule*, 93
British Commonwealth, 7, 32, 33, 94, 95, 96, 105, 125
  bibliographies, 53, 122
  higher education, 85
  history of education, 113
  literature, 11–23
  material in England, 122
British Council, 122
British Museum, 125
British National Bibliography, 126
Bulgaria, 64
  abstracting services, 120
Buildings, 29
  Africa, 97
  West Germany, 61
Burma, 31, 45, 74, 105
  abstracting services, 121
  bibliographies, 45
  higher education, 45
  politics and education, 74, 78
  research, 121
Bushranging, 16

California university, 115
Cambodia, 105
Cambridge, 132
Canada, 5, 31, 37–39, 74, 85, 115, 130, 131
  administration of schools, 38
  aid, 74
  bibliographies, 38
  church and education, 38, 74
  curriculum, 38
  democracy and education, 38
  educational change, 38
  educational theory, 38, 74

Canada—*contd.*
  equality of opportunity, 74
  French-Canadian education, 74
  history of education, 38
  language problems, 85
  literature, 18–19
  Ontario, 133
  planning, 133
  Quebec, 133
  reports on education, 38
  research, 134
  social change, 38
  state and education, 74
  statistics, 37, 38
  women's education, 38
Canberra, 105
Carnegie Corporation, 97, 98
Caribbean Countries
  higher education, 108
  literature, 12
Case studies. *See* National case studies
Catalogues, 125
Catholicism, 5
Catholic orders, 5
Centre for Information on Language Teaching, 122
Ceylon, 31, 46, 74, 115
  administration of education, 46
  aims of education, 46
  control of education, 46
  curriculum, 46
  democracy and education, 46
  finance of education, 46
  higher education, 45
  history of education, 46, 113
  legislation, 46
  missionary education, 99
  organization of education, 46
  western education, 46
Change. *See* Educational, social change.
Character education, USSR, 66
Charter Act 1698, 47
Chicago University, School of Education, Comparative Education Centre, 93, 115, 136
Children's literature
  USSR, 66
Chile, 31, 43
  administration of education, 43
  aid, 43
  bibliographies, 43
  curriculum, 98
  economics and education, 43
  examinations, 98
  higher education, 43, 98
  history of education, 43
  organization of education, 43
  social change, 43
  vocational education, 43

SUBJECT INDEX

China, 5, 7, 31, 64, 74, 107, 108, 131, 135
  bibliographies, 46
  Communism, 46, 108
  educational theory, 46
  engineering education, 74
  higher education, 74, 82
  history of education, 46
  indoctrination, 46
  planning, 44
  politics and education, 46
  reform, 74, 107–108
  social change, 46
Christian Churches, 5
Church and education, 5, 93, 95
  Australia, 52
  Belgium, 74
  Brazil, 42
  Canada, 38, 74
  England, 56, 75, 77, 84
  France, 59, 75, 77, 79
  Italy, 75, 79
  Netherlands, 80
  Tanganyika, 82
  USA, 40, 77, 84
  See also Religion and education
Citizenship education, 93, 124
  Europe, 102
  Iran, 71
  Poland, 64
Class. *See* Social class
Co-education
  UAR, 72
  USSR, 66
Columbia, 5
Colombo Plan for Co-operative Economic Development in South and South-East Asia, 105
Colonies, 93
  See also Great Britain—colonies, France—colonies, etc.
Columbia University, 109, 115, 128, 135
  Bureau of Applied Research, 70
  Teachers' College, 3, 92, 111, 114
  Teachers' College International Institute, 93
Commercial education
  Belgium, 56
  England, 77, 123, 124
Commonwealth
  Books exhibition, 53
  British. *See* British Commonwealth
  co-operation in education, 48
  education conference, 58
  studies, 122
Communication media, 95
Communism, 64
  Africa, 81
  China, 46

Community development
  Africa, 37
Comparative education
  aims, 1, 8, 113, 116, 130
  history, 2, 3, 5, 7, 8, 116, 130, 132
  methodology, 1–4, 5, 6, 8, 113, 116, 117, 126, 127, 130, 131, 132
  teaching, 1–8, 112–136
Comparative Education Societies, 73, 104, 114, 115
Comparative Education Society in Europe, 113–114, 115, 128–130
  British section, 11, 130
Comparative Education Society, USA, 65, 115, 127–128
Comprehensive schools, 2
  England, 57, 77, 86
  Nigeria, 36
  Norway, 86
  Sweden, 69–70
  USA, 86
  USSR, 66
Compulsory education
  Asia, 45
  England, 77
  New Zealand, 53
  Pakistan, 49
  UAR, 72
  Western Europe, 55
Congo, 75
  Belgian, 56
  higher education, 97
Constitution, Italy, 62
Control of education, 5, 6, 7, 27, 57
  Africa, 34
  bibliographies, 58
  Ceylon, 46
  England, 58
  Germany, 61
  Nigeria, 36
Convictism, 15–16
Correspondence education
  New Zealand, 53
Cost of education
  Spain, 63
Council for Education in World Citizenship, 124
Council of Europe, 55, 100, 102, 103, 112, 132
  Council of Cultural Co-operation, 100, 119
Council on Higher Education in the American Republics, 108
Counselling. *See* Guidance
Cross-cultural studies, 2, 3, 4, 11, 24, 29, 32, 87–106, 128, 136
  in literature, 21, 22
Cross-national studies, 87, 88, 97, 98, 100–106, 132, 136
Cultural bias, 4

SUBJECT INDEX

Culture contact, 12, 34
  England, 77
  Japan, 109
  USA, 109
Curriculum, 6, 9, 29, 96, 124
  Africa, 97
  Australia, 52
  Austria, 55
  Brazil, 42, 98
  Canada, 38
  Ceylon, 46
  Chile, 98
  England, 98
  Europe, 101
  France, 60, 98
  Ghana, 98
  India, 47, 98
  Japan, 48, 98
  Latin America, 44
  New Zealand, 53, 98
  Nigeria, 36
  Norway, 69
  Pakistan, 44
  Poland, 65
  primary education, 27, 93
  secondary education, 6, 27, 95
  Senegal, 98
  South Africa, 98
  Sweden, 70
  UAR, 98
  USA, 40, 98
  USSR, 6, 66, 67, 98
  West Germany, 61
  Western Europe, 55
  Yugoslavia, 67
Curriculum control, 4
Cyprus, missionary education, 99
Czechoslovakia, 7, 31, 64
  apprenticeship schools, 64
  higher education, 64, 114
  pre-primary education, 64
  social factors and education, 64
  statistics, 64

Danish Information Service, 32, 68
Democracy and education, 5, 6, 92
  Australia, 52
  Canada, 38
  Ceylon, 46
  England, 56
  France, 59
  India, 48
  Japan, 109
  USA, 40
Denmark, 7, 31, 32, 54, 68–69, 75
  administration of education, 54
  bibliographies, 69
  folk high schools, 75, 82
  glossaries, 54
  history of education, 69

Denmark—*contd.*
  'New Gymnasiums', 69
  primary education, 69
  private schools, 69
  reform, 68
  school organization, 69
  secondary education, 69
  statistics, 69
  teacher, salaries, 54
  teacher training, 69
  teaching methods, 69
Developing Countries, 1, 6, 7, 11, 45, 71, 91, 92, 98, 99, 126
  aid, 92, 98
  bibliographies, 99
  economics and education, 98, 99
  planning, 41, 98
  research centres, 131
  social factors and education, 98
  technology, 98
Discipline
  USSR, 66
Dissenting academies, 5

East Africa
  literature, 19
  teachers, 73
East Asia. *See* Asia
East European studies
  West Germany, 76
East Germany, 64, 75–76
  bibliographies, 64
  educational theory, 64
  extra-curricular activities, 76
  higher education, 114
  indoctrination, 76
  science education, 64
East India Comany, 47
Eastern Europe, 63–68, 75
  bibliographies, 64, 67–68
  juvenile delinquency, 75
  nationalism, 63
  research, 134
  vocational education, 120
East-West Major Project on mutual appreciation of Eastern and Western cultural values, 50
Economics and education, 5, 6, 36, 57, 63, 91, 92, 95, 96, 100, 115, 123
  Africa, 33–34
  Belgium, 56
  bibliographies, 123
  Brazil, 42
  Chile, 43
  developing countries, 98, 99
  England, 58
  France, 59
  Ghana, 88
  indexing services, 123
  Latin America, 41, 80, 105

SUBJECT INDEX

Economics and education—*contd.*
  Mexico, 43
  Pakistan, 49
  Philippines, 81
  Scandinavia, 68
  Spain, 63
  Turkey, 72
  USA, 40
  USSR, 66, 83
  Western Europe, 54, 55, 75
Edge Hill College of Education Dept. of Sociology, 123
Education Associations, 94, 118
Educational change, 7, 27, 28, 29, 57, 133
  Canada, 38
  England, 57
  Germany, 60
  Italy, 62
  Sweden, 86
Educational theory, 94, 95, 96, 116, 134
  Asia, 44
  Canada, 38, 74
  China, 46
  East Germany, 64
  Poland, 64
  USA, 39, 40, 74
  USSR, 65
Egypt, 70, 100
  missionary education, 99
  See also UAR
Eire. *See* Ireland
Elites, 6, 97, 99
  France, 59
  Pakistan, 78, 81
El Salvador, Worker's education, 107
Emigrants, 12
Engineering education
  China, 74
England, 3, 5, 6, 7, 10, 15, 20, 21, 30, 31, 56–58, 77, 86, 94, 95, 96, 131, 133
  administration of education, 56, 57, 58
  adult education, 123
  agricultural education, 123
  bibliographies, 58
  British Commonwealth material in, 122
  church and education, 56, 75, 77, 84
  commercial education, 77, 123, 124
  comprehensive schools, 57, 77, 86, 112
  compulsory education, 77
  control of education, 58
  Crowther Report, 53, 112
  culture contact, 77
  curriculum, 98
  democracy and education, 56

England—*contd.*
  economics and education, 58
  educational change, 57
  equality of opportunity, 77
  examinations, 98
  extra-curricular activities, 102
  finance, 56, 57
  further education, 56, 58, 123
  glossaries, 58
  higher education, 57, 58, 77, 86, 98, 112, 114
  history of education, 57, 58, 77
  industrial education, 123, 124
  industry and education, 57
  language teaching, 74, 76, 77, 80
  legislation, 56
  literature, 12
  local authorities and education, 56, 58
  music education, 77
  periodicals, 58, 116
  planning, 133
  politics and education, 77, 84
  primary education, 58
  public schools, 58
  research, 77
  Robbins Report, 112, 132
  secondary education, 58, 77, 86
  social factors and education, 56, 57, 58
  special education, 56, 58
  state and education, 56, 58
  statistics, 132
  teacher training, 56, 57
  teacher methods, 57
  technical education, 57, 77, 123
  technology, 57
  theses, 134
  welfare services, 56, 58
English education
  USA, 83, 84
  USSR, 83, 84
English teaching
  abstracting services, 122
  bibliographies, 122
  India, 48
  West Germany, 61
  Information Centre, 122
Enrolment, 6, 25, 26, 27
  Asia, 45
  Pakistan, 49
  Philippines, 81
  Spain, 63
  Sweden, 70
  West Germany, 76
Equality of opportunity, 6
  Canada, 74
  England, 77
  Sweden, 82
Equipment, 29

SUBJECT INDEX

Eritrea
 Bibliographies, 37
Ethiopia, 75
 bibliographies, 37
 higher education, 75, 97
 reform, 75
Europe, 2, 3, 6, 7, 10, 11, 13, 30, 31, 34, 54–68, 75, 91, 94, 99, 100, 101, 102–103, 107, 112, 114, 129, 130, 135
 abstracting services, 120
 aid, 100
 bibliographies, 119
 biology, 103
 citizenship education, 102
 curriculum, 101
 extra-curricular activities, 102
 higher education, 97, 100
 language teaching, 103
 learning, 101
 legislation, 119
 Leisure, 102
 manpower, 101
 out-of-school education, 100
 physical education, 103
 planning, 91, 101
 primary education, 103, 119
 research, 100, 101, 103, 132
 research centres, 131
 science, 101
 science teaching, 101
 secondary education, 103, 119, 124, 134
 sport, 103
 teacher training, 102
 teaching, 101
 teaching aids, 103
 technical education, 100, 134
 vocational education, 103, 134
 See also Eastern, Western Europe; also under individual countries
European Communities, 101
European Cultural Centre, 102
European Free Trade Association, 101
European Ministers of Education, Second Conference, Third Conference, 55
Examinations, 6, 9, 27, 124
 Australia, 52
 Brazil, 98
 Chile, 98
 England, 98
 France, 98
 Ghana, 98
 India, 98
 Japan, 98
 NewZealand, 98
 Pakistan, 56
 Senegal, 98
 South Africa, 98

Examinations—*contd.*
 UAR, 98
 USA, 98
 USSR, 98
Excellence, 95
Experiments in education
 Germany, 60
 New Zealand, 53
Extra-curricular activities
 East Germany, 76
 England, 102
 Europe, 102
 France, 102
 Iran, 71
 Netherlands, 102
 Scotland, 59
 Switzerland, 102
 USSR, 66
 West Germany, 102

Factor approach, 88, 98
Far East, 75. *See also* under individual countries
Federal authorities, 5
Feudalism, 6
Films
 USA, 40
Finance, 29
 Africa, 34, 97
 Austria, 55
 Ceylon, 46
 England, 56, 57
 India, 44
 Pakistan, 44
 Scotland, 59
 Sweden, 70
 USSR, 109–110
Finance of higher education, 28
Finance of schools, 5
Finland, 31, 54, 75
 bibliographies, 69
 glossaries, 54
 higher education, 54
 legislation, 75
 pre-school education, 54
 primary education, 54
 research, 67
 secondary education, 54
 statistics, 54
 teacher training, 54
 technical education, 54
Florence, 114
Folk high schools
 Denmark, 75, 82
 Sweden, 75, 82
Ford Foundation, 72, 105
France, 1, 5, 6, 7, 10, 30, 31, 54, 59–60, 75, 86, 96, 107, 119, 120, 131, 135
 administration of education, 54, 59, 60

SUBJECT INDEX

France—*contd.*
  bibliographies, 59, 60
  church and education, 59, 75, 77
  colonies, 5, 30, 37, 73, 97
  curriculum, 60, 98
  democracy and education, 59
  economics and education, 59
  elites, 59
  examinations, 98
  extra-curricular activities, 102
  glossaries, 54
  guidance, educational, 60
  higher education, 60, 98, 114, 119
  history of education, 59, 60, 126
  humanities, 59
  influence in Africa, 34
  Langevin-Wallon Commission 1947, 59
  literature, 18
  local authorities and education, 60
  manpower, 60
  nursery education, 60
  organization of education, 59
  parent education, 110
  planning, 86
  politics and education, 59
  primary education, 60
  reform, 59, 60, 75, 88, 119
  religion and education, 59
  science, 59
  secondary education, 60, 86
  social factors and education, 59, 60
  state and education, 60
  teacher salaries, 54
  teacher training, 60, 75
  technology, 59
  theses, 119
  vocational education, 60
Frankfurt, Hochschule für Internationale pädagogische Forschung, 93
French Africa
  Literature, 19
French-Canadian education
  Canada, 74
Fundamental education, 126
  Americas, 104
  Latin America, 106
  Mexico, 107
  Middle East, 100
Further education
  Africa, 33
  England, 56, 58, 123

Geneva, 24, 28, 82, 84, 114, 120
Geographic factors, 5, 30, 88
Geographical factors and education
  Pakistan, 49
  Western Europe, 75
George Peabody College, 115

Germany, 2, 5, 7, 10, 30, 31, 60–61, 96, 107, 120, 131, 135
  administration of education, 61
  bibliographies, 60, 61
  control of education, 61
  educational change, 60
  experiments in education, 60
  higher education, 61, 114
  history of education, 60, 61, 126
  influence in Africa, 34
  language teaching, 74, 76, 77, 80
  organization of education, 60
  reform, 60
  selection, 132–133
  social factors and education, 61
  teachers, 60
  See also East Germany, West Germany
Germany, Democratic Republic. *See* East Germany
Germany, Federal Republic. *See* West Germany
Ghana, 31, 34, 35, 37, 76, 107
  Agriculture, 35
  curriculum, 98
  economics and education, 88
  examinations, 98
  higher education, 98
  politics and education, 34
  reform, 76
  secondary education, 35, 88
  social change, 35
  technology, 35
Ghent, 129, 133
Gifted children, 95, 96
  USSR, 66
Glossaries, 117, 130
  Austria, 54
  Belgium, 54
  Brazil, 42
  Denmark, 54
  England, 58
  Finland, 54
  France, 54
  Italy, 54, 62
  Japan, 49
  Luxembourg, 54
  Netherlands, 54
  Norway, 54
  Peru, 43
  Portugal, 54
  Rumania, 65
  Sweden, 54, 60
  Turkey, 72
  USA, 39
  West Germany, 54, 61
  Western Europe, 54
Gordonstoun, 61
Great Britain, 6, 7, 16, 52, 53, 56–59, 132, 135

SUBJECT INDEX

Great Britain—*contd.*
  American studies, 85
  bibliographies, 57, 97, 126
  colonies, 30, 35, 73
  Crowther Report, 77, 112
  high commission territories in Africa, 85
  higher education, 96, 97
  immigrants, 125
  indexing services, 118
  influence in Africa, 34
  international education, 124
  literature, 18
  Malaya, education policy in 80, 81
  parent education, 110
  planning, 133
  Public Record Office, 126
  reports on education, 57, 112, 132
  research, 134
  Robbins Report, 112, 132
  secondary education, 6
  theses, 135
  See also England, Northern Ireland, Scotland
Greece, 6, 31, 61–62, 77, 107
  administration of education, 62
  Anavryta National School, 61
  Children's Colonies, 61
  higher education, 61
  Ministry of Religious and National Culture, 62
  pre-school education, 61
  primary education, 61
  secondary education, 61, 77
  youth, 62
Greenland, 69
Guatemala, 77–78
  primary education, 78
  Teachers, 78
Guidance, 29, 95
  France, 60
  UAR, 72
  Western Europe, 55
Guinea, 78
  politics and education, 78

Hamburg, 114, 130
Handicapped children, USSR, 65
Health education, 89
Hebrew, 71
Hellenic patterns, 6
Higher education, 5, 7, 26, 28, 57, 91, 92, 93, 95, 96, 97, 99, 127, 129
  admission to, 28, 92, 98, 99
  Africa, 33, 34, 85, 96, 97, 106
  Americas, 104
  Asia, 45, 105–106
  Australia, 52, 73, 85, 108
  Austria, 55, 114
  Belgium, 114

Higher education—*contd.*
  Bibliographies, 28
  Brazil, 98, 108
  British Commonwealth, 85
  Burma, 45
  Caribbean, 108
  Ceylon, 45
  Chile, 43, 98
  China, 74, 82
  Congo, 97
  Czechoslovakia, 64, 114
  East Germany, 114
  England, 57, 58, 77, 86, 98, 112, 114
  Ethiopia, 75, 97
  Europe, 97, 100
  Finance, 28
  Finland, 54
  France, 60, 98, 114, 119
  Germany, 61, 114
  Ghana, 89
  Great Britain, 96, 97
  Greece, 61
  History of, 97, 108
  History teaching, 134
  India, 47, 78, 96, 97, 98
  Indonesia, 45
  Ireland, 58
  Italy, 62, 79, 114
  Japan, 98
  Latin America, 41, 42, 79, 80, 84, 108
  Mexico, 43, 108
  Netherlands, 114
  New Zealand, 98
  Nigeria, 36
  Norway, 69
  Pakistan, 50
  Philippines, 45
  Poland, 114
  Rumania, 65
  Scandinavia, 114
  Scotland, 115
  Senegal, 98
  South Africa, 97, 98
  Sudan, 82
  Sweden, 70
  Switzerland, 114
  Thailand, 45
  UAR, 72, 98
  Uruguay, 85
  USA, 40, 80, 84, 98, 108, 114, 115
  USSR, 66, 74, 82, 83, 98, 114
  West Germany, 76
  West Indies, 44
  Western Europe, 54
  Yugoslavia, 114
Historical method, 5, 6, 7, 8, 93, 94, 113
History of education, 113
  Africa, 34

SUBJECT INDEX

History of education—*contd.*
  Americas, 42, 104
  Australia, 51
  Austria, 55
  Belgium, 56, 126
  Canada, 38
  Ceylon, 46, 113
  Chile, 43
  China, 46
  Denmark, 69
  England, 57, 58, 77
  Europe, 97
  France, 59, 60, 123
  Germany, 60, 61, 126
  higher education, 97, 108
  India, 47, 97, 113
  Iran, 71
  Ireland, 58
  Israel, 71
  Italy, 62
  Japan, 48, 49
  Mexico, 43
  New Zealand, 53
  Nigeria, 35, 36
  Pakistan, 49, 50, 113
  Poland, 65
  Scotland, 57, 59
  Sweden, 70
  USA, 39, 40
  USSR, 65, 66
  West Germany, 76
  West Indies, 44
History teaching, 89, 124, 126, 134
  higher education, 134
  West Germany, 76
Holland, *See* Netherlands
Home economics
  Netherlands, 62
Hong Kong, 78
Hull university, 110
Humanism, 5
Humanities
  France, 59
Hungary, 64, 86
  Planning, 86

Ibadan, International school, 36
Iceland, 59, 103
  teacher training, 103
Imaginative literature, 9–23
Immigrants
  Australia, 16
  Bibliographies, 125
  Great Britain, 125
  Israel, 71
  USA, 39
Indexing services, 116, 117, 118, 123
  Australia, 121
  economics and education, 123
  Great Britain, 118

Indexing services—*contd.*
  manpower and education, 123
  theses, 135
  USA, 118
India, 5, 7, 31, 47–48, 78, 91, 96, 105, 115, 131
  abstracting services, 120
  administration of education, 47, 48
  bibliographies, 47, 51, 97
  Calcutta University Commission, 97
  curriculum, 47, 98
  democracy and education, 48
  Education Commission 1822, 47
  English teaching, 48
  examinations, 98
  finance, 44
  higher education, 47, 78, 96, 97, 98
  history of education, 47, 97, 113
  Independence Act 1947, 47
  international understanding, 48
  Kashmir, 99
  Kerala, 99
  language, 48
  language problems, 47
  literature, 19, 21–23
  material in London, 121
  medium of instruction, 47
  missionary education, 47, 99
  periodicals, 120
  planning, 44, 47, 48
  politics and education, 47
  primary education, 47
  reform, 97
  secondary education, 47
  social factors and education, 47
  special education, 48
  sport, 48
  students, 78
  teacher training, 48
  technical education, 78
  University Commission 1902, 47
Indoctrination, 4
  China, 46
  East Germany, 76
  Indonesia, 78
  USSR, 83
Indonesia, 78, 105
  higher education, 45
  indoctrination, 78
  nationalism, 78
  planning, 44
  politics and education, 74, 78
  social factors and education, 78
Industrial development, 5
Industrial education, 91
  England, 123, 124
Industry and education, 95, 131, 132
  England, 57
Innsbruck, 114
Inspection, 29

SUBJECT INDEX

Institute of Inter-American Affairs, Division of education, 107
International agencies, 4, 24–30, 48, 58, 89–92, 100, 101, 106–107, 110-111, 124, 129, 131
International Association for the Advancement of Educational Research, 132
International Association of Universities, 92, 98
International Atomic Energy Agency, 110–111
International Bureau of Education, 4, 24, 28, 29, 94, 102, 117, 118, 129
International Co-operation, 91, 104
International Co-operation Year in Education, 85
International education, 95, 97, 123, 124, 128, 129, 130, 135
   Austria, 73
   Great Britain, 124
   Nigeria, 36
   USA, 97
International Education Institute, 92–93
International Federation of Library Associations, 50
International Institute for Educational Planning. *See* UNESCO International Institute, etc.
International Labor Office, 120
International Monetary Fund, 111
International Project for the Evaluation of Educational Achievement, 90
International schools, 36, 73
International understanding, 90, 124, 125, 126, 131, 132
   bibliographies, 124
   India, 48
International Vocational Training Information Centre, 120
Iran, 31, 70, 71, 78
   citizenship education, 71
   extra-curricular activities, 71
   history of education, 71
   legislation, 71
   medical education, 71
   missionary education, 71
   physical education, 71
   secondary education, 78
   social change, 71
   social factors and education, 71
   teachers, 71
Iraq, 70
Ireland, 5, 31, 58–59, 78
   bibliography, 59
   higher education, 58
   history of education, 58
   legislation, 59

Ireland—*contd.*
   primary education, 58
   secondary education, 58
   statistics, 59
   theses, 135
   vocational education, 58
Islam, 6, 50, 72, 81
Israel, 31, 71, 78, 107
   Agriculture education, 71
   Arab education, 71
   history of education, 7
   immigrants, 71
   Kibbutz education, 71
   language teaching, 71
   religion and education, 78
   statistics, 71
   youth, 71
Italy, 5, 7, 10, 31, 54, 62, 79
   administration of education, 54, 62
   bibliographies, 62
   church and education, 75, 79
   constitution, 62
   educational change, 62
   Fanfani 10-year plan, 62
   glossaries, 54, 62
   Gonella Plan, 62
   higher education, 62, 79, 114
   history of education, 62
   Latin question, 62
   planning, 79
   reform, 62, 76, 79
   state and education, 75, 79
   teacher salaries, 54
   teacher training, 62
   technical education, 62
   television, 62
   vocational education, 62

Japan, 5, 6, 7, 10, 31, 48–49, 79, 96, 107, 109, 115, 130, 131
   ability, 48
   achievement, 48
   bibliographies, 49, 51, 79
   culture contact, 109
   curriculum, 48, 98
   democracy and education, 109
   examinations, 98
   glossaries, 49
   higher education, 98
   history of education, 48, 49
   moral education, 6, 48, 49, 79
   planning, 49
   politics and education, 48, 49
   reform, 109
   research, 132
   social class, 49
   social factors and education, 49, 68
   society for the study of education, 131
   Soviet studies, 82

SUBJECT INDEX

Japan—*contd.*
  statistics, 49
  students, 79
  Tokugawa education, 79
  Western education, 48
Jewish education
  Scotland, 59
Jordan, 70
Judaic Christian literature, 10
Juvenile delinquency
  Eastern Europe, 75
  USSR, 83

Karachi Plan, 45, 105
Kashmir
  Missionary education, 99
Kenya
  planning, 79
Kerala, Missionary education, 99
Kibbutz education
  Israel, 71
Kiev, 65
Kindergarten. *See* Nursery education
King's College. *See* London University
  King's College
Korea, 79
Kuala Lumpur, 106
Kwakiutl children, 74

Language, 1, 4, 19, 29, 88
  India, 48
  Pakistan, 50
  UAR, 72
Language education
  Africa, 37
Language policy, 5
Language problems
  Asia, 106
  Canada, 85
  India, 47
Language teaching, 89, 122
  Belgium, 74, 76, 77, 80
  England, 74, 76, 77, 80
  Europe, 103
  Germany, 74, 76, 77, 80
  Israel, 71
  Netherlands, 74, 76, 77, 80
  USA, 75, 84
  West Germany, 61
  Western Europe, 75, 84
Laos, 105
Latin America, 5, 7, 41-44, 79-80, 91,
    94, 96, 104, 107, 115
  administration of education, 42
  American schools, 80
  bibliographies, 41, 44
  curriculum, 44
  economics and education, 41, 80,
    105
  fundamental education, 100

Latin America—*contd.*
  higher education, 41, 42, 79, 80,
    84, 108
  organization of education, 42
  planning, 41-42, 104-105
  politics and education, 41, 104-105
  radio schools, 80
  science education, 42
  secondary education, 80
  social class, 79
  social factors and education, 41,
    104-105
  socio-economic aspects, 104
  See also under individual countries
Learning
  Europe, 101
  UAR, 72
  USA, 40
Lebanon, 70
Leeds University, 12
Legislation, 4, 26, 27, 28
  Africa, 34
  Ceylon, 46
  England, 56
  Europe, 119
  Finland, 75
  Iran, 71
  Ireland, 59
  Netherlands, 80
  Norway, 69
  Pakistan, 49
  South Africa, 81
  Switzerland, 63
  USA, 115
  Yugoslavia, 67
Leisure, 90
  Europe, 102
Leningrad, 65, 66
Liberal education, 94
Libraries, 12, 31, 32, 115, 116-127
  Africa, 51, 121
  Asia, 51
Linguistic factors, 5
Linguistic minority education
  USA, 83, 84
  USSR, 83, 84
Literacy, 25, 91
  Pakistan, 49, 50
  Peru, 43
Literature
  Africa, 18-19
  Asia, 51
  Australia, 14-18, 19
  Belgium, 108
  British Commonwealth, 11-23
  Canada, 18-19
  India, 19, 21-23
  New Zealand, 13-14, 19
Liverpool University
  Dept. of Adult Education, 123

SUBJECT INDEX

Liverpool University—*contd.*
  Dept. of Social Science, 123
  School of Education, 123
Local authorities and education, 5
  England, 56, 58
  France, 60
London, 128, 129
  Indian material in, 121
London University, 114, 136
London University Institute of Education, 3, 92, 93, 99, 113, 128, 136
  Comparative education library, 1, 33, 117
  Department of Education in Tropical Areas, 121
  Education in Tropical Areas Library, 36
London University King's College, 3, 92
Los Angeles, 115
Luxembourg, 31, 54
  Administration of education, 54
  glossaries, 54
  teacher salaries, 54

McGill, 115
Madrid, 114
Malaya, 80, 105
  British educational policy in, 80, 81
  literature, 12
Malaysia, 105
Manpower
  Asia, 106
  Europe, 101
  France, 60
  indexing services, 123
  Mexico, 43
  Puerto Rico, 81
  Spain, 63
Maoris, 13, 14, 53
Marshall Plan, 100
Max-Planck-Gesellschaft, Institut für Bildungs forschung, 86, 93
Medical education
  Iran, 71
Medium of instruction
  India, 47
Melbourne, 115
Methodology, comparative, 73, 87, 88, 108, 113, 126, 127, 130, 132
Mexico, 7, 31, 43, 100
  economics and education, 43
  fundamental education, 107
  higher education, 43, 108
  history of education, 43
  manpower, 43
  planning, 43
  secondary education, 43

Michigan University
  Dept. of Education, 93, 115
  School of Education, 136
Middle East, 7, 31, 50, 70–72, 80, 102
  bibliographies, 70
  fundamental education, 100
  research, 134
  See also under individual countries
Missionary education, 96, 99
  Bahamas, 99
  Ceylon, 99
  Cyprus, 99
  Egypt, 99
  India, 47, 99
  Iran, 71
  Kashmir, 99
  Kerala, 99
  Nigeria, 36, 99
Modern languages, 29
Mongolian People's Republic, 80
Moral education, 6, 96, 132
  Japan, 6, 48, 49, 79
  USSR, 66
Moscow, 65, 66, 83, 93
Multi-racial societies, 5
Music education
  England, 77
  Sweden, 70

Nashville, 115
National case studies, 2, 3, 6, 11, 24, 26, 27, 28, 30–33, 33–89, 95, 106–111, 113, 118, 136
National character, 7, 9–10
National Education Assocation, 39
National Foundation for Educational Research England and Wales, 125, 135
National systems of education, 2, 3, 4, 7, 87, 90, 96
Nationalism, 5, 12, 22, 110
  Indonesia, 78
  Nigeria, 36
  Eastern Europe, 63–64
Native education
  South Africa, 81
Natural factors, 5
Negro Education Grant
  West Indies, 44
Nepal
  teacher training, 86
Netherlands, 3, 5, 7, 31, 54, 62, 80, 96, 132
  administration of education, 54
  agriculture education, 62
  bibliographies, 62
  church and education, 80
  extra-curricular activities, 102
  glossaries, 54

SUBJECT INDEX

Netherlands—*contd.*
  higher education
  home economics, 62
  language teaching, 74, 76, 77, 80
  legislation, 80
  organization of education, 62
  primary education, 80
  reform, 80
  school hygiene, 62
  secondary education, 80
  statistics, 62
  teacher salaries, 54
  technical education, 62
New media, 91, 96
New York, 114, 128, 130
New York University, 115, 135
  School of Education, 127
New Zealand, 5, 31, 52–53, 80, 86, 105, 115, 130
  agriculture, 53
  arithmetic teaching, 80, 84
  bibliographies, 53, 54
  compulsory education, 53
  correspondence education, 53
  Council for Educational Research, 52
  curriculum, 53
  Currie Report 1962, 53
  examinations, 98
  experiments in education, 53
  higher education, 98
  history of education, 53
  literature, 13–14, 19
  Parry Report 1959, 53
  primary education, 80
  reform, 53
  religious education, 80
  reports on education, 53
  research, 52–53
  rural education, 53
  school-leaving age, 53
  secondary education, 53
  statistics, 52
  teacher status, 80
  teacher training, 53
  Thomas Report 1944, 53
Nigeria, 21, 31, 35–36
  aid, 110
  Archer Report, 110
  Ashby Commision Report, 110
  bibliographies, 36
  comprehensive schools, 36
  control of education, 36
  curricula, 36
  Eastern, 99
  higher education, 36
  history of education, 35, 36
  international education, 36
  missionary education, 36, 99
  northern, 20, 110

Nigeria—*contd.*
  Oldman Report, 110
  organization of education, 36
  Phelps-Stokes Commission Report, 35, 36
  planning, 36, 109, 110
  primary education, 110
  reports on education, 110
  teacher training, 36
  Western, 36
  1944 Education Act, 56
Non-Russian education
  USSR, 82
North America, 7, 37–41, 135
Northern Ireland
  theses, 135
Norway, 5, 7, 31, 32, 68, 69, 81, 86
  administration of education, 54, 69
  bibliographies, 69
  comprehensive education, 86
  curriculum, 69
  glossaries, 54
  higher education, 69
  legislation, 69
  organization of education, 69
  periodicals, 69
  pre-school education, 69
  reform, 68, 81
  statistics, 69
  teacher salaries, 54
  teacher training, 69
Nursery education
  France, 60
  Rumania, 65
  Scandinavia, 68

Oakland, 82, 84
Oceania, 135
OECD, 91, 92, 100, 101, 107, 111, 112–113, 131, 132
  Committee for Research Co-operation, 101
  Committee for Science Policy, 101
  Committee for Scientific and Technical Personnel, 101
Ohio State University College of Education, 131
Ontario Institute for Studies in Education, 133
Oregon University, 133
Organization for Europe Economic Co-operation, 100
Organization of American States, 104
Organization of education, 6, 26, 29
  Ceylon, 46
  Chile, 43
  France, 59
  Germany, 60
  Latin America, 42
  Netherlands, 62

SUBJECT INDEX

Organisation of education—*contd.*
  Nigeria, 36
  Norway, 69
  Poland, 64–65
  Spain, 63
  UAR, 72
  USA, 39, 40
  USSR, 65
  Yugoslavia, 67
  See also School organization
Oriental education, 8
Oslo, 132
Out-of-School Education
  Europe, 100
Oxford University, 77
  Department of Education, 114

Pakistan, 31, 49–50, 81, 105
  administration of education, 50
  bibliographies, 49, 50, 51
  compulsory education, 49
  curriculum, 44
  economics and education, 49
  elites, 78, 81
  enrolment, 49
  examinations, 50
  finance, 44
  geographical factors and education, 49
  higher education, 50
  history of education, 49, 50, 113
  language, 50
  legislation, 49
  literacy, 49, 50
  planning, 44, 109
  primary education, 44, 49
  religion and education, 49
  research, 50
  social factors and education, 49
  statistics, 50
  syllabi, 51
  teacher salaries, 49
  teacher training, 44
  universal education, 49
  women's education, 44
Palestine, 70
Pan-American Union, 104, 107
  Dept. of Culture, 104
Parent education, 90, 110
  bibliographies, 110
  France, 110
  Great Britain, 110
  USA, 110
  West Germany, 110
Paris, 24, 41, 104, 114, 131
Parliamentary Group for World Government, 124
Pastoralists, 16
Pennsylvannia University, 115

Periodicals, 8, 27, 31, 114, 116, 118, 119, 120, 126, 130, 131, 134
  Africa, 37, 121
  Australia, 121
  England, 58, 117
  India, 120
  Norway, 69
  Poland, 65
  social factors and education, 123
  USA, 117, 118
  USSR, 120
Peru, 31, 42, 43, 104
  adult education, 43
  aid, 43
  bibliographies, 43
  glossaries, 43
  literacy, 43
  statistics, 43
Phi Delta Kappa Symposium on Educational Research, 132
Philadelphia, 76, 85
Philippines, 81, 91, 105, 131
  American educational policy in, 80, 81
  Economics and education, 81
  Enrolment, 81
  higher education, 45
  planning, 44
Philosophy of education. *See* Educational theory
Physical education
  Europe, 103
  Iran, 71
Pittsburgh University, 115
  Dept. of Education, 93
Planning, 28, 63, 90, 91, 92, 95, 96, 104, 133
  Africa, 33, 34
  Americas, 104
  Asia, 44, 45
  China, 44
  developing countries, 41, 98
  England, 133
  Europe, 91, 101
  France, 86
  Great Britain, 133
  Hungary, 86
  India, 44, 47, 48
  Indonesia, 44
  Italy, 79
  Japan, 49
  Latin America, 41–42, 104–105
  Mexico, 43
  Nigeria, 36, 109, 110
  Pakistan, 44, 109
  Philippines, 44
  Puerto Rico, 81
  Scandinavia, 68
  Senegal, 109
  Spain, 63

SUBJECT INDEX

Planning—*contd.*
  Tanzania, 109
  Thailand, 82
  Uganda, 109
  USA, 133
  West Germany, 76
Poland, 5, 31, 64–65, 120
  attitudes, 64
  bibliographies, 65
  citizenship education, 64
  curriculum, 65
  educational theory, 64
  higher education, 114
  history of education, 65
  organization of education, 64–65
  periodicals, 65
  reform, 65
  research, 120
  school organization, 65
  statistics, 65
  teacher training, 64–65
  textbooks, 65
Political culture, 6
Political education
  USA, 82, 84
  USSR, 82, 84
  West Germany, 61
Political philosophy. *See* Citizenship education
Politics and education, 6, 87, 88, 93, 94, 96, 97, 100
  Africa, 33–34, 73
  Australia, 52
  Belgium, 56, 108
  Burma, 74, 78
  China, 46
  England, 77
  France, 59
  Ghana, 34
  Guinea, 78
  India, 47
  Indonesia, 74, 78
  Japan, 48, 49
  Latin America, 41
  USA, 77, 84
Polytechnical education
  USA, 83, 84
  USSR, 65, 66, 67, 83, 84
Portugal, 31, 63
  administration of education, 54
  bibliographies, 63
  glossaries, 54, 63
  teacher salaries, 54
Pre-primary education, 26, 27
  Czechoslovakia, 64
  Rumania, 65
Pre-school education, 5, 26, 99
  Finland, 54
  Greece, 61
  Norway, 69

Pre-school education—*contd.*
  Sweden, 70
  Western Europe, 54
Primary education, 4, 5, 7, 26, 27, 89, 91, 96, 99
  Africa, 33
  Asia, 45
  bibliographies, 27
  Brazil, 74
  curriculum, 27, 93
  Denmark, 69
  England, 58
  Europe, 103, 119
  Finland, 54
  France, 60
  Greece, 61
  Guatemala, 78
  India, 47
  Ireland, 58
  Netherlands, 80
  New Zealand, 80
  Nigeria, 110
  Pakistan, 44, 49
  Rumania, 65
  Switzerland, 82, 84
  teacher training, 29
  textbooks, 29
  UAR, 72
  USA, 82, 84
  West Germany, 60
  Western Europe, 54, 55
  Western Samoa, 81
Primitive societies, 6
Private schools
  Australia, 52
  Denmark, 69
  Switzerland, 63
  USA, 39, 40
Problem approach, 87, 88
Progressive education, 7
Prussia, 2, 3
Psychology, 134
  Australia, 121
  Educational, 135
  USSR, 107, 132
Public schools
  England, 5, 58
Puerto Rico, 81
  manpower and education, 81
  planning, 81
Puritanism, 5

Rabat, 106
Race relations, 5, 17
  USA, 39
Racial factors, 5, 88
Radio schools
  Latin America, 80
Rahmenplan, 61

SUBJECT INDEX

Reading Institute of Education, 130
Reading University, 130
  Dept. of Education, 114, 130
Recruitment, 6
Reference works, 24–30, 112, 116, 118, 122, 133
Reform, 4, 6, 30, 95, 112, 113, 129
  China, 74, 107–108
  Denmark, 68
  Ethiopia, 75
  France, 59, 60, 75, 88, 119
  Germany, 60
  Ghana, 76
  India, 97
  Italy, 62, 76, 79
  Japan, 109
  Netherlands, 80
  New Zealand, 53
  Norway, 68, 81
  Poland, 65
  Rumania, 65
  Spain, 81
  Sweden, 68, 69, 70, 86
  USSR, 67, 83, 109
  West Germany, 61, 76, 79
  Western Europe, 54, 55
  Yugoslavia, 67
Regional Fundamental Education Centre in Latin America, 100
Religion, 134
Religion and education, 5, 36
  Israel, 78
  Pakistan, 49
  See also Church and education
Religious education
  New Zealand, 80
  West Germany, 61
Reports on education, 117
  Africa, 35, 37, 97
  Canada, 37
  Great Britain, 57, 112, 132
  Nigeria, 110
Research, 28, 90, 91, 108, 112–136
  Africa, 121, 134
  Americas, 134
  Asia, 134
  Australia, 51
  Burma, 121
  Canada, 134
  Eastern Europe, 136
  England, 77
  Europe, 101, 103, 132
  Finland, 69
  Great Britain, 134
  Japan, 132
  Middle East, 134
  New Zealand, 52–53
  Pakistan, 50
  Poland, 120
  social factors and education, 123

Research—*contd.*
  USA, 132-133, 135
  USSR, 84, 120, 134
  Western Europe, 134
  Yugoslavia, 120
Research aids, 115, 116–127, 130, 133
Research Centres, 5, 112, 131, 134
  Africa, 131
  Americas, 131
  Asia, 131
  developing countries, 131
  Europe, 131
  USA, 135
Researchers, 131
  USA, 131
Rhodesia, 81
  Native education, 81
Robbins Report, 55, 112
Rome, 114
Royal Commonwealth Society, 125
Rumania, 31, 64, 65
  bibliographies, 65
  glossaries, 65
  higher education, 65
  nursery education, 65
  pre-primary education, 65
  primary education, 65
  reform, 65
  secondary education, 65
  teachers, 65
  technical education, 65
  textbooks, 65
  vocational education, 65
  Youth, 65
Rural education, 29, 89, 94
  New Zealand, 53
  South Africa, 81

Saudi Arabia, 131
Scandinavia, 7, 31, 68–70, 96
  administration of education, 68
  bibliographies, 68
  cultural commission, 68
  economics and education, 68
  expert committee on educational research, 68
  higher education, 114
  nursery education, 68
  planning, 68
  social factors and education, 68
  teacher training, 68
  technical education, 2
  unity school, 68
  vocational education, 2
  See also under individual countries
School holidays
  USSR, 66
School hygiene
  Netherlands, 62

174

SUBJECT INDEX

School-leaving age
  New Zealand, 53
  Western Europe, 55
School organization, 6, 9
  Denmark, 69
  Poland, 65
  Sweden, 70
  USSR, 66
  See also Organization of education
School psychology
  West Germany, 76
School systems, 5
School welfare services, 26, 27
Schools Council, 133
Science, 91, 92, 104
  Europe, 101
  France, 59
Science education
  Americas, 104
  East Germany, 64
  Latin America, 42
Science teaching
  Africa, 106
  Europe, 101
Scotland, 31, 59, 77
  aims of education, 59
  bibliographies, 59
  extra-curricular activities, 59
  finance of education, 59
  higher education, 115
  Jewish education, 59
  ministry of education, 57, 59
  secondary education, 77
  teacher training, 59
  teachers, 59
  teaching methods, 59
  See also Great Britain
Secondary education, 3, 5, 6, 7, 25, 26, 27, 91, 93, 96, 98, 99
  Africa, 33
  Americas, 104
  Australia, 85
  bibliographies, 27
  curriculum, 6, 27, 95
  Denmark, 69
  England, 58, 77, 86
  Europe, 103, 119, 134
  Finland, 54
  France, 60, 86
  Germany, 3
  Ghana, 35, 88
  Greece, 61, 77
  India, 47
  Iran, 78
  Ireland, 58
  Latin America, 80
  Mexico, 43
  Netherlands, 80
  New Zealand, 53
  Rumania, 65

Secondary education—*contd.*
  Scotland, 77
  Spain, 81
  Sweden, 70, 86
  teacher training, 29
  UK, 6
  USA, 83, 84, 86
  USSR, 65, 67, 83, 84
  West Germany, 60, 76
  West Indies, 44
  Western Europe, 54, 55
  Yugoslavia, 67
Secular factors, 5
Segregated education
  South Africa, 81
  USA, 40
Selection, 6, 95, 96
  Germany, 132
  Sweden, 82
Senegal
  curriculum, 98
  examinations, 98
  higher education, 98
  planning, 109
Sèvres International Institute, 129
Sex education
  USSR, 66
Singapore, 105
Social change, 10, 11, 95
  Africa, 34
  bibliographies, 123
  Canada, 38
  Chile, 43
  China, 46
  Ghana, 35
Social change in literature, 12, 17, 19, 20, 21
  Iran, 71
  USSR, 83
  Western Europe, 54
Social class, 4, 14, 16, 22, 88
  Asia, 45
  Japan, 49
  Latin America, 79
  USA, 39
Social education, 132
Social factors and education, 57, 87, 95, 96, 100, 113, 132
  abstracting services, 123
  Africa, 33, 36
  Asia, 105
  Australia, 52
  Brazil, 42, 74
  Czechoslovakia, 64
  developing countries, 98
  England, 56, 57, 58
  France, 59, 60
  Germany, 61
  India, 47
  Indonesia, 78

SUBJECT INDEX

Social factors and education—*contd.*
  Iran, 71
  Japan, 49, 86
  Latin America, 41, 104–105
  Pakistan, 49
  periodicals, 123
  research, 123
  Scandinavia, 68
  Turkey, 72
  USA, 40
  USSR, 65, 66
Social mobility
  Asia, 106
Socialism, 5
Society for Research into Higher Education Ltd., 135
Socio-economical factors, 4, 87, 93, 94, 97, 98
Socio-economic aspects
  Asia, 45
  Brazil, 42
  Latin America, 104
  USA, 85
Somalia, 81
South Africa, 5, 81
  curriculum, 98
  examinations, 98
  higher education, 97, 98
  legislation, 81
  literature, 12, 19
  native education, 81
  rural education, 81
  segregated education, 81
South America, 135
Southampton University Institute of Education, 120
Southeast Asia. *See* Asia
Soviet studies, 128
  Japan, 82
  West Germany, 76
Space for Youth Foundation, 102
Spain, 5, 7, 63, 81–82, 107
  administration of education, 63
  cost of education, 63
  economics and education 63
  enrolment, 63
  higher education, 114
  manpower, 63
  organization of education, 63
  planning, 63
  reform, 81
  secondary education, 81
  statistics, 63
Special education
  England, 56, 58
  India, 48
  Sweden, 70
  USSR, 65–66
Sport
  Europe, 103

Sport—*contd.*
  India, 48
Standing Conference on Library Materials on Africa, 121
Stanford University, 115
State and education, 5, 93, 95
  Belgium, 74
  Brazil, 42
  Canada, 74
  England, 56, 58
  France, 60, 75, 79
  Italy, 75, 79
  Turkey, 72
  UAR, 72
Statistics, 25, 26, 27, 28, 29, 87, 92, 94, 116, 117
  Asia, 45
  Canada, 37, 38
  Czechoslovakia, 64
  Denmark, 69
  England, 132
  Finland, 54
  Ireland, 59
  Israel, 71
  Japan, 49
  Netherlands, 62
  New Zealand, 52
  Norway, 69
  Pakistan, 50
  Peru, 43
  Poland, 65
  Spain, 63
  Turkey, 72
  UAR, 72
  Uganda, 109
  USSR, 67
  West Germany (Berlin), 60
  Western Europe, 54, 55
Strasbourg, 103
Strasbourg University, 103
Students, 92, 129
  India, 78
  Japan, 79
  Uruguay, 85
  Yugoslavia, 85
Sudan, 82
  higher education, 82
Sweden, 31, 68, 69–70, 82, 86, 132
  administration of education, 54, 70
  art education, 70
  bibliographies, 70
  comprehensive schools, 69–70, 112
  curriculum, 70
  educational change, 86
  enrolment, 70
  equality of opportunity, 82
  finance, 70
  folk high schools, 75, 82
  glossaries, 54, 70
  higher education, 70

SUBJECT INDEX

Sweden—*contd.*
  history of education, 70
  music education, 70
  pre-school education, 70
  reform, 68, 69, 70, 86
  school organization, 70
  secondary education, 70, 86
  selection, 82
  special education, 70
  teacher salaries, 54
  television, 70
  vocational education, 70
Switzerland, 5, 63, 132
  bibliographies, 63
  extra-curricular activities, 102
  higher education, 114
  legislation, 63
  primary education, 82, 84
  private schools, 63
  teacher training, 63
  vocational education, 63
Sydney, 115
Syllabi, 29
  Nigeria, 36
  Pakistan, 50
  USSR, 66
Syracuse University, 115
Syria, 70, 82

Tanganyika, 6, 82
  church and education, 82
  See also Tanzania
Tanzania,
  planning, 109
  See also Tanganyika
Tashkent, 65
Teacher associations, 94, 118
Teacher performance, 4
Teacher salaries
  Austria, 54
  Belgium, 54
  Denmark, 54
  France, 54
  Italy, 54
  Luxembourg, 54
  Netherlands, 54
  Norway, 54
  Pakistan, 49
  Portugal, 54
  Sweden, 54
  USSR, 82, 110
  West Germany, 54
Teacher status, 26, 95
  Africa, 34
  New Zealand, 80
Teacher training, 5, 6, 7, 29, 33, 94, 95, 96, 127, 130, 134
  Africa, 33, 34, 37
  Asia, 106

Teacher training—*contd.*
  Australia, 52, 73
  Denmark, 69
  England, 56, 57
  Europe, 102
  Iceland, 103
  Finland, 54
  France, 60, 75
  India, 48
  Italy, 62
  Nepal, 86
  New Zealand, 53
  Nigeria, 36
  Norway, 69
  Pakistan, 44
  Poland, 64–65
  Scandinavia, 68
  Scotland, 59
  Switzerland, 63
  Turkey, 72
  UAR, 72
  USA, 6, 40, 86
  USSR, 66
  vocational education, 120
  West Germany, 61
  Western Europe, 54
Teachers, 27, 29
  Africa, 37
  East Africa, 73
  Germany, 60
  Guatemala, 78
  Iran, 71
  Rumania, 65
  Scotland, 59
  USA, 73
  USSR, 83
  West Germany, 61
  West Indies, 44
Teachers' College. *See* Columbia University, Teachers' College
Teaching, 94, 114, 129
  Brazil, 42
  Europe, 101
Teaching aids, 125
  Europe, 103
Teaching methods, 9, 27, 29, 94
  Africa, 37
  Australia, 52
  Denmark, 69
  England, 57
  Nigeria, 36
  Scotland, 59
  West Germany, 61
  Western Europe, 55
Technical education, 5, 7, 99, 123
  Africa, 37
  Americas, 104
  Australia, 52
  Belgium, 56
  England, 57, 77, 123

SUBJECT INDEX

Technical education—*contd.*
  Europe, 100, 103, 134
  Finland, 54
  India, 78
  Italy, 62
  Netherlands, 62
  Rumania, 65
  Scandinavia, 2
  USSR, 67
  Western Europe, 54, 75
Technology, 91, 92, 124
  bibliographies, 124
  developing countries, 98
  England, 57
  France, 59
  USSR, 66
  Western Europe, 54
Television
  Italy, 62
  Sweden, 70
  USA, 86
Tertiary education. *See* Higher education
Tests and testing
  Australia, 51
Textbooks, 2, 3, 4–8, 25, 29, 87, 116
  Asia, 51
  Poland, 65
  primary education, 29
  Rumania, 65
  West Germany, 76
Thailand, 82
  higher education, 45
  planning, 82
Theory of education. *See* Educational theory
Theses, 115, 116, 133, 134–136
  bibliographies, 133–136
  England, 134
  France, 119
  Great Britain, 135
  indexing services, 134
  Ireland, 135
  Northern Ireland, 135
  USA, 134
Tokugawa education
  Japan, 79
Trinidad, 22
Turkey, 6, 7, 31, 70, 72, 82, 107
  bibliographies, 72
  economics and education, 72
  glossaries, 72
  social factors and education, 72
  state and education, 72
  statistics, 72
  teacher training, 72
  'village institutes', 82
  Western education, 72
  women, 72

UAR, 31, 72, 84, 91
  administration of education, 72
  bibliographies, 72
  co-education, 72
  compulsory education, 72
  curriculum, 98
  examinations, 98
  guidance, 72
  higher education, 72, 98
  language, 72
  learning, 72
  organization of education, 72
  primary education, 72
  state and education, 72
  statistics, 72
  teacher training, 72
  See also under individual countries
Uganda, 82
  planning, 109
  statistics, 109
Unesco, 4, 24, 28, 29, 48, 49, 50, 58, 89–91, 94, 98, 100, 102, 104, 106, 112, 117, 118, 124, 129, 130
  Dept. of School and Higher education, 130
  East-West Major Project on mutual appreciation of Eastern and Western cultural values, 50
  Institute for Education, Hamburg, 73, 89, 90, 110, 124, 128, 129
  International Institute for Educational Planning, 41, 90, 91, 104, 106
Union of Soviet Socialist Republics. *See* USSR
United Arab Republic. *See* UAR
United States of America. *See* USA
United Nations, 89, 91, 110
United Nations Trust Territories, 84
Universal education
  Pakistan, 49
University Microfilms Inc., 134
Uruguay
  higher education, 85
  students, 85
USA, 1, 2, 5, 6, 7, 10, 30, 31, 34, 39–41, 46, 71, 74, 84–85, 86, 94, 95, 96, 97, 99, 107, 112, 115, 130, 131, 135
  administration of education, 39, 40
  adult education, 40
  American schools in Latin America, 80
  arithmetic teaching, 80, 84
  attitudes, 40
  bibliographies, 39, 40, 41
  church and education, 40, 77, 84
  comprehensive schools, 86, 112
  culture contact, 109
  curriculum, 40, 98

SUBJECT INDEX

USA—*contd.*
democracy and education, 40
Dept. of Health, Education and Welfare, Office of Education, 119, 120, 121
Dept. of State, Office, of External Research, 134
economics and education, 40
educational theory, 39, 40, 74
English education, 83, 84
examinations, 98
films, 40
glossaries, 39
higher education, 40, 80, 84, 98, 108, 114, 115
history of education, 39, 40
history of schools, 10
immigrants, 39
indexing services, 118
influence of education, 40
international education, 97
language teaching, 75, 84
learning, 40
legislation, 115
linguistic minority education, 83, 84
literature, 18
organization of education, 39, 40
parent education, 110
periodicals, 117, 118
Philippines, educational policy in, 80, 81
planning, 133
political education, 82, 84
politics and education, 77, 84
polytechnical education, 83, 84
primary education, 82, 84
private schools, 39, 40
race relations, 39, 40
research, 132–133, 135
research centres, 135
researchers, 131
secondary education, 83, 84, 86
segregated education, 40
social class, 39
social factors and education, 40
socio-economic aspects, 85
teacher training, 6, 40, 86
teachers, 73
television, 86
theses, 134
Wiesbaden-Philadelphia Reading Study, 76, 85
USSR, 2, 5, 6, 7, 10, 30, 31, 65–67, 82–84, 91, 96, 109, 112, 120, 128
Academy of Pedagogical Sciences, 66
athletics, 83
bibliographies, 66, 110
boarding schools, 66
character education, 66

USSR—*contd.*
children's literature, 66
co-education, 66
comprehensive schools, 66
curriculum, 6, 66, 67, 98
discipline, 66
economic education, 83
economics and education, 66
educational theory, 65
English education, 83, 84
examinations, 98
extra-curricular activities, 66
finance, 109–110
gifted children, 66
handicapped children, 65
higher education, 66, 74, 82, 83, 98, 114
history of education, 65, 66
introduction, 83
juvenile delinquency, 83
linguistic minority education, 83, 84
moral education, 66
non-Russian education, 82
organization of education, 65
periodicals, 120
political education, 82, 84
polytechnical education, 65, 66, 83, 84
pyschology, 107, 132
reforms, 67, 83, 109
research, 84, 120, 134
school holidays, 66
school organization, 66
secondary education, 65, 67, 83, 84
sex education, 66
social change, 83
social factors and education, 65, 66
Soviet Pedagogical Institute, 83
special education, 65–66
statistics, 67
syllabi, 66
teacher salaries, 82, 110
teacher training, 66
teachers, 83
technical education, 67
technology, 66
vocational education, 83
youth, 65
Uzbekistan, 83

Vancouver, 115
Vienna, 73, 114
Vietnam, 105
'Village Institutes' Turkey, 82
Visits abroad, 4
Vocational education, 7, 99, 120
Africa, 37
Americas, 104

SUBJECT INDEX

Vocational education—*contd.*
  Chile, 43
  Eastern Europe, 120
  Europe, 103, 134
  Finland, 54
  France, 60
  Ireland, 58
  Italy, 62
  Rumania, 65
  Scandinavia, 2
  Sweden, 70
  Switzerland, 63
  USSR, 83
  Western Europe, 54, 120

Wales. *See* England
War
  effects on education, 95
Washington, 107
  Brookings Institute, 91
Welfare services
  England, 56, 58
West Africa
  literature, 12, 19
West Germany, 5, 6, 60–61, 76, 86, 107, 119, 130
  administration of education, 54
  American studies, 76
  bibliographies, 61
  Bremer plan, 76
  buildings, 61
  curriculum, 61
  East European studies, 76
  English teaching, 61
  enrolment, 76
  extra-curricular activities, 102
  glossaries, 54, 61
  higher education, 76
  history of education, 76
  history teaching, 76
  language teaching, 61
  parent education, 110
  planning, 76
  political education, 61
  primary education, 60
  Rahmen plan, 76
  reform, 61, 76, 79
  religious education, 61
  school psychology, 76
  secondary education, 60, 76
  Soviet studies, 76
  statistics (Berlin), 60
  teacher salaries, 54
  teacher training, 61
  teachers, 61
  teaching methods, 61
  textbooks, 76
  Wiesbaden-Philadelphia Reading study, 76, 85

West India Library, 125
West Indies, 1, 22, 31, 37, 44
  higher education, 44
  history of education, 44
  Negro Education Grant, 44
  secondary education, 44
  teachers, 44
Western education, 8
  Ceylon, 46
  Japan, 48
  Nigeria, 36
  Turkey, 72
Western Europe, 54–63, 75
  compulsory education, 55
  curriculum, 55
  economics and education, 54, 55, 75
  geographic factors and education, 75
  glossaries, 54
  guidance, 55
  higher education, 54
  language teaching, 75, 84
  pre-school education, 54
  primary education, 54, 55
  reform, 54, 55
  research, 134
  school leaving age, 55
  secondary education, 54, 55
  social change, 54
  statistics, 54, 55
  teacher training, 54
  teaching methods, 55
  technical education, 54, 75
  technology, 54
  vocational education, 54, 120
  See also under individual countries
Western European Union, 101
Western Samoa, 81
  primary education 81
White House Conference 1955, 40
Wiesbaden, 76, 85
Wisconsin University, 115
Women, 25
  Turkey, 72
Women's education
  Africa, 37
  Canada, 38
  Pakistan, 44
Workers' education
  El Salvador, 107
World Health Organization, 89

Youth, 126
  Greece, 62
  Israel, 71
  Rumania, 65
  USSR, 66
  Yugoslavia, 85

SUBJECT INDEX

Youth education, 5
Yugoslavia, 64, 66, 85, 91, 107, 120
  administration of education, 67
  bibliographies, 67, 120
  curriculum, 67
  higher education, 114
  legislation, 67

Yugoslavia—*contd.*
  organization of education, 67
  reform, 67
  research, 120
  secondary education, 67
  students, 85
  youth, 85